They Teach That in College
Second Edition

College & Career Press
Chicago, Illinois

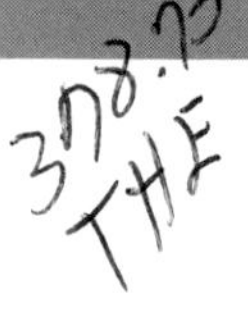

Project Staff

Managing Editor: Andrew Morkes

Additional Editorial Assistance: Amy McKenna, Felicitas Cortez

Interior Design: The Glasoe Group

Cover Design: Meyers Design, Inc.

Photo Credits

Front Cover (top left to right): Photos to Go Unlimited (#1, #2), iStockPhoto (#3)
Front Cover (teacher): iStockPhoto
Back Cover (bottom): Photos to Go Unlimited

ISBN 10: 0-9745251-7-0
ISBN 13: 978-0-9745251-7-4

Published and distributed by

College & Career Press, LLC
PO Box 300484
Chicago, IL 60630
773/282-4671 (phone/fax)
amorkes@chicagopa.com
www.collegeandcareerpress.com

Printed in the United States of America

08-01

Acknowledgments

The editors of *They Teach That in College!?*
would like to extend their sincerest appreciation
to the educators and associations that provided their time
and expertise to assist us in the creation of this book.

Other Titles in the *They Teach That in College!?* series:

They Teach That in Community College!?
They Teach That in College!?-Midwest Edition (print and electronic editions)
They Teach That in College!?-East Edition (ebook only)
They Teach That in College!?-West Edition (ebook only)
They Teach That in College!?-South Edition (ebook only)

Other Products Available From College & Career Press:

College Exploration on the Internet
College Spotlight newsletter
The CAM Report newsletter

Table of Contents

Introduction

Business, Social Sciences/History, and Education are the most popular college majors today, but not every student has the interest or aptitude to be successful in these fields. Additionally, many of these fields are glutted with graduates who are forced to take lower-paying jobs or positions that are unrelated to their field of study.

They Teach That in College!? provides information about interesting, lucrative, and cutting-edge college majors unknown to many counselors, educators, and parents. It includes profiles of more than 95 college majors, course listings, potential employers, contact information for colleges and universities that offer these programs, contact information for professional associations that offer career information about these fields, interesting sidebars, photographs, and interviews with college educators.

How This Book is Organized

They Teach That in College!? has 96 main chapters—which focus on unique and interesting majors. What is a unique major?' We used two official criterion to select majors to include in this book: 1) the major had to be fast-growing and offer good employment and salary prospects for students, and 2) the major had to be offered at less than 25 percent of colleges and universities in the United States. A third unofficial criterion was that the major had to capture our imagination—in short it had to be fun and, hopefully, interesting to our readers.

The following paragraphs provide an overview of the specific subsections that are contained in the chapters:

The unique major chapters have the following subsections: 1) an opening paragraph that details the major in question, classroom activities, and the typical educational path for students who pursue study in this field; 2) a list of typical courses that students will take if they study the major; 3) a list of potential employers of students who study the major; 4) a list of colleges and universities that offer the major (each entry includes contact information and the degree levels—such as certificate, associate, bachelor's, master's, and doctorate—that are available for the major; and, 5) a list of professional associations and organizations that you can contact for more information (job shadowing, free publications, financial aid, etc.) on the field.

Additionally, the articles occasionally feature interviews with college educators. These educators offer an overview of their programs, suggest high school classes that will help you prepare for college, present information on the future of their fields, and other useful advice.

In addition to the aforementioned sections, *They Teach That in College!?* also features a school index, a schools by state index, and an association/organization index.

What's New in the Second Edition?
We have made many improvements and additions to the second edition of *They Teach That in College!?* We have:
✔ Increased the number of majors covered from 68 in the last edition to 96 in the second edition.
✔ Added nearly 40 new majors to the book, including Nanoscience/Nanotechnology, Sustainable Agriculture, Mechatronics Systems Engineering, Horticultural Therapy, Forensic Accounting, Satellite Communications, Ecotourism, and Comic Book Art, to name just a few.
✔ Added many new interviews with educators, as well as new sidebars.
✔ Thoroughly updated the articles, including contact information for colleges and universities and professional associations.
✔ Added photographs.

Finally . . . Important Issues to Keep in Mind

Majors Are Always Changing. Remember that the world of education is constantly changing: majors may be renamed, available degree levels may change, programs may be dropped due to budget cuts, etc. Use this book as a starting place for your career and college exploration, but be sure to contact the school in which you are interested in attending for the latest program information.

The Internet Is Always Changing. You probably know this already, but websites are constantly updated—course schedules change, contact information is revised, majors are added or deleted. . . . you get the idea. If you have trouble locating any of the websites listed in this book, try shortening the web address to its basic address. For example, if you are having trouble reaching the University of Wisconsin's art therapy website (www.uwsuper.edu/admissions/factsheets/art_therapy.htm), shortening the address to the University's most basic address (e.g., http://www.uwsuper.edu) will usually allow you to access the site and locate the information at the site's home page or by using its search feature. If this doesn't work, try a keyword search using the name of the college or call the college or association to ask for its current website address and other information.

The Importance of Accreditation. Accreditation is the process of determining whether an educational institution or academic program meets standards set by regional or national organizations of professionals. All quality colleges are accredited, and most, but not all, academic programs (such as those in petroleum engineering or art therapy, for example) also receive accreditation from accrediting bodies. We have made every attempt to list accredited programs in this book (but also list unaccredited programs to provide you with a wide selection of education options). Since a good education is key to success in the workplace, be sure to investigate the accreditation status of the program in which you are interested. Attending an unaccredited program MAY limit your ability to transfer credits (if you are attending a two-year college and plan to transfer to a four-year program to continue your education) and perhaps reduce employment opportunities.

Online Education. Some of these programs may be available online, but, due to the fast-changing nature of online education, we have largely excluded mention of these programs from the book. If you are interested in online educations options, visit the program's website or contact the admissions offices of colleges in which you are interested in attending for more information.

We hope that *They Teach That in College!?* becomes a valued and trusted resource as you navigate the challenges of selecting a college major! We wish you the best in all of your future endeavors!

The Editors

Agricultural Education

Ask almost anyone to name typical agricultural careers, and you might hear "farmer" and "farm manager." While these careers remain very important to our food industry, today's agriculture and agricultural education involves much more than farming and managing farms. Agriculture students can now pursue dozens of majors that are far removed from planting crops and managing farms—majors as diverse as agricultural communications, finance, marketing, and sales; biochemistry; biological and food process engineering; food industry marketing and management; food manufacturing; international agronomy; landscape architecture; public horticulture; quantitative agricultural economics; turf science; and wood products manufacturing technology. Degrees range from associate degrees to the doctorate.

Typical Courses:

> Varies by major

Potential Employers:

> Agricultural industry
> Food industry
> Broadcasting industry
> Financial industry
> Government agencies (e.g., U.S. Department of Agriculture)
> Virtually any other industry that specializes in agricultural-related products and services

Available At:

The following programs are just a sampling of the unique opportunities that are available to students interested in agricultural careers. Agricultural education programs are available at two- and four-year colleges and universities throughout the United States. Visit the websites of schools in your area to learn more about unique majors that are offered.

Cornell University (Ithaca, NY)
607/255-2036
http://www.cals.cornell.edu
Degrees available: Bachelor's degree, master's degree, doctorate degree (more than 20 agricultural majors are available)

Kirkwood Community College (Cedar Rapids, IA)
800/332-2055
agsci@kirkwood.edu
http://www.kirkwood.edu/agrisciences
Degrees available: Certificate, diplomas, associate degrees (15 fields of study)

University of Missouri (Columbia, MO)
573/882-8301
http://cafnr.missouri.edu
Degrees available: Bachelor's degree, master's degree, doctorate degree (more than 15 agricultural majors are available)

Purdue University (West Lafayette, IN)
765/494-8392
GOinAG@purdue.edu
http://www.agriculture.purdue.edu or
http://www.agriculture.purdue.edu/goinag/qanda.html
Degrees available: Associate degree, bachelor's degree (nearly 50 agricultural majors are available)

Texas A&M University (College Station, TX)
979/845-4747
http://coals.tamu.edu
Degrees available: Bachelor's degree, master's degree, doctorate degree (nearly 50 agricultural majors are available)

University of Wisconsin-Madison (Madison, WI)
608/263-2400
http://www.wisc.edu/academics/majors.php
Degrees available: Bachelor's degree, master's degree, doctorate degree (25 agricultural majors are available)

For More Information:

American Farm Bureau Federation
202/406-3600
http://www.fb.org

American Society of Agronomy
608/273-8080
http://www.agronomy.org

National FFA Organization
317/802-6060
http://www.ffa.org

U.S. Department of Agriculture
202/720-2791
http://www.usda.gov

Interview: Dale Whittaker

The editors of *They Teach That in College!?* discussed the changing world of agriculture and agricultural education with Dale Whittaker, Associate Dean and Director of Academic Programs and Professor of Agricultural and Biological Engineering at Purdue University's College of Agriculture. Purdue offers nearly 50 undergraduate and preprofessional programs in agriculture.

Q. How has agriculture changed over the years?

A. After the green revolution/chemical revolution of post-World War II, agriculture became more mechanized and farmers were able to be more productive with the same amount of land. Over the past several decades, the focus has shifted from a production-oriented focus to a consumer-oriented focus. Today's agriculture is less about producing more with what we have and much more about producing the right products, getting them safely and cleanly packaged, and getting them to market and doing it in a sustainable way in a manner that the consumer desires. This focus has led to the rise of organic products, targeted health products, and more diversity in what is produced.

Q. How has agricultural education been affected by these changes?

A. In terms of agricultural education, there is much more of a focus on what the consumer wants, so there is more study in agricultural economics, international trade, entrepreneurship, engineering, processing, and packaging. A good example of this change in focus is in our agronomy program, where 50 percent of students are pursuing study in turf grass, sports field, lawn, and golf course management. The other 50 percent are interested in crop production.

Structural changes have also occurred in education. In the '50s and '60s, we had programs such as animal husbandry where students mainly took animal science classes. In the '70s, we started seeing more diversification in the curricula and selection of majors. At Purdue, that meant a larger selection of majors introduced. More recently, our students have focused on a very diverse curricula, with strong humanities, foreign languages, basic science, and areas of specialization. Today, our students are using more minors and double majors, and a much higher percentage are going on to graduate work.

Q. What are the most popular majors in the School of Agriculture?

A. Some of the majors that have experienced growth include food science, landscape architecture, landscape horticulture, turf grass management, pre-veterinary medicine, agricultural sales and marketing, wildlife, fisheries and aquatic sciences, and biological engineering. We have also had a very dramatic enrollment growth recently in biochemistry. And more students are becoming interested in companion animal management and the study of animals as models of human health.

Q. What nontraditional career options are available to agricultural majors?

A. Many of our students are pursuing careers in resource management. We have students who are managing fisheries in Alaska, students who are managing forests on the West Coast, and students who are managing professional football stadiums.

In terms of food science, many of the interesting new products, packaging, flavors, and prepared products are being developed by students with strong food science, as well as strong biology and chemistry, backgrounds. We also see a lot of our students going into medical school. A few are starting to go into law school. We see some students going into education. We have a core in our entomology major that teaches science education. We are also seeing a growing interest in forensic entomology (which uses the stages and development of insects to determine time and cause of death).

Some of our graduates also work for the government as regulators for the Environmental Protection Agency. Others go to work for companies and write impact statements and permitting statements for these regulators. So, we have students regulating other students. A small number of our graduates are farming. About 7 percent go on to manage family farms or large corporate farms. And corporate farming is an international career; these students find jobs all over the world.

Q. What does the future hold for agricultural education?

A. Agricultural education will continue to move toward a consumer-driven focus. The next educational focus in agriculture will be on human health. That's really where food science, biochemistry, and the animal sciences have gone. Even in our natural resources department, one of the fastest-growing programs is humans in the environment and managing natural and urban landscapes. I also think we will continue to see the basic sciences, such as plant science, molecular science, proteomics, ionomics, and genomics, move into the undergraduate curriculum.

American Sign Language/ Interpreter Training

Approximately 32.5 million people in the United States are deaf or hard of hearing, according to the U.S. Census Bureau. As government, and society as a whole, has become more aware of the rights and needs of people who are deaf, exciting career opportunities have emerged for persons interested in professional work in deaf-related fields. To meet this demand, colleges are adding or improving their deaf studies programs, which teach students about deaf history, culture, and sign language. The academic discipline of deaf studies is a growing field, as increased understanding of the deaf community—within the broader national and international community—is necessary.

Typical Classes:

- Basic Sign Language
- Introduction to American Sign Language
- Sign Mime and Creative Movement
- Introduction to Deaf Studies
- Structure of American Sign Language
- Deaf Art/Deaf Artists
- Deaf Theater History
- Organizational Communication and the Deaf Employee
- Deaf Culture and Community
- Introduction to American Sign Language Teaching
- Civil Rights and Deaf People

Potential Employers:

- Human services organizations
- Government agencies
- Schools
- Deaf-related associations and organizations
- Employment agencies that serve the deaf or hard of hearing

Available At:

The following programs are just a sampling of the unique opportunities that are available to students interested in ASL/deaf studies..Education programs are available at two- and four-year colleges and universities throughout the United States. Visit the websites of schools in your area to learn more about deaf studies programs.

Boston University (Boston, MA)
617/353-2300 (undergraduate) 617/353-3205 (Voice/TTY, graduate)
http://www.bu.edu/sed/prospectivestudents.htm
Degrees available: Bachelor's degree, master's degree, doctorate

California State University-Northridge
818/677-5116 (Voice), 818/677-4973 (TTY)
deaf.studies@csun.edu
http://www.csun.edu/~sch_educ/dfst/index.html
Degrees available: Bachelor's degree

Gallaudet University (Washington, DC)
202-651-5814 (Voice), 202/651-5814 (TTY)
http://deafstudies.gallaudet.edu
Degrees available: Bachelor's degree, master's degree

LaGuardia Community College (Long Island City, NY)
718/482-7200
http://www.lagcc.cuny.edu/majors
Degrees available: Associate degree

Rochester Institute of Technology (Rochester, NY)
National Technical Institute for the Deaf
585/475-6809 (Voice/TTY), 585/475-6851 (TTY)
http://www.rit.edu/programs-level.html
Degrees available: Certificate, bachelor's degree

Seattle Central Community College (Seattle, WA)
206/344-4347 (Voice), 206/344-4347 (TTY)
http://seattlecentral.edu/proftech/PROdeafstudies.php
Degrees available: Associate degree

Towson University (Towson, MD)
410/704-2436 (Voice/TTY)
http://wwwnew.towson.edu/main/academics/degreeprograms/index.asp
Degrees available: Bachelor's degree

For More Information:

Alexander Graham Bell Association for the Deaf and Hard of Hearing
202/337-5220 (Voice), 202/337-5221 (TTY)
info@agbell.org
http://www.agbell.org

American Speech-Language-Hearing Association
800/638-8255, 301/296-5650 (TTY)
actioncenter@asha.org
http://www.asha.org

Animation

When many people think of animation, they instantly think of the Saturday morning cartoons they watched as children. But animation has come a long way in the last couple of decades, with significant computerized software advances that have created a much broader range of opportunities in today's animation field. Television and film animation is still a viable career option, but animation is also used in many other applications—computer game development, medical simulations, advertising, industrial and architectural design, and more. Housed in most college art departments, this major requires artistic vision and creativity along with an aptitude for computers and technology. Business savvy and communication skills are also important. Since this field offers diverse opportunities for graduates, it is a good choice for the individual who wants a well-rounded education that is marketable across a variety of industries and applications, but which is also specialized enough to provide significant direction in post-graduation job seeking.

Typical Courses:

> Fundamentals of Design
> Rendering and Modeling Techniques
> Cartooning
> Storyboarding
> Digital Design with Photoshop
> Design for Advertising
> Multimedia Flash
> Digital Layout, Imaging, and Editing
> Television Video/Studio Production
> 3D Animation and Commercial Applications

Potential Employers:

> Television and film production companies
> Corporations and small businesses
> Advertising agencies
> Architectural firms
> Web design consulting firms

Available At:

The following programs are just a sampling of the opportunities that are available to students interested in animation. Visit the websites of schools in your area to see if they offer study options in the field.

University of the Arts (Philadelphia, PA)
800/616-ARTS
www.uarts.edu/academics/cad/ma/bfaanim.html
Degrees available: Bachelor's degree

Bristol Community College (Fall River, MA)
www.bristol.mass.edu/Catalog/degree/dp_animation_motion.cfm
Degrees available: Associate's degree

Columbia College Chicago (Chicago, IL)
312/344-6700
http://www.filmatcolumbia.com/animation.html
Degrees available: Bachelor's degree

Columbus College of Art & Design (Columbus, OH)
614/224-9101
http://www.ccad.edu/majors-ms.htm
Degrees available: Bachelor's degree

DePaul University (Chicago, IL)
312/362-8381
http://www.cti.depaul.edu/admissions/undergraduate/undergrad_majorsMinors.asp
Degrees available: Bachelor's degree

Johnson County Community College (Overland Park, KS)
913/469-8500
http://www.jccc.net/home/catalog/default/toccareerprograms/careerprograms/AAS-ANIMATN
Degrees available: Associate degree

Lake Washington Technical College (Kirkland, WA)
425/739-8100
http://lwtchost.ctc.edu/programs2/mmdp
Degrees available: Associate degree

Minneapolis College of Art and Design (Minneapolis, MN)
612/874-3700
http://www.mcad.edu
Degrees available: Bachelor's degree, master's degree

Mohawk Valley Community College (Utica, NY)
315/792-5446
http://www.mvcc.edu/academics/degree.cfm
Degrees available: Associate degree

New Hampshire Technical Institute (Concord, NH)
603/271-7757
http://nhti.edu/academics/academicprograms/degaggp.html
Degrees available: Associate degree

The Ohio State University (Columbus, OH)
614/292-6746
http://www.design.osu.edu/dept_grad.html
Degrees available: Master's degree

Purdue University (West Lafayette, IN)
765/494-7505
http://www.tech.purdue.edu/cgt
Degrees available: Associate, bachelor's degree, master's degree

Rhode Island School of Design (Providence, RI)
401/454-6233
http://www.risd.edu/pdf/facts/fav.pdf
Degrees available: Bachelor's degree

Santa Ana College (Santa Ana, CA)
714/564-5600
http://www.sac.edu/degrees/sac/Art-3-D_Animation.htm
Degrees available: Certificate

For More Information:

Animation World Network
323/606-4200
http://www.awn.com

International Animated Film Society
818/842-4691
http://www.asifa-hollywood.org

Aquaculture

Aquaculture is similar to agriculture, but instead of growing crops or raising typical farm livestock, fish and shellfish are raised. The study of aquaculture is growing in popularity for a number of reasons: the rise in demand for seafood by health-conscious consumers, the need to combat overfishing in the wild, and the need to find economical and efficient ways of providing food sources for the world's burgeoning population. Most fish raised through aquaculture are for human consumption or are used to stock ponds, rivers, and lakes for recreational fishing. Catfish, salmon, trout, tilapia, crayfish, and shrimp are just some of the many species that are cultivated through aquaculture. The fish are typically raised in pens not only in coastal areas, but inland as well, by utilizing natural or man-made water structures. Students interested in aquaculture can focus on the biological, technical, or managerial aspects of the industry. Aquaculture is practiced all over the world and is expected to provide new employment opportunities in the near future.

Typical Courses:

- Introduction to Fisheries Management
- Aquatic Ecology
- Diseases of Fish
- Nutrition of Fish
- Fish Reproduction
- Introduction to Computer Concepts and Applications
- Aquacultural Organisms
- Aquacultural Laboratory Techniques
- Aquacultural Field Techniques
- Aquacultural Management Practices

Potential Employers:

- Commercial fisheries
- Aquariums
- Colleges and universities
- State or federal organizations (such as the U.S. Fish and Wildlife Service)

Available At:

The following programs are just a sampling of the opportunities that are available to students interested in aqaculture. Visit http://www.was.org for more aquaculture programs.

Auburn University (Auburn, AL)
334/844-4786
www.ag.auburn.edu/fish
Degrees available: Bachelor's degree, master's degree

Delaware Technical and Community College-Owens Campus (Georgetown, DE)
856/5400
www.dtcc.edu/owens/programs
Degrees available: Certificate

Hillsborough Community College-Brandon Campus (Tampa, FL)
813/253-7802
www.hccfl.edu/by/aquaculture
Degrees available: Certificate, associate degree

Morrisville State College (Morrisville, NY)
315/684-6237
www.morrisville.edu/Academics/Ag_NRC/NRC/html/AquacultureAAS.htm
Degrees available: Associate degree

University of Rhode Island (Kingston, RI)
401-874-1000
www.uri.edu/cels/favs/FAV_Aquacult.html
Degrees available: Bachelor's degree, master's degree, doctorate

College of Southern Idaho (Twin Falls, ID)
800/680-0274
www.csi.edu/prospectivestudents
Degrees available: Certificate, associate degree

Texas A&M University-Corpus Christi
361/825-2676
http://lsci.tamucc.edu/mari/
Degrees available: Master's degree

For More Information:

American Fisheries Society
http://www.fisheries.org

Aquaculture Network Information Center
http://aquanic.org

World Aquaculture Society (U.S. Branch)
http://www.was.org

Art Conservation

Imagine the *Mona Lisa* marred by soot, smoke, and water damage as a result of a fire. A Civil War-era photograph disintegrating with age. Or just the vibrant colors of a beloved family painting dulled by time. The world would be a far less beautiful and interesting place without art. *Art conservators* protect paintings, photographs, sculpture, works of art on paper, textiles, architecture, books, ethnographic and archaeological objects, and other types of artwork from damage inflicted by temperature and humidity extremes, excessive light, pests, pollutants, poor handling practices, natural disasters, and accidental damage. They work to prevent damage to at-risk objects and attempt to conserve artwork that has been damaged. A master's degree in art conservation is required to work in this field. Only a few colleges and universities in the United States offer degrees in art conservation.

Typical Courses:

- Introduction to Art Conservation
- Techniques of Examination and Documentation
- Conservation Science: Properties and Behavior of Materials
- Structure of Works of Art
- Methods of Analysis
- Technology and Conservation of Paintings
- Professionalism in Conservation

Potential Employers:

- Museums
- Conservation centers
- Private collectors
- Art and antique dealers
- Government agencies
- Galleries
- Auction houses

Available At:

Buffalo State College (Buffalo, NY)
716/878-5025
artcon@buffalostate.edu
Degrees available: Master's degree, advanced certificate

University of California-Los Angeles
310/825-9407
acordts@ucla.edu
http://ioa.ucla.edu/conservation
Degrees available: Master's degree

University of Delaware (Newark, DE)
302/831-3489
art-conservation@udel.edu
www.artcons.udel.edu
Degrees available: Bachelor's degree, master's degree, advanced certificate, doctorate

New York University (New York, NY)
212/992-5800
conservation.program@nyu.edu
www.nyu.edu/gsas/dept/fineart/ifa/curriculum/conservation.htm
Degrees available: Master's degree

State University College of New York-Buffalo
716/878-5025
gradoffc@buffalostate.edu
http://www.buffalostate.edu/gradprog.xml?bpid=133
Degrees available: Master's degree

University of Texas-Austin
512/471-3821
www.gslis.utexas.edu/programs/certificates/conservation.php
Degrees available: Master's degree (combined with a certificate in the Conservation of Library and Archival Materials or a certificate in the Preservation Administration of Library and Archival Materials)

For More Information:

American Institute for Conservation of Historic and Artistic Works
202/452-9545
info@aic-faic.org
http://aic.stanford.edu

Interview: Vicki Cassman

Dr. Vicki Cassman is the Director of Undergraduate Art Conservation Studies at the University of Delaware in Newark, Delaware. The University offers one of the few art conservation programs in the United States. Dr. Cassman discussed her school's program and the education of students in this field with the editors of *They Teach That in College!?*

Q. Please tell us about your program.

A. We offer a bachelor of arts in material culture preservation, a master of science in art conservation and a certificate in conservation, and a doctor of philosophy in preservation studies.

The bachelor of arts in material culture preservation prepares students for graduate-level study in a formal recognized conservation training program. In addition to course work, internships are encouraged. Undergraduates who do not go on for graduate work have taken jobs in museums and related institutions as collections managers, conservation technicians, curatorial assistants, or registrars in museum-related institutions. The undergraduate program is housed in the historic building known as Old College at the University of Delaware, Newark campus.

The master of Ssience in art conservation and a certificate in conservation is one of the few recognized graduate training programs in the U.S., and it prepares students for careers as practicing conservators in museums, regional centers, or private practice. Faculty and students use 26 well-equipped conservation studios, laboratories, examination rooms, and workshops in the Louis du Pont Crowninshield Research Building at Winterthur Museum and Country Estate. This building houses one of the country's largest and best-equipped museum analytical laboratories and conservation studios.

The doctor of philosophy in preservation studies is an interdisciplinary doctoral course of study involving the philosophies, research methodologies, and policies informing preservation efforts focused on art, architecture, landscapes, and material culture. The program makes use of faculty and physical resources in the Colleges of Arts and Sciences, Agriculture, Engineering, Human Services, Education, Public Policy, and Marine Studies at the University of Delaware, and the faculty and resources of the Winterthur Museum and Country Estate.

Q. What type of internship opportunities are provided by your program?

A. BA-Material Culture Preservation. There are two required internships for the undergraduate program. The first internship should be completed under the supervision of University of Delaware faculty after completing two semesters of Care and Preservation of Cultural Property I-II, usually taken during the sophomore year. We encourage students to take one of the "in-house" internships either at the Winterthur Museum or the University of Delaware in art

Fast Fact

Recommended undergraduate classes, according to the American Institute for Conservation of Historic and Artistic Works, include science, the humanities (art history, anthropology, and archaeology), and studio art.

conservation or collection management. The second internship is usually at another institution to gain a different experience and perspective.

MS-Art Conservation. The entire third year of the three-year program is an internship. It is spent under the supervision of a conservation professional(s) at one or more host institution(s) or private laboratories, where the student should function as a cooperative and productive staff member. The fundamental objectives are to broaden the student's exposure to specialty object problems and treatments, refine hand skills, build confidence in object assessment and decision making, improve report-writing skills, and develop responsible professionalism.

Q. What high school subjects/activities should students focus on to be successful in this major?

A. A high school student should strive to obtain as strong a chemistry background as possible since often freshmen struggle with university-level chemistry requirements. Chemistry is the make or break factor for most students in the major. Volunteering in museums is a good preparatory experience as well.

Q. What are the most important personal and professional qualities for art conservation majors?

A. We often speak about the four-legged stool that represents the field of conservation and the skills needed by our majors. Our field requires excellent hand skills; a specialized knowledge of the history of materials and techniques that one gains from anthropology, art history, or history; and chemistry knowledge to understand deterioration and materials used to treat artifacts. The fourth leg of the stool represents ethical considerations. Students must have a passion for artifacts, technology, and materials, as well as have infinite patience and ability to work with their hands. An understanding of chemistry and how it is applied to the field of conservation has always been important but it is becoming of even greater importance to the field in general.

Q. What is the employment outlook for the field of art conservation? How will the field change in the future?

A. With a B.A. in material culture preservation you are not considered a conservator; however, it does allow you to work as a conservation technician in a conservation lab, art handler, or as an assistant collection manager or assistant registrar within a museum or similar institution. The field of collection management is a hybrid between conservation and registration, and it is becoming more common in museums. Collection managers have not had a professional organization, but the American Institute for Conservation of Historic and Artistic Works is now formally accepting and encouraging collections managers to join since the fields are so closely allied. However, by far the greatest needs are currently in the area of preservation professionals for libraries and archives.

With a M.S. in art conservation we have had 100 percent employment for our graduate students, and almost all have stayed in the profession. Though there are positions available for graduates, they must be able to move to where the jobs are since these are often in large urban centers. There are far greater numbers of jobs available for conservators in libraries and archives, but the University of Texas provides the recognized training for jobs in this specialty. Accreditation and certification of conservation professionals soon will start in the United States and it has already begun in the United Kingdom.

Art Therapy

Artists have been using creative self-expression as an outlet to express their feelings and emotions since the beginning of time. But you don't have to be a famous painter or sculptor to understand the basic premise behind the discipline of art therapy—expressing oneself can be an emotional, healing, and therapeutic process. Art therapy is a health profession that is built upon this fundamental principle that the creative process can enhance a person's physical, mental, and emotional well-being. The *art therapist* serves as the facilitator in guiding a client through the process of resolving conflicts and problems, developing interpersonal skills, reducing stress, increasing self-esteem, and coming to a sense of self-understanding—by means of personal artistic expression. People who enter the field have a strong commitment to working with people in one-on-one situations. They believe in the nurturing and healing power of art and its importance in helping people resolve personal issues resulting from a variety of life challenges such as physical or mental illness, grief, or trauma. A master's degree in art therapy is required for professional certification in art therapy. Students entering master's programs may have undergraduate degrees in areas such as art, education, or psychology.

Typical Courses:

- Theories of Art Therapy, Counseling, and Psychotherapy
- Ethics and Standards of Practice
- Assessment and Evaluation
- Individual, Group, and Family Techniques
- Human and Creative Development
- Research Methods
- Drawing
- Painting
- Sculpting
- Clinical Practice: Counseling Skills in Art Therapy Practice

Potential Employers:

- Hospitals (medical and psychiatric)
- Clinics
- Public and community agencies
- Wellness centers
- Educational institutions
- Businesses

> Private practices
> Outpatient counseling clinics
> Residential treatment facilities
> Halfway houses
> Prisons
> Domestic violence and homeless shelters
> Correctional facilities
> Nursing homes
> Hospice programs

Available At:

Nearly 30 colleges and universities in the United States are approved by the American Art Therapy Association (AATA). Here is just a small selection of approved schools. Visit the AATA's website, www.arttherapy.org/staep.html, for a complete list of approved schools, as well as other schools with programs.

School of the Art Institute of Chicago (Chicago, IL)
312/899-7481
arttherapy@saic.edu
Degrees available: Master's degree

Emporia State University (Emporia, KS)
620/341-5317
www.emporia.edu/psyspe/arttherapy/athp.html
Degrees available: Master's degree

University of Louisville (Louisville, KY)
502/852-6884
etemail@louisville.edu
www.louisville.edu/edu/ecpy/et/ArtThx.htm
Degrees available: Master's degree

Marylhurst University (Marylhurst, OR)
800/634-9982, ext. 6244
studentinfo@marylhurst.edu
www.marylhurst.edu/arttherapy/index.php
Degrees available: Master's degree, advanced certificate

Marywood University (Scranton, PA)
570/348-6278
swise@marywood.edu
www.marywood.edu/departments/art/grad/grad.html#at
Degrees available: Master's degree

Mount Mary College (Milwaukee, WI)
414/258-4810, ext. 301
www.mtmary.edu/at.htm or
www.mtmary.edu/arttherapy.htm

Degrees available: Bachelor's degree (women students only), master's degree (male/female students)

New York University (New York, NY)
212/998-5726
ia4@nyu.edu
http://education.nyu.edu/depts/art/programs/5
Degrees available: Master's degree

Southern Illinois University-Edwardsville
618/650-2000
jgausep@siue.edu
www.siue.edu/ART/areas/art_therapy
Degrees available: Master's degree, advanced certificate

Southwestern College (Santa Fe, NM)
877/471-5756
admissions@swc.edu
www.swc.edu/programs/MA_art_therapy.htm
Degrees available: Master's degree, advanced certificate

Ursuline College (Pepper Pike, OH)
888/URSULINE
gradsch@ursuline.edu
www.ursuline.edu/academics/graduate/atc
Degrees available: Master's degree, advanced certificate

For More Information:

American Art Therapy Association
888/290-0878
info@arttherapy.org
www.arttherapy.org

National Coalition of Arts Therapies Associations
www.nccata.org

Interview: Bruce Moon

Dr. Bruce Moon is the Graduate Program Director of the Art Therapy Department at Mount Mary College in Milwaukee, Wisconsin. He discussed his program and the education of art therapy students with the editors of *They Teach That in College!?*

Q. Please provide a brief overview of your program.

A. Art therapy is a challenging and exciting career choice that allows individuals to combine skills in art making with the desire to help persons who are suffering with emotional, physical, or developmental challenges. At Mount Mary College the

Did You Know?

Art therapists earn annual median salaries of approximately $45,000, according to the American Art Therapy Association.

art therapy program is housed in the Art and Design Division and is a vital and dynamic component of graduate education.

Our approach to art therapy education is uniquely art-based and experiential, and we endeavor to provide a creative integration of artistic, academic, and clinical education. In every way possible we attempt to live-out our program mission, "Art Therapy: Compassion in Action."

The Graduate Art Therapy Program utilizes an art-based and experiential approach to graduate level art therapy education. The faculty and students strive to create a community of learners in which all members share a commitment to meaningful participation in graduate level academic, artistic, clinical, and intra- and inter-personal study.

Classes are offered at times designed to accommodate students' needs. Students may choose from among daytime, evening, and weekend classes. The course of study combines disciplined artistic inquiry with intensive academic investigation of art therapy and counseling theories and techniques, and hands-on clinical practicums and supervision. These elements provide students with a thorough and rich educational experience.

In addition to our nationally known full-time faculty, part-time faculty members who are actively working in the field enrich the program. Each semester, guest lecturers—national leaders and innovators of the profession—contribute diversity to the program with exciting, current topics in art therapy that broaden and enrich the students' perspectives. Small group, experiential, and art-based learning is a key strength of the program. Students have the opportunity to select from a wide range of practicums through which they develop their skills in real-life treatment settings.

Q. What high school subjects should students focus on to be successful in this major?

A. It is important to note that art therapy is a master's degree level of entry profession. High school students can begin to prepare for their undergraduate work and later graduate education by taking the maximum number of studio art classes and psychology/social science classes. It is also important to develop good writing skills and to become well versed in metaphoric language. English composition and literature courses, in addition to art and psychology courses, help to prepare students for the rigors of undergraduate and graduate study.

Q. What are the most important personal and professional qualities for art therapy (AT) majors?

A. I believe that the most important personal and professional qualities for art therapy students are twofold: 1) a genuine love of art making, and 2) a deep commitment to humanity and a longing to make the world a better place. Of course it is important also to have some measure of artistic skill, a capacity to articulate ideas in a coherent manner, and the discipline to succeed as an art therapy scholar and practitioner.

Q. What advice would you offer AT majors as they graduate and look for jobs?

A. It is often important for art therapists to have an entrepreneurial spirit and to be willing to sell themselves to potential employers. Art therapy is a unique and potent treatment modality, but it is a little less well known than some other helping professions. It helps to be able to confidentially and clearly describe the profession to potential employers and to be able to make a strong case for why art therapy is needed in a particular setting.

I also always advise graduates to not let the ideal be the enemy of the good. By that I mean there are few 'perfect' jobs out in the world, and sometimes it is important to just get your foot in the door so that they can prove their worth.

Q. How will the field of art therapy change in the future?

A. I've been in the profession for more than 30 years now, and the field of art therapy has made many changes in that time. Many years ago the majority of art therapists worked in psychiatric hospitals. Today, however, the field has expanded to include art therapists in nursing homes, prisons, schools, community counseling agencies, hospice programs, rehabilitation hospitals, oncology units, and residential treatment facilities. I suspect that over the next 10 to 20 years ever more new applications of art therapy will emerge.

Another significant change will come about as more states codify licensure procedures for art therapists, which will result in art therapists routinely receiving third party payment for their services. All things considered, this is an exciting time to consider entering the profession of art therapy.

Automotive Engineering Technology

If you have a passion for cars, and an aptitude for engineering, a degree in automotive engineering technology might be right up your alley. While your in-class work will focus on design, development, and testing of all kinds of motorized vehicles, most programs will also require a significant amount of time getting practical, hands-on experience in a variety of settings. Of the career paths available to automotive engineers, all require an interactive, people-focused personality—you'll be working daily with customers and personnel from other departments. Careers in automotive engineering are plentiful; most graduates find jobs with major automotive manufacturers.

Typical Courses:

- Calculus
- Statistics
- DC Circuits
- Computer-Aided Drafting
- Material Processing and Metallurgy
- Automotive Drivability and Diagnosis
- Fluid Power Systems
- Automotive Thermodynamics and Engine Design
- Automotive Technology and Systems

Potential Employers:

- Automotive manufacturers
- Engineering firms

Available At:

Ferris State University (Big Rapids, MI)
231/591-2655
www.ferris.edu/automotive-engineering-college-degree.htm
Degrees available: Bachelor's degree

Lawrence Technological University (Southfield, MI)
248/204-2563
www.ltu.edu/engineering/mechanical/
engineering_mechanical__master_3.asp
Degrees available: Master's degree

Did You Know?

There were 21,200 dealerships selling new cars in the United States in 2006, according to the National Automobile Dealers Association.

University of Michigan (Ann Arbor, MI)
734/763-1134
autoeng@umich.edu
http://interpro.engin.umich.edu/auto
Degrees available: Bachelor's degree

Minnesota State University (Mankato, MN)
507/389-6383
http://cset.mnsu.edu/aet
Degrees available: Bachelor's degree

For More Information:

American Society for Engineering Education
202/331-3500
www.asee.org

Junior Engineering Technical Society
703/548-5387
info@jets.org
www.jets.org

Aviation Management

Aviation management prepares students to work in the airline industry in management, marketing, finance, sales, personnel, public relations, and other related areas. Programs can often have different areas of emphasis, based on the department in which they are housed. Some programs are designed for students interested in a curriculum containing a strong engineering science and analysis component, while others are for those who prefer a liberal arts background and a broader base of social sciences or business management principles. Some programs require actual flight training, while others do not. Degrees are available at all academic levels.

Typical Courses:

- Introduction to Aviation Management
- National Airspace Systems
- Air Traffic Control
- Aviation Law
- Airport Planning
- Airport Management
- Airline Management
- Airline Marketing
- General Aviation Operations
- Aviation Industry Regulation
- Aviation Management Writing and Communication
- Aviation Management Practices and Processes
- Air Transport Labor Relations
- Fiscal Aspects of Aviation Management
- Aviation Industry Career Development

Potential Employers:

- Airlines
- Commercial service airports (e.g., Chicago O'Hare International, Detroit Metro, and Los Angeles International)
- General aviation and reliever airports (e.g., Teterboro Airport, New Jersey, or DuPage Airport, Illinois)
- Federal Aviation Administration
- Transportation Security Administration
- Aviation/aerospace manufacturers (e.g., Lockheed-Martin, B. F. Goodrich Aerospace, Bell Helicopters-Textron, and The Boeing Company)
- General aviation companies (e.g., Cessna Aircraft Company, Signature Flight Support)

Available At:

The following list of aviation management programs is not exhaustive. Check with academic institutions near you to determine if majors, minors, or concentrations are available in aviation management. Additionally, for more information on accredited schools, contact the University Aviation Association (www.uaa.aero) and the Council on Aviation Accreditation (www.caaaccreditation.org/programs.html).

Auburn University (Auburn, AL)
cobweb@auburn.edu
http://business.auburn.edu/academicdepartments/aviation
Degrees available: Bachelor's degree, master's degree

Eastern Michigan University (Ypsilanti, MI)
734/487-1161
www.emich.edu/sts/aviation_management.htm
Degrees available: Bachelor's degree

Embry-Riddle Aeronautical University (Daytona Beach, FL)
386/226-6100 (undergraduate), 800/388-3728 (graduate)
www.erau.edu/db/degrees/b-aviationmgt.html
Degrees available: Bachelor's degree, master's degree

Indiana State University (Terre Haute, IN)
812/237-2641
http://aerospace.indstate.edu
Degrees available: Bachelor's degree

Louisiana Tech University (Ruston, LA)
318/257-2691
www.latech.edu/aviation
Degrees available: Bachelor's degree

Miami Dade College (multiple campuses, Florida)
https://sisvsr.mdc.edu/ps/sheet.aspx
Degrees available: Associate degree

The Ohio State University (Columbus, OH)
614/292-2405
aviation@osu.edu
http://aviation.osu.edu/considering_aviation/
degree_aviationmanage.php
Degrees available: Bachelor's degree

Southern Illinois University-Carbondale
618/453-8898
www.aviation.siu.edu
Degrees available: Bachelor's degree, master's degree

For More Information:

Air Transport Association of America
www.airlines.org

Council on Aviation Accreditation
www.caaaccreditation.org/programs.html

Federal Aviation Administration
www.faa.gov

University Aviation Association
www.uaa.aero

Interview: David NewMyer

Dr. David NewMyer, Professor and Chair of Aviation Management and Flight at Southern Illinois University Carbondale, discussed his program and the education of aviation management students with the editors of *They Teach That in College!?*

Q. Please provide an overview of your program.

A. The bachelor of science in aviation management program offered at Southern Illinois University Carbondale is a 48-semester-hour major consisting of the following:

1. A 12-semester hour set of core aviation management classes including such individual courses as Aviation Management Writing and Communication, Aviation Management Practices and Processes, Air Transport Labor Relations, Fiscal Aspects of Aviation Management, and Aviation Industry Career Development. A student enrolled in the Aviation Management program is required to take four of these five courses.
2. A 15-semester-hour set of Aviation Management major classes including Introduction to Aviation Management, Air Traffic Control, Airport Planning, Aviation Industry Regulation, Airport Management, Airline Management, General Aviation Operations, Legal Aspects of Aviation, Aviation Maintenance Management, Aviation Safety Management, Aviation Security Management and Regulation, National Airspace Systems and Aircraft Product Support Management. A student in the program must take five of these classes.
3. A nine-hour set of Aviation Management electives taken from the above list of classes or from a selected list of elective classes from other departments including psychology, marketing, information management systems, and many more.
4. A 12-hour set of internship, cooperative education, independent study, or approved equivalent classes. This requirement allows students the chance to go out and work in the aviation industry for college credit in any aviation industry segment (aviation manufacturing, airlines, general aviation and aviation-related government jobs).

A student in this major must also have either a technical background upon entry or must fulfill a 31-semester-hour approved career elective requirement that relates to the student's career objectives to enter a segment of the aviation industry.

Finally, a student in this major must complete a 41-semester-hour university core curriculum that includes mathematics, composition, public speaking, science, social science, humanities, fine arts, PE/health, and multicultural and interdisciplinary classes.

Students graduating with this major go on to work to all parts of the aviation industry: manufacturing, airlines, general aviation, government (including airports), and the military. Key job titles held by alumni include business operations professional, cost estimator, technical writer, aircraft product support specialist, facilities programmer, pilot/flight officer, aviation maintenance manager, on-board crew specialist, crew scheduler, dispatcher, ramp manager, customer service manager, airport manager, airport operations specialist, airport marketing representative, air traffic control specialist, general manager, director of corporate aviation, flight department manager, chief pilot, vice president (in several locations in the industry), and many more.

Q. How will the field change in the future?

A. The field of aviation management will change with the aviation industry as a whole. For example, one must follow aircraft technology trends (the Airbus A-380 and the Boeing 787 'Dreamliner'), the Very Light Jet phenomenon, and the explosion in the number of regional jets over the last decade. Also, one must follow what is going on operationally in the aviation industry; there have been many mergers of aerospace manufacturers, airlines, and general aviation companies over the past two decades. Also, low-cost carriers such as Southwest Airlines, jetBlue Airways, AirTran Airways, and Frontier Airlines are changing how airlines are managed and operated. Another area of opportunity is the Air Traffic Control field, a specialty field within aviation management. This field will experience growth in opportunities as Federal Aviation Administration air traffic controllers hired in the 1980s begin to retire. Finally, airports are expanding tremendously . . . consider the multi-million or multi-billion dollar expansions underway or just completed at St. Louis Lambert International and Chicago O'Hare International. All of these changes create opportunities for future aviation management majors. Future aviation management students wanting to know more should consult the latest Federal Aviation Administration (FAA) Aerospace Forecast at the FAA website, www.faa.gov

Bioinformatics

If you are interested in computer science and biology, then the new field of bioinformatics might be for you. Bioinformatics can be generally described as the application of cutting-edge computer science to analyze and manage biological information. Bioinformatics played a significant role in the Human Genome Project, and it has also helped shorten the research and development time for pharmaceuticals. Experts predict that bioinformatics will be used in the future to create designer drugs and treatments that will be much more effective for individual patients. Degrees in bioinformatics, sometimes known as biostatistics, are available at all levels, but advanced degrees are typically required for the best positions in the field.

Typical Courses:

- Fundamentals of Biology
- Genetics
- Cell and Molecular Biology
- Biochemistry
- Bioinformatics
- Bioethics
- Computer Science
- Database Design
- Fundamentals of Chemistry
- Organic Chemistry
- Calculus
- Statistics
- Data Structures
- Discrete Mathematics
- Algorithms

Potential Employers:

- Pharmaceutical companies (such as Sanofi Aventis, Bristol-Myers Squibb, Merck & Co., Pfizer, and Wyeth)
- Research laboratories
- Colleges and universities
- Government agencies
- Software companies

Available At:

Only a few colleges offer associate and bachelor's degrees in bioinformatics. For a list of colleges that offer graduate degrees in bioinformatics, visit www.colorado.edu/chemistry/bioinfo.

Boston University (Boston, MA)
617/358-0752
bioinfo@bu.edu
www.bu.edu/bioinformatics
Degrees available: Master's degree, doctorate degree

University of California-Santa Cruz
831/459-2158
www.soe.ucsc.edu/programs/bioinformatics
Degrees available: Bachelor's degree, master's degree, doctorate degree

Canisius College (Buffalo, NY)
716/888-2430
www.canisius.edu/bif
Degrees available: Bachelor's degree

University of Colorado (Denver, CO)
303/315-9030
http://pmb.uchsc.edu/biostatistics
Degrees available: Master's degree, doctorate degree

University of Denver (Denver, CO)
303/871-2453
www.cs.du.edu
Degrees available: Bachelor's degree

Howard Community College (Columbia, MD)
410/772-4827
www.howardcc.edu/academics/program_information/catalog/web/programs/ScienceTechnology/bioinformatics.html
Degrees available: Associate degree

University of Idaho (Moscow, ID)
208/885-6242
bcb@uidaho.edu
www.sci.uidaho.edu/biosci/BCB
Degrees available: Master's degree, doctorate degree

Indiana University (Indianapolis, IN)
317/278-4636
http://informatics.iupui.edu
Degrees available: Bachelor's degree, master's degree

Iowa State University (Ames, IA)
800/262-3810
www.iastate.edu/depts
Degrees available: Bachelor's degree, master's degree

Loyola University Chicago (Chicago, IL)
773/508-3640
hlaten@luc.edu
www.luc.edu/bioinformatics
Degrees available: Bachelor's degree

University of Minnesota (Minneapolis, MN)
612/626-3500
sph-ssc@umn.edu
http://www.biostat.umn.edu
Degrees available: Master's degree, doctorate degree

State University of New York-Buffalo
716/829-3690
sphhp-biostat@buffalo.edu
http://sphhp.buffalo.edu/biostat
Degrees available: Master's degree, doctorate degree

Northeastern University (Boston, MA)
617/373-2260
gradbio@neu.edu
www.bioinformatics.neu.edu
Degrees available: Master's degree

Ramapo College of New Jersey (Mahwah, NJ)
201/684-7722
http://bioinformatics.ramapo.edu
Degrees available: Bachelor's degree

Rochester Institute of Technology (Rochester, NY)
585/475-2532
http://bioinformatics.rit.edu
Degrees available: Bachelor's degree, master's degree

University of the Sciences (Philadelphia, PA)
215/596-8800
www.usip.edu/bioinformatics
Degrees available: Bachelor's degree, master's degree

University of Texas-El Paso
915/747-8484
bioinformatics@utep.edu
www.bioinformatics.utep.edu
Degrees available: Master's degree

For More Information:

American Association for the Advancement of Science
202/326-6400
www.aaas.org

Biotechnology Industry Organization
202/962-9200
www.bio.org

Interview: Howard Laten

Dr. Howard Laten, director of the Bioinformatics Program at Loyola University Chicago, discussed his program and the education of bioinformatics students with the editors of *They Teach That in College!?*

Q. Tell us about your program.

A. Bioinformatics is a new, four-year, interdisciplinary bachelor of science program in the College of Arts and Sciences at Loyola University Chicago. Bioinformatics is a discipline characterized by the collection, management, and analysis of massive biological and biochemical datasets utilizing computer hardware and software technologies. Bioinformatics creates knowledge from the mining of complex data relationships that only computer algorithms can evaluate. The Loyola curriculum features upper-level courses in genetics, biochemistry, computer science, and statistics that provide students with the knowledge and tools to enter this arena. Students will learn the fundamentals and applications in a field that is fueling revolutionary advances in medicine, agriculture, and environmental science, and leading to new discoveries in cell biology, genetics, and evolution. Students will also be exposed to the serious ethical issues this knowledge raises.

Q. Can you briefly detail a few medical and scientific breakthroughs that have been prompted by developments in bioinformatics?

A. Bioinformatics is directly responsible for the success of the Human Genome Project and all other genome projects—from fruit flies, to rice, to bird flu. Bioinformatics is directly responsible for new cancer diagnostic tools and treatment programs, and for the advent of personalized medicine—prescribing drugs based on patients' genetic and/or gene expression profiles. Bioinformatics has led to the discovery of the root causes of many genetic diseases, including Huntington's, muscular dystrophy, familial breast cancer, familial colon cancer, and is hot on the trail of others like Parkinson's, diabetes, and obesity. Improved varieties of corn, soybean, rice, and cotton are all outcomes of bioinformatics. Our understanding of the evolutionary relationships among all life on earth has been greatly enhanced by bioinformatics, and bioinformatics has enabled scientists to examine the complex relationship between the health of our bodies and the food and air we consume.

Q. What high school subjects/activities should students focus on to be successful in this major?

A. Students should take and enjoy science and math classes, and should embrace the power of computers in their everyday lives.

Q. Where do bioinformatics graduates find employment?

A. While many graduates continue their educational training in M.S., Ph.D., and applied health professions programs, immediate employment opportunities for graduates are found in academic, medical, and government research labs; in the pharmaceutical and biotechnology industries; and in scientific computing and health informatics companies.

Q. How will the field of bioinformatics change in the future?

A. The field will continue to expand and diversify for many years to come as scientists refocus their bioinformatics tools from the level of understanding the complexities of the genome to understanding the complexities of the organism. New technologies for data acquisition and for data storage and manipulation, as well as the continuing application of the technology to human health and agriculture, will influence these directions.

Biomedical Equipment Technology

Students who are mechanically inclined may enjoy working in the field of biomedical equipment technology. *Biomedical equipment technicians* maintain and repair important medical equipment such as lasers, x-ray equipment, and machines used to perform tests such as EKGs, CT scans, and MRIs. They may also modify or operate some medical instruments or equipment. They may work in laboratories and hospitals, medical equipment manufacturers, and in other locations that use medical equipment. Biomedical equipment technicians must be able to think quickly and work effectively under pressure, as they may be called to repair lifesaving equipment in time-sensitive situations. In addition to being mechanically inclined, workers in the field of biomedical equipment technology should also have good computer skills and communication skills. Demand for biomedical equipment technicians is expected to grow faster than the average for all occupations, according to the U.S. Department of Labor.

Typical Courses:

> Algebra and Trigonometry
> AC and DC Circuit Analysis
> Physiological Transducers
> Biomedical Instrumentation and Systems
> Biomedical Equipment Laboratory
> Computer Calculations for Electronics
> Analytic Geometry & Calculus
> Medical and Clinical Equipment
> Medical Technology Management
> Medical Equipment Troubleshooting
> Microprocessor Systems

Potential Employers:

> Hospitals
> Shared service organizations
> Other medical facilities

Available At:

The following programs are accredited by the Technology Accreditation Commission for the Accreditation Board for Engineering and Technology.

Chattahoochee Technical College (Marietta, GA)
770/528-4465
www.chattcollege.com/Default.aspx?tabid=43
Degrees available: Associate degree

Cuyahoga Community College (Cleveland, OH)
800/954-8742
www.tri-c.edu/programs/docs/subjects/engtech.htm
Degrees available: Associate degree

DeVry University (Decatur, GA)
www.devry.edu/programs/biomedical_engineering_technology/about.jsp
Degrees available: Bachelor's degree

DeVry University (Phoenix, AZ)
www.devry.edu/programs/biomedical_engineering_technology/about.jsp
Degrees available: Bachelor's degree

Pennsylvania State University-New Kensington Campus
888/968-7297
www.nk.psu.edu/Academics/Degrees/bet.html?cn215
Degrees available: Associate degree

The following schools offer training in biomedical equipment technology, but are not accredited by the Technology Accreditation Commission for the Accreditation Board for Engineering and Technology:

Cincinnati State Technical and Community College
(Cincinnati, OH)
513/861-7700
www.cincinnatistate.edu/FutureStudent/Academics/AcademicDivisions/EngineeringTechnologies/BMET.htm
Degrees available: Associate degree

Dakota County Technical College (Rosemount, MN)
651/423-8232
www.dctc.edu/prospStudents/programs/bioEquip.cfm
Degrees available: Certificate, associate degree

Delgado Community College-City Park Campus
(New Orleans, LA)
504/671-5012
enroll@dcc.edu
http://faculty-web.dcc.edu/busstud/technology/bio.htm
Degrees available: Associate degree

Howard Community College (Columbia, MD)
410/772-4827
www.howardcc.edu/academics/degrees_certs
Degrees available: Certificates, associate degree

Inver Hills Community College (Inver Grove Heights, MN)
(offered in partnership with Anoka-Ramsey Community College)
651/450-8500
www.inverhills.edu/AcademicPrograms/CareerPrograms/index.aspx
Degrees available: Certificate, associate degree

Linn State Technical College (Linn, MO)
800/743-8324
www.linnstate.edu/academic/bio/default.asp
Degrees available: Associate degree

Owens Community College-Toledo Campus (Toledo, OH)
800/466-9367, ext. 7000
www.owens.edu/academic_dept/iet/programs.html
Degrees available: Associate degree, advanced certificate

Southeast Technical Institute (Sioux Falls, SD)
800/247-0789
www.southeasttech.com
Degrees available: Associate degree

Texas State Technical College-Waco (Waco, TX)
254/867-4885
www.waco.tstc.edu/bet
Degrees available: Associate degrees

For More Information:

American Society for Healthcare Engineering
312/422-3800
ashe@aha.org
www.ashe.org

Association for the Advancement of Medical Instrumentation
703/525-4890
www.aami.org

Medical Equipment and Technology Association
www.mymeta.org

Interview: Myron Hartman

Myron Hartman is an instructor and the program coordinator for Pennsylvania State University's Biomedical Engineering Technology program, one of only five programs of its kind in the nation to be accredited by the Technology Accreditation Commission for the Accreditation Board for Engineering and

Technology. He discussed his program and the field of biomedical engineering technology (BET) with the editors of *They Teach That in College!?*

Q. Tell us about your program.

A. The BET program at Penn State University, New Kensington campus is a two-year associate program. The major prepares the BET graduates who, during the first few years of professional practice, will be able to: 1) Perform preventive maintenance and assurance and safety inspections on a wide range of medical devices; 2) Understand use, application, and operation on a wide range of medical equipment and systems, with normal/abnormal outcomes/measurements; 3) Demonstrate a broad knowledge of electrical and electronic engineering technology fundamentals, components, and circuits; 4) Apply basic mathematical and scientific principals to identify, analyze, and solve technical problems on a wide range of medical equipment and systems; 5) Understand use and application of applicable test equipment, simulators, and tools required to [perform] preventive maintenance and service medical equipment and systems; 6) Be aware of, understand, and apply codes, standards, and regulations regarding medical equipment support; 7) Perform and assist with application design, installation, and acceptance testing for medical equipment and systems; 8) Work with fellow technicians, clinical professionals, and other related professionals by functioning effectively on committees and teams, and by independent work; 9) Properly document actions and follow required procedures, policies, and regulatory requirements; 10) Communicate effectively with fellow technicians, clinical professionals, and other related professionals; 11) Continue professional development by participating in education and training on medical equipment and systems; 12) Participate in quality improvement programs that support medical equipment and systems; and 13) Participate in recognizing, reporting, and monitoring improvements to medical equipment and the related profession, as required by regulation and on a professional voluntary basis.

Q. What classes should high school students take to prepare for postsecondary BET programs?

A. For high school students preparing to enter any technical program, the following courses are essential: math (algebra and trigonometry), English, physics, chemistry, and any other science-related studies.

Q. What qualities do students need to be successful in their careers?

A. The number one skill to be successful in the BET field is customer skills. You must be able to work well with other people, and able to communicate, empathize with people's situations, understand the who-what-where-when-why of situations, and have a good attitude and smile. You also must be a self starter and be able to work independently, as most BMETs set their priorities for each work day and to what must be completed. Next would be the technical ability of problem solving—the ability to use electronic test equipment, computers, software, and tools to diagnose, dissemble, repair, calibrate, and test medical equipment. One additional skill would be creativity in problem solving. Many problems must be solved in short time frames, so being able to think quickly, know your resources, read technical manuals, contact and communicate with technical support departments, and solve the problem to meet the needs of the customer [are key].

Q. What is the future employment outlook for biomedical equipment technicians?

A. I think the employment opportunity is the best it has ever been. With only five ABET-accredited schools in the nation and fewer BET programs in general, there are fewer qualified people entering the profession. Individuals who started in the field in the late 70s are approaching retirement age, with some advancing to management and other related positions. Some hospitals have hired individuals with electronics or computer science degrees, but these individuals do not have the necessary fundamentals to be proficient as a BMET. Since I have been at Penn State, the employment placement is close to 100 percent. Graduates make good starting salaries, and advancement normally happens within a year or so after employment.

One of the biggest problems in getting more people interested in the field is that very few know it exists. Guidance counselors, high school teachers, and the public in general are not even aware of the profession. It is so specific, with very few schools offering programs, it is the best-kept secret for a rewarding field. Most people discover the program through a neighbor or relative who works in the field. But for those who do discover it, it is a very rewarding professional career. If you have good people skills, a good attitude, are open to relocation, and have passing grades and fairly good technical skills, you will get a job in this profession.

Biomedical Photography

Students who are interested in the biological sciences and photography may want to learn more about careers in biomedical photography. Students in biomedical photography programs explore the field by learning more about digital and traditional photography and their uses in science, medicine, technology, and industry. Classroom topics include black and white and color photography, close-up and high-magnification photography, lighting, ophthalmic photography, imaging technologies, desktop publishing software, computer graphics, techniques for biomedical news and public relations photography, equipment and techniques for magnified images, and planning, executing and presenting a professional portfolio. Some colleges offer specialized areas of concentration such as photography of the patient for medical documentation, public relations, standardization of lighting in the studio, close-up photography, photomicrography, digital imaging, and video and audio-visual presentation. The Rochester Institute of Technology offers the only bachelor's degree in the field.

Typical Courses:

- Black and White Photography
- Color Photography
- Biomedical Photography
- Photography and the Microscope
- Digital Media
- Biology
- Desktop Publishing
- Creating a Portfolio

Potential Employers:

- Hospitals
- Colleges and universities
- Medical publishers
- Medical examiners' offices
- Forensic laboratories
- Pharmaceutical companies
- Health care and medical research centers
- Ophthalmic practices
- Producers of multimedia and web publishing

Available At:

Randolph Community College (Asheboro, NC)
336/633-0200
www.randolph.cc.nc.us/edprog/curr/bioph.html
Degrees available: Associate degree

Rochester Institute of Technology (Rochester, NY)
biomed@rit.edu
http://biomed.rit.edu
Degrees available: Bachelor's degree

For More Information:

BioCommunications Association
919/245-0906
office@bca.org
www.bca.org

Health and Science Communications Association
860/376-5915
www.hesca.org

Ophthalmic Photographers' Society
ops@opsweb.org
www.opsweb.org

Interview: Michael Peres

The Rochester Institute of Technology (RIT) is the only school in the United States that grants a bachelor of science in this exciting field. The editors of *They Teach That in College!?* discussed the field of biomedical photography with Professor Michael Peres, Chair of RIT's Biomedical Photographic Communications Department.

Q. What is biomedical photography?

A. Biomedical photography might be defined as photodocumentation that is applied to the biological sciences. The biological sciences might include human and veterinary medicine with sub-specialties in ophthalmology and forensic science (medical examiner's office), as well as bio-research (e.g., agriculture, entomology, pharmaceuticals, etc.). In these various applications/industries, the images that are created represent data and/or scientific facts. One might characterize this type of photography as information imaging. It can include both still- and motion/time-based photography, as well as other computer imaging.

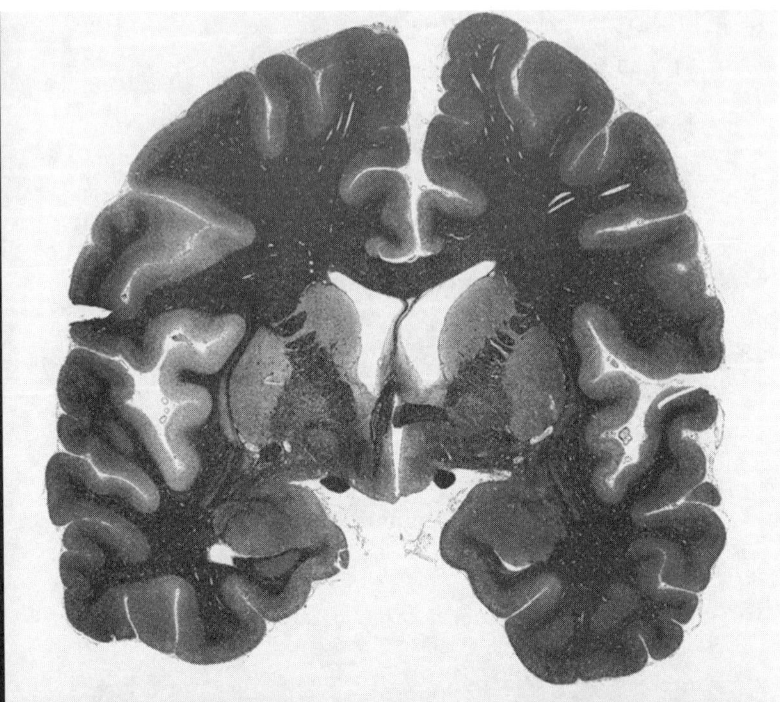

A coronal section of human cerebellum. Photographed at life size at capture. (Image courtesy of Professor Michael Peres, Rochester Institute of Technology)

Q. What are some examples of the types of biomedical subjects that are frequently photographed?

A. People who are having plastic surgery, including their pre- and post-operative conditions, might be representative of subjects of this type of photography. In dermatology, there is pre-screening photography for skin cancer where changes in moles are monitored photographically to monitor changes in color and/or size. In ophthalmic photography, retinal images are made in large numbers in a test called a fluorescein angiogram. In laboratory work, using a microscope is also common for subjects smaller than a rice grain. Depending on the application/industry, anything might be a subject.

Q. Please describe a typical student in your program.

A. The typical student is both creative and technical. He or she loves to solve problems that requires the use of tools (cameras/lights) and processes that are both analytical and conceptual. An example of this might be how to develop and use a system to photograph a round transparent subject such as a contact lens, or how to create a solution to photograph something invisible such as a headache.

He or she is also self directed, like science, love photography and pictures, have analytical minds, and like using the computer to enhance and to distribute the work either through the web, through print, or with multimedia. He or she also enjoys working with people and is interested in a career in the photographic services industry.

Q. What type of co-ops or internships are available to students in your program?

A. All students are required to complete at least one work study block. The minimum co-op requirement suggests an eight-week duration that is paid and a minimum of 20 hours per week. Almost all students find a 10-week block that is full-time. We often will have approximately 20 students on co-op during a typical summer. Over the course of the last few years, some traditional sponsors include the Veterans Administration medical centers across the country, various research labs in the Smithsonian Institute, Columbia University Hospital, The Mayo Clinic, Cleveland Clinic, Zeiss MicroImaging, FujiFilm, and Johns Hopkins Hospital, to name a few.

Q. What types of career options are available to graduates of your program?

A. After they graduate, students are fairly open minded to many options in the job market. Ophthalmic photography continues to be the dominant career option for biomed students. There is often one job opportunity per week anywhere in the United States—with a starting salary of approximately $38,000.

Other positions exist in the pharmaceutical industry, in human medicine, in forensic labs, in and veterinary schools; some graduates work as visual imaging specialists for the military or industrial sectors. Job titles include ophthalmic photographer, visual imaging expert, medical photographer, graphics specialist, technical services representative, photographic researcher, and multimedia specialist.

Q. What is the future for your program and biomedical photography in general?

A. The future for our program seems stable. Biomed is a small department, so finding employment for 12-15 highly motivated, smart imaging experts seems more than achievable. For now, the department is fixed in its capacity to take and place more students because of space, faculty and the equipment realities.

Biomedical photography in the United States has undergone significant changes as a consequence of nationally recognized changes in the health care industry and reimbursement procedures, as well as the complete integration of digital photography into that same industry. Ophthalmic photography is experiencing growth for now, and although this trend may slow in the next years, the industry is readily accepting highly skilled people. We have also observed easy placement of our graduates into the "instructional media industry," such as companies that produce home school educational products.

Biometric Systems

Fingerprinting has been used for more than a century to identify people, primarily in the field of law enforcement, since it was determined that every human being has a unique set of fingerprints. But did you also know that our eyes, voices, and even our faces all contain unique, one-of-a-kind signatures that can be electronically measured and used for identification purposes? Today, manual fingerprinting is replaced by digital imaging, and a whole new field of study is being devoted to the development of technologies to identify humans by unique physical characteristics, no longer just for the purpose of law enforcement. This technology is used to restrict access in buildings where security is top priority, but it is also increasingly be used for other purposes. Banking centers are beginning to use biometric systems hoping to make pin numbers a thing of the past and decrease identity theft. Businesses use this technology as a means to clock in employees or check in members. The potential uses and applications of this technology continue to grow. The bachelor's program in biometric systems at West Virginia University is currently the only program in the country dedicated to the study of this fascinating discipline.

Typical Courses:

> Biology
> Chemistry
> Physics
> Calculus
> Microprocessor Systems
> Computer Security
> Bioengineering
> Economics
> Forensic Statistics
> Electrical Circuits
> Biometric Systems

Potential Employers:

> Law enforcement agencies
> Scientific laboratories
> Government agencies
> Private companies that build biometric systems or that integrate biometric systems into their existing products

Available At:

West Virginia University (Morgantown, WV)
304/293-LANE, ext. 2515
www.wvu.edu/~forensic
Degrees available: Bachelor's degree, advanced certificate

For More Information:

The Biometric Consortium
www.biometrics.org

Biometrics Catalog
www.biometricscatalog.org

National Biometric Security Project
http://nationalbiometric.org

Interview: Lawrence Hornak

Dr. Lawrence Hornak is a professor and biometrics advisor in the Lane Department of Computer Science and Electrical Engineering at West Virginia University (WVU), which is located in Morgantown, West Virginia. He discussed his program and the education of biometrics students with the editors of *They Teach That in College!?*

Q. What is biometrics?

A. Biometrics is a convergence of many disciplines, which is part of its attraction to students and faculty alike. Basically, a biometric system is a set of hardware and software that is optimized to capture information about a person, process it, reduce it to its bare essentials, and then compare it to previously enrolled information to see if there is a match. It is through this process that a person's identity is either ascertained or is verified. This is what biometrics is all about. Currently, the information available comes from sensors, which are basically cameras or use other data capture systems that capture aspects of the person's physiology (iris pattern, fingerprint, face, hand, voice). Eventually, one can envision this moving to a molecular realm as devices advance for this purpose.

Q. Please provide an overview of your biometrics program.

A. The biometric systems program at WVU is the only B.S. program in existence specifically focused on this very important area. The required curriculum of the bachelor of science degree in biometric systems is 130 credit hours.

Biometric identification is a highly interdisciplinary field. Designers work with the physics of the sensor to obtain measurements of the biometric defined by human physiology. Signal and image processing techniques are applied to the sensor signal and pattern recognition employed to extract features usable for identification. Databases combined with artificial intelligence enable rapid storage, retrieval, and pattern matching, while decision theory supports the mechanisms whereby systems can provide the needed identification results. Underlying the entire system is a foundation of statistics and mathematics that provides the language for implementing and evaluating biometric technology and systems. Given the interdisciplinary nature of the field, the program provides students with a firm foundation in electrical and computer engineering and computer science meshed with an understanding of biology, physiology, forensics, and the interaction between living and nonliving materials and systems necessary to design, implement, and evaluate biometric systems. This foundation is built on a strong framework of mathematics, statistics, and physical sciences complemented by an appropriate general studies component including psychology and physiology to give students an understanding of the human factors involved in acceptance and use of biometric systems.

Emphasis areas established through choice of specific course sets in the junior and senior year enable students to tailor their degree to follow their interests in key areas of biometric system development. Currently designated areas of emphasis are Sensors and Circuits, Signal Processing, Statistics, and Software Systems.

Engineering design experiences are a central part of many of the curriculum's courses beginning in the very first semester of the program. The design experience concludes with a capstone two-semester design course in the senior year in which students form teams to plan and build biometric systems and subsystems of their own design.

Q. What are the most important qualities for biometrics majors?

A. The most successful students have a great drive to not only explore but, once they start down a path, to complete a job they have started. During the program, students who develop a mix of strong technical and interpersonal skills are the most successful. Students think engineers and systems designers work in solitary. This could not be further from the truth. In fact, most of the time they spend is in managing and working with others to effectively achieve a goal.

Q. What advice would you offer biometrics majors as they graduate and look for jobs?

A. Keep the big picture and know that there is tremendous opportunity for you to shape the future, given the fact that biometrics technology can have application in virtually all areas of day-to-day living to enable convenience, privacy, and security. Moreover, always keep in mind that especially in the area of biometrics, your greatest technical solution is only as good as people's willingness to accept it. So work on building acceptance in parallel with building the system.

Q. How is the field of biometrics changing the world in which we live?

A. As for the impact of biometrics, it is significant. Irrespective of the technological era, trust and privacy are the cornerstones of a free and democratic society. Long term, the pervasiveness achieved by information technology within our society will be enabled or inhibited by the degree to which society perceives that it secures and strengthens these cornerstones. Whether the supporting technology be parchment or quantum electronics, the underlying process to be upheld remains the same. Whether the individual is boarding a plane, purchasing online, or accessing medical records, the efficacy of the supporting technology will be judged by its ability to promote and preserve trust among parties through its transparency, preservation of privacy, and resistance to attack. To date, information technology has demonstrated a tremendous potential to provide the framework for such trusted processes on a global scale while at the same time opening new opportunities for freedom of access to information, services, and products. However, realizing this potential in an environment of rising security requirements hinges critically upon achieving robust authentication of individual users. Biometric authentication moves beyond faceless logins and passwords to authentication that tightly binds user actions to the individual physical identity of the user. This is not a short-term need precipitated by current world events but a long-term direction prerequisite to the needed establishment of trust and preservation of privacy early in the evolution of Information Technology. As embedded computing and wireless technology extends processing power and network connectivity to virtually every object and space with which we interact, transparent, automated human biometric identification will be enable to achieve the trusted processes essential for the acceptance by society of this truly pervasive and ubiquitous computing environment.

Biotechnology

The Biotechnology Industry Organization defines biotechnology as the use of cellular and molecular processes to solve problems or make products, such as vaccines, diagnostic tests, disease-resistant crops, and so forth. Since the anthrax attacks of 2001, which made the general public aware of the threat of bioterrorism, the biotech field has gained attention. Biotech workers, after all, are the ones who work on developing ways of detecting the presence of infectious diseases as well as developing the antidotes to save us. Of course, not every biotech worker walks around in a contamination suit passing out vaccines. Areas of the industry include research and development, clinical research, manufacturing, and quality control. Since many specialties exist in biotechnology, there are many ways to train for the field. For example, scientists working in research and development may have a Ph.D. in a science field, an M.D., or both. Others who work in research and development may include laboratory assistants, research assistants, and plant breeders. These workers do not need advanced degrees such as a Ph.D. In fact, many may have diplomas or associate degrees in biotechnology. Workers in clinical research, also known as testing or validation, usually have science degrees or nursing degrees. Those in administrative positions may have more advanced degrees. Engineers in manufacturing and quality control need at least a bachelor's degree in their specialty; technicians need associate degrees. The biotechnology industry in the United States has grown rapidly, nearly quadrupling in revenues from 1992 to 2003, according to the Biotechnology Industry Organization.

Typical Courses:

- General Biology
- General Biology Laboratory
- Cell Biology
- Molecular Biology
- Immunology
- Microbiology
- High Performance Computing for Bioinformatics
- Ethical Issues in Medicine and Biology
- Genetic Engineering
- Genomics
- Bioinformatics

Potential Employers:

- > Biotechnology companies
- > Agriculture industry
- > Food industry
- > Pharmaceutical industry
- > Government agencies
- > Health care industry

Available At:

The following list of biotechnology programs is not exhaustive. For a list of graduate programs in biotechnology, visit www.gradschools.com.

Camden County College (Camden, NJ)
865/227-7200, ext. 4479
www.camdencc.edu/departments/biotechnology
Degrees available: Associate degree

Columbia University (New York, NY)
212/854-2313
www.columbia.edu/cu/biology/pages/ma-biotech/pro/intro
Degrees available: Master's degree

East Stroudsburg University of Pennsylvania (East Stroudsburg)
570/422-3704
www.esu.edu/biotech/index.html
Degrees available: Bachelor's degree

Houston Community College (multiple campuses, Texas)
www.hccs.edu/discipline/Bitc/bitc.htmL
Degrees available: Certificate, associate degree

Iowa State University (Ames, IA)
800/262-3810
www.biotech.iastate.edu
Degrees available: Bachelor's degree

Kent State University (Kent, OH)
330/672-3613
dstroup1@kent.edu
http://bioweb.biology.kent.edu
Degrees available: Bachelor's degree

Niagara University (Niagara, NY)
800/778-3450
www.niagara.edu/biology
Degrees available: Bachelor's degree

Rochester Institute of Technology (Rochester, NY)
585/475-2411
www.rit.edu/~932www/ugrad_bulletin/colleges/cos/biotech.html
Degrees available: Bachelor's degree

For More Information:

Biotechnology Industry Organization
202/962-9200
info@bio.org
www.bio.org

National Center for Biotechnology Information
301/496-2475
info@ncbi.nlm.nih.gov
www.ncbi.nlm.nih.gov

BioWorld Online
www.bioworld.com

Interview: Diane Stroup

Dr. Diane Stroup, director of biotechnology and an associate professor of chemistry at Kent State University in Kent, Ohio, discussed her program and the education of biotechnology students with the editors of *They Teach That in College!?*

Q. Please provide an overview of your program.

A. Kent State University offers a four-year program that leads to a bachelor of science degree in biotechnology. This challenging curriculum includes courses in biology, chemistry, recombinant DNA, and bioinformatics. A notable feature of the program is the amount of hands-on laboratory experience acquired through an individual laboratory project or external internship.

Q. What type of internship opportunities are provided by your program?

A. Students enrolled in the program can receive up to nine credit hours towards completion of their degree through their work in an approved internship. Students have the choice of working with one of the Kent State University researchers on campus, or off-site in a private or government laboratory. The projects vary according to the student's interests.

Q. What classes should high school students take to be successful in this major?

A. Students should have a good foundation in mathematics, preferably pre-calculus. Chemistry is fundamental to all of

Get Started in High School

To prepare for a career in biotechnology, take as many health, biology, anatomy and physiology, mathematics, biology, chemistry, physics, English, and speech classes in high school as you can. You can also read books and visit websites about biotechnology or talk with your counselor or teacher about setting up a presentation by a biotechnology worker.

the natural sciences, so preparation in this subject useful. Students who acquire foreign language skills have an advantage in that they can test out of part of the university foreign language requirement.

Q. What are the most important personal and professional qualities for biotechnology students?

A. Biotechnology is a diverse field, attracting people with wide ranges of talents. However, they all share one dominant characteristic: a strong desire to improve the world. Biotechnology is transforming the way food is produced, speeding the development of new medical treatments, restoring contaminated environments to their original condition, and providing alternative sources of fuel. People working towards this brighter future are flexible and can adapt to change.

Q. How will the field of biotechnology change in the future?

A. A better question would be how biotechnology is changing the future. The main thrust of biotechnology is to provide solutions to problems that threaten human life and the environment. The field is characterized by making things better, faster, and cleaner. The Kent State University B.S. in biotechnology is designed to prepare individuals for the rapidly changing opportunities and to grow in pace with the improvements that they have helped bring about.

Bowling Industry Management

Training in all phases of bowling center operations—from sales and marketing to pinsetter maintenance—makes a degree in bowling industry management a unique educational investment. In today's exceedingly competitive recreational industry, such highly specialized training programs position the future bowling industry manager ahead of the crowd. Vincennes University is the only college in the United States to offer a degree in bowling industry management.

Typical Courses:

> Accounting
> Lane and Pinsetter Maintenance
> Marketing
> Computer Science
> Business English
> Pro Shop Operations
> Personal Fitness Management
> Psychology
> Management

Potential Employers:

> Self-employment (opening your own bowling center)
> Company-owed recreational facilities
> Equipment manufacturers

Available At:

Vincennes University (Vincennes, IN)
812/888-4428
www.vinu.edu
Degrees available: Associate degree

For More Information:

Professional Bowlers Association
www.pba.com

Bowl.com
www.bowl.com

Interview: Gary Sparks

Gary Sparks is the director of the Bowling Lanes Management Program at Vincennes University in Vincennes, Indiana. He is also the coach of the Vincennes University bowling program and a member of the National Junior College Athletic Association's Hall of Fame. Mr. Sparks discussed his program and the education of students in the field with the editors of *They Teach That in College!?*

Q. Tell us about your program.

A. The program offers either an A.S. or A.A.S. degree in Bowling Industry Management, depending on what level of some of the general education classes that are taken. The degree itself is a comprehensive program that goes through all aspects of the operation of a bowling center, including mechanics, maintenance, and the "core" operations of building lineage and leagues, including dealing with employees and all the financial obligations that go with running a business.

Q. What are the most important personal and professional qualities for bowling industry management majors?

A. Good bowling center managers are those who have good "people" skills. A good personality, the ability to work and interact with others, leadership qualities, and decision-making qualities are all strong components of being a successful center manager.

Q. Where do bowling industry management graduates find employment?

A. Graduates have many opportunities in the entire bowling industry field for potential employment. The "management" side is still the biggest core, getting directly into managing a center or being an assistant manager for a time before moving up. But we also place many graduates into sales, marketing, and technical positions within the industry. Some graduates have went out into the pro shop business area, so that becomes a potential area as well.

Broadcast Meteorology

F5 tornadoes, hurricanes, floods, scorching heat, blizzards. Weather plays a significant role in how we live our daily lives. And the reporting of weather conditions has become a major part of television and radio newscasts. There is even an entire television channel—The Weather Channel—devoted to keeping people informed about weather conditions around our country and the world. As a result, college programs have sprung up to train interested students in broadcast meteorology. Students should be prepared for a solid core of classes in both meteorological science and communication. While some programs offer or require a larger set of classes with a focus on media and broadcasting, all programs require a strong aptitude in the science of meteorology. Only a handful of colleges and universities in the United States offer degrees in broadcast meteorology.

Typical Courses:

> Algebra
> Calculus
> Physics
> News Writing
> Atmospheric Structure
> Global Physical Climatology
> Commercial Meteorology
> Speech Composition and Presentation
> Weather Analysis and Forecasting
> Television Production

Potential Employers:

> Affiliate television stations
> Cable television stations
> Public and private forecasting firms
> Environmental consulting firms
> National Weather Service
> Airlines

Available At:

Mississippi State University (Mississippi State, MS)
662/325-3915
www.msstate.edu/dept/geosciences/broadcast-meteorology.htm
Degrees available: Bachelor's degree, master's degree

Did You Know?

Meteorology is one of the oldest of modern sciences. The word itself was coined by Aristotle more than 2,000 years ago for the first textbook on the science of "things lifted up."

State University of New York-Albany
518/442-4556
www.atmos.albany.edu
Degrees available: Bachelor's degree

Pennsylvania State University (University Park, PA)
814/865-0478
www.met.psu.edu/dept/undprog
Degrees available: Bachelor's degree, master's degree, doctorate

Valparaiso University (Valparaiso, IN)
219/464-5000
www.valpo.edu/geomet/met/met.html
Degrees available: Bachelor's degree

For More Information:

American Meteorological Society
www.ametsoc.org

Broadcast Education Association
www.beaweb.org

National Association of Broadcasters
www.nab.org

National Weather Association
www.nwas.org

National Weather Service
www.nws.noaa.gov

Interview: Paul Knight

Paul Knight is the director of the Weather Forecasting and Communications Option in the Department of Meteorology at Pennsylvania State University in University Park, Pennsylvania. He discussed his program and the education of broadcast meteorology students with the editors of *They Teach That in College!?*

Q. Please provide an overview of your program.

A. The Weather Communication option for a bachelor of science degree in meteorology from Penn State allows students in their last two years of undergraduate study to specialize in courses related to the communications of weather information. Students in this option, which is indicated on their diploma, are required to take approximately 20 credits of both core and elective courses in this field. The core courses include Weather Prediction, Mesoscale Meteorology, Weather Communications Part 1 And 2, and an intensive writing course.

Q. What high school subjects/activities should students focus on to be successful in this major?

A. High school students interested in pursuing a career in weather communications would be well advised to take both physics and calculus. Any options for advanced earth science courses would be recommended as well as experience in communications (school newspaper, radio, or television). Performing in theater and musical talent would also help prepare for this major.

Q. What are the most important personal and professional qualities for broadcast meteorology majors?

A. The ability to speak in front of varying size groups of people is required. It is even better if you enjoy it! A good sense of humor is necessary since everyone's forecasts go awry, and dealing with criticism in a healthy and constructive way is very important. Gaining confidence in your abilities to make a highly visible presentation as well as being willing to improve one's personal appearance are useful qualities. Ultimately, the most important is a passion for learning, especially the science of the atmosphere.

Q. How will the field of broadcast meteorology change in the future?

A. As broadcasting becomes narrow-casting due to the convergence of the Internet and television as well as the advent of hi-definition television, the opportunities for communicating weather information will increase. Computer skills related to web interface development and database management will become an important need in this field.

Comic Book Art

Career opportunities in comic book art are as varied as the genres of comic books currently published—ranging from humorous to horror fantasy to graphic novels that combine many elements. *Cartoonists* and *comic illustrators* draw comic strips and caricatures for publications, calendars, greeting cards, or clothing lines. *Comic writers and editors* combine their artwork with plotlines and dialogue in order to tell a story, many times using humor or irony. The background layout of many comic strips and cartoons are completed by a team of artists including *colorists* or *background artists;* who color the background scenes; *letterers,* who fill comic balloons with dialogue or interjections; and *inkers* who outline figures and background to add dimension. While a talent for drawing is a plus, comic book art programs teach students the importance of character and plot development and storyboarding in creating believable characters. The popularity and scope of cartoons and anime is greater than ever, especially since many artists use the Internet to create and display their work.

Typical Courses:

> Comic Art
> Illustration
> Introduction to Animation
> Drawing: Observation
> Drawing: Color
> Drawing: Figure
> Professional Practice
> Internship

Potential Employers:

> Comic book publishers
> Graphic design firms
> Publishing companies
> Newspapers and magazines

Available At:

Center for Cartoon Studies (White River Junction, VT)
802/295-3319
www.cartoonstudies.org
Degrees available: Certificate, master's degree

Minneapolis College of Art and Design (Minneapolis, MN)
800/874-6223
www.mcad.edu/showPage.php?pageID=1058
Degrees available: Bachelor's degree, master's degree

Rhode Island School of Design (Providence, RI)
800/364-RISD
www.risd.edu/ce_comic.cfm
Degrees available: Certificate

For More Information:

National Cartoonists Society
www.reuben.org

Compressed Air and Gas Systems

Hocking College in Nelsonville, Ohio, offers the only two-year Compressed Air & Gas Systems (CAGS) program in the nation. Hocking's Compressed Air and Gas Systems Program currently offers an associate in applied science degree in compressed air and gas systems as well as certificates in rotary screw compressors, reciprocating compressors, and pneumatics. "Compressed air systems," according to Steve West, the instructional coordinator of Hocking's CAGS program, "are used in industry to power pneumatic tools and devices ranging from air impact guns, to sand blasters, to air starters on gas engines, to linear pneumatic cylinders. Compressed gas systems are also, in some cases, used to power pneumatic devices, although compressed natural gas is pressurized into pipelines and distributed throughout the country to industries and households for energy purposes."

Typical Courses:

- Compressor Practicum
- Hydraulics And Pneumatics
- Compressed Air Applications
- Air System Design
- Precision Instruments
- Centrifugal Compressors
- Compressed Air Systems Troubleshooting
- Vacuum Pumps/Blowers
- Rotary Screw Compressors
- Basic Refrigeration

Potential Employers:

- Distributorships
- Repair centers
- Any industry that used compressed air and gas systems

Available At:

Hocking College (Nelsonville, OH)
877/462-5464
www.hocking.edu/academics/schools/industrial_technology

For More Information:

Compressed Air and Gas Institute
216/241-7333
cagi@cagi.org
www.cagi.org

Interview: Steve West

Steve West is the instructional coordinator of the Compressed Air & Gas Systems Program at Hocking College in Nelsonville, Ohio. Mr. West discussed his school's program and the education of students in this field with the editors of *They Teach That in College!?*

Q. What are compressed air and gas systems?

A. The definition of a compressed air/gas system would be the distribution network of a compressed air/gas plant including the compressor that produces the compressed air/gas, the dryers that remove moisture from the compressed air/gas, filters that remove contamination from the compressed air/gas, and the piping that distributes the compressed air or gas to a point of use.

Students who graduate from Hocking College's CAGS Program receive training in the maintenance and repair on all the components of the compressed air/gas network including the compressor, the dryer, the filtering system, and the piping system.

The general public is probably not aware that compressed air is, for all intents and purposes, a utility. Many manufacturing plants are dependent upon compressed air as much as they are upon electricity, water, or steam. Just as an example, one automobile assembly plant in the state of Ohio has indicated that it loses over $600,000 per hour with a total loss of compressed air capability. It goes without saying that it will take some very responsible and technically savvy service technicians to provide a seamless and non-ending supply of compressed air to industries and plants such as the one mentioned above.

Q. What high school subjects/activities should students focus on to be successful in this major?

A. The Compressed Air and Gas Systems Program typically has students from both vocational and regular high schools.

Vocational training that includes refrigeration, electrical, or plumbing skills is excellent preparation for the CAGS Program. Conversely, the CAGS Program has had students who had no experience in any of the above-cited skills, who have graduated and been successful as technicians.

Q. What are the most important personal and professional qualities for CAGS students?

A. The most important requisite personal and professional qualities for students interested in becoming CAGS technicians are "hands-on" abilities with tools and equipment and customer service skills. Students must also be interested in continuing their technical education after graduation through corporate-sponsored training and Internet based types of training.

Q. Where do compressed air and gas systems graduates find employment?

A. Graduates of Hocking College's CAGS Program have been successful obtaining service technician positions at distributorships and repair centers for Ingersoll-Rand, Atlas-Copco, Gardner-Denver, CompAir, and more. Starting wages for technicians range from $10 to $15 per hour. Technicians who complete additional company-sponsored training/certification programs can eventually earn more than $100,000 per year.

Computer and Digital Forensics

A new field of study is emerging from two hot career areas—computers and forensics. Computer and digital forensics combines computer know-how with the meticulous methods of forensic science. Due to the prevalence of computers in society today, many criminal activities utilize computers—creating a need for the *computer and digital forensic specialist.* Computer and digital forensic specialists work to find evidence of such things as the tampering, destruction, or copying of files, email, or instant messages. They also track such things as Internet usage and the use of restricted programs or databases. In many cases they must be careful to extract the sought-after computer data without destroying the original version, and to preserve the data in question in such a way that it will hold up in a court of law.

Typical Courses:

- Analysis of Digital Media
- Investigative Interviewing
- Computer Forensics
- Criminal Investigation
- Introduction to Statistics
- Computer and Network Security
- Financial Accounting
- Forensic Accounting
- Criminal Law
- Preserving/Documenting Evidence

Potential Employers:

- Law enforcement agencies
- Government agencies
- U.S. military
- Corporations
- Law firms
- Accounting firms

Available At:

The following list of colleges and universities that offer programs in computer and digital forensics is not exhaustive. Visit the website of the

American Academy of Forensic Sciences (www.aafs.org) for a complete list of schools that offer training in computer forensics and other forensics-related specialties. Visit the website (www.e-evidence.info/education.html) for additional schools with developing programs in computer forensics and/or courses and minors in computer forensics.

California State University-Fullerton
www.csufextension.org/Classes/Certificate
Degrees available: Advanced certificate

Champlain College (Burlington, VT)
802/865-6460
http://digitalforensics.champlain.edu
Degrees available: Certificate, bachelor's degree

George Washington University (Washington, DC)
703/248-6208
www.gwu.edu/~mastergw/programs/crime_commerce
Degrees available: Master's degree

Iowa Lakes Community College (Estherville, IA)
712/362-7981
www.iowalakes.edu/programs_study/social_human/criminal_justice/computer_forensics.htm
Degrees available: Associate degree

Johns Hopkins University (Columbia, MD)
410/516-4234
http://carey.jhu.edu/undergraduate-programs/bsis/digital-forensics-concentration
Degrees available: Bachelor's degree

North Carolina Wesleyan College (Rocky Mount, NC)
877/629-2237
http://annex.ncwc.edu/adult%5Fdegree/certificate/certificate.htm
Degrees available: Certificate

Community College of Philadelphia (Philadelphia, PA)
215/751-8010
www.ccp.edu/site/academic/degrees/computer_forensics.php
Degrees available: Associate degree

Southern Utah University (Cedar City, UT)
435/586-7700
www.suu.edu/ciet/csis/cs_degrees_bachelor.html
Degrees available: Bachelor's degree

Utica College (Utica, NY)
866/295-3106
http://www.utica.edu/academic/ssm/cybersecurity
Degrees available: Bachelor's degree, master's degree

For More Information:

American Academy of Forensic Sciences
www.aafs.org

IEEE Computer Society
www.computer.org

National Association of Forensic Accountants
www.nafanet.com

National Center for Forensic Science
http://ncfs.ucf.edu/home.html

Interview: Gary Kessler

The Computer and Digital Forensics program at Champlain College in Burlington, Vermont, offers certificates and associate and bachelor's degrees in the discipline. The editors of *They Teach That in College!?* spoke with Gary Kessler, associate professor and program director of the Computer and Digital Forensics program at Champlain College, about this interesting field.

Q. What is computer and digital forensics?

A. "Digital forensics" is the discovery, collection, and analysis of evidence found on computers, cell phones, PDAs, digital cameras, and other digital devices and networks. "Computer forensics" usually refers to the analysis of computer devices, and "network forensics" refers to the analysis and interpretations of network traffic, logs, etc.

Q. Please describe your program.

A. Champlain College offered its first computer forensics course in Fall 2002. The Computer and Digital Forensics program started in fall 2003. Since fall 2004, all courses in the program have been available online, as well as on campus.

Champlain College's Computer and Digital Forensics program combines aspects of criminal justice, computer technology, and cybercrime. In addition to the broad general education courses, students take courses in:

✓ Criminal Justice (Basic Criminal Law and Investigation)

✓ Computer Technology (Data Communications, Computers & Telecommunications, Operating Systems, and Information Security)

✓ Cybercrime and Forensics (Computer Forensics I & II, Analysis of Digital Media, White Collar Crime, and Forensic Accounting)

The National Security Agency and the Department of Homeland Security announced in 2007 the designation of Champlain College as a National Center of Academic Excellence in Information Assurance Education. The program has also been named by the National Institute of Justice Electronic Crime Partnership Initiative as the model undergraduate curriculum for e-crime education.

Q. Where will future graduates find employment opportunities?

A. We anticipate graduates finding opportunities in a number of areas:

✓ Law enforcement, either as a police officer or a civilian employee of law enforcement. This area also includes government and military. Applications here would include criminal investigations and antiterrorism intelligence gathering.

✓ As part of an organization's information security team, specializing in incident response, recovery, and remediation.

✓ Civilian work working for third party examiners such as those at a data recovery organization, legal defense team, or accounting firm.

Q. What personal qualities should students have to be successful in your program and in their post-college career?

A. Individuals in this field need to possess an array of skills and be educationally well-rounded. More specifically, they must:

✓ Be technically knowledgeable about computers and networks

✓ Enjoy troubleshooting and solving puzzles

✓ Be aware of the legal constraints and organizational policies that guide what they can and cannot do

✓ Be willing to constantly learn about new technologies and laws

✓ Be able to communicate in both written and oral form, and be particularly able to present technical information to non-technical audiences (e.g., judges, juries, and attorneys)

Q. What is the future of computer and digital forensics? In what new areas/industries will it be used in the future?

A. Because computers and the Internet are the fastest-growing technologies being adopted by criminals and terrorists, digital forensics is and will remain a growth industry; more and more analysts will be needed in the public and private sectors.

This is a field that is also unlikely to be outsourced, particularly in the public sector where national security issues are paramount.

Computer and Internet Security

Computer systems of all sizes and complexity are vulnerable. They are vulnerable to the threat of hackers who may have devious intentions—to access highly confidential data, to steal money electronically, or to infect a system with a destructive virus. In today's computerized world, businesses—small and large—need to be protected against such threats. The *computer and Internet security professional*'s job is to keep computer systems secure at all times. They must stay on top of the latest high-tech advancements in order to always be one step ahead of the latest virus, worm, or hacker. Individuals who enter this field should have a strong interest in math, computer science, and computer programming, with a desire to be lifelong problem solvers. Security situations can change without notice, and computer and Internet security professionals must periodically update and execute strategies to ensure safe networks for companies. This individual's position is increasingly important as our world continues to become more and more dependent on computerized records in all areas of business, and as more business is conducted over the Internet.

Typical Courses:

- Linux/UNIX Fundamentals
- Managing Network Security
- Managing Web Servers
- Network Security Design
- Internet Connectivity
- Introduction to Routers
- Information Technology and Data Assurance
- Information Technology Hardware Essentials
- Information Technology Operating Systems
- Managing Local Area Network Hardware
- Security Awareness
- High Technology Crime

Potential Employers:

- Corporations and small businesses
- Government agencies
- Schools and university systems

> Computer networking consulting firms
> Nearly any organization that uses computers

Available At:

The following programs are just a sampling of the opportunities that are available to students interested in computer and Internet security. Contact schools in your area to see if they offer study options in the field.

Dakota State University (Madison, SD)
888/DSU-9988
www.dsu.edu/undergraduate_degrees.htm
Degrees available: Bachelor's degree

East Stroudsburg University (East Stroudsburg, PA)
570/422-3666
compusec@esu.edu
www.esu.edu/compusec/education.html
Degrees available: Bachelor's degrees

Ferris State University (Big Rapids, MI)
231/591-2434
http://catalog.ferris.edu/programs/538
Degrees available: Advanced certificate, master's degree

ITT Technical Institute
(available at more than 60 campuses in 28 states)
www.itt-tech.edu/teach/list/iss.cfm
Degrees available: Bachelor's degree

Madison Area Technical College
(available at the following Wisconsin campuses: Madison, Truax)
608/246-6232
http://matcmadison.edu/matc/asp/programlist.asp
Degrees available: Certificate, associate degree

Milwaukee Area Technical College
(available at the following Wisconsin campuses: Downtown Milwaukee, Mequon)
www.matc.edu/landing_ps.html
Degrees available: Associate degree

Missouri Tech (Creve Coeur, MO)
800/960-TECH
www.motech.edu/network-administration-security-bachelors.html
Degrees available: Bachelor's degree

Moraine Valley Community College (Palos Hills, IL)
708/974-5454
www.morainevalley.edu/programs/program_list.htm
Degrees available: Certificate, associate degree

Purdue University-West Lafayette (West Lafayette, IN)
765/494-7841
www.cerias.purdue.edu/education/graduate_program
Degrees available: Master's degree, doctorate

Rochester Institute of Technology (Rochester, NY)
585/475-2411
www.rit.edu/~932www/ugrad_bulletin/colleges/ccis/security.html
http://csia.rit.edu
Degrees available: Bachelor's degree, master's degree

For More Information:

CERT Coordination Center
www.cert.org

Computer Security Institute
www.gocsi.com

Computer Game Development

In the days of Pong and Pac-Man in the 1970s and 1980s, kids could only dream of designing their own computer games. Since then, computer games have grown from a novelty to a multi-billion-dollar industry. The Interactive Digital Software Association estimates that approximately 60 percent of the U.S. population plays computer and video games, and this growing interest has created a demand for computer game developers, programmers, and other professionals. In 1994, DigiPen Institute of Technology became the first school in North America to offer a two-year degree in video game programming. Today, the Institute offers associate and bachelor's degrees. In addition to DigiPen, a growing number of colleges and universities offer courses or degrees in game design and development.

Typical Courses:

> Introduction to Game Design and Production
> High Level Programming
> Algebra and Trigonometry
> Linear Algebra and Geometry
> Calculus and Planar Analytic Geometry
> Computer Graphics
> Game Implementation Techniques
> Discrete Math and Combinatorics
> 3D Computer Animation Production
> Advanced Animation and Modeling

Potential Employers:

> Computer game companies
> Educational publishers
> Any industry that requires computer simulations

Available At:

The following list of colleges that offer degrees in computer and video game development is not exhaustive. For a complete list of schools that offer computer and video game development degrees, visit www.igda.org/breakingin/resource_schools.php or www.gamasutra.com/education.

Art Institutes International (locations nationwide)
888/624-0300
www.artinstitutes.edu
Degrees available: Associate degree, bachelor's degree

University of Baltimore (Baltimore, MD)
410/837-5473
http://iat.ubalt.edu/sde
Degrees available: Bachelor's degree

Champlain College (Burlington, VT)
800/570-5858
www.champlain.edu/majors/egame or
www.champlain.edu/majors/egame-prog
Degrees available: Bachelor's degree

University of Denver (Denver, CO)
303/871-2453
www.cs.du.edu
Degrees available: Bachelor's degree

DePaul University (Chicago, IL)
312/362-8381
www.cti.depaul.edu/programs
Degrees available: Bachelor's degree

DigiPen Institute of Technology (Redmond, WA)
866/478-5236
www.digipen.edu/main.html
Degrees available: Associate degree, bachelor's degree, master's degree

Ferris State University (Grand Rapids, MI)
800/998-3425
www.ferris.edu
Degrees available: Bachelor's degree

Houston Community College Southwest (Houston, TX)
713/718-6743
http://swc2.hccs.edu/digigame
Degrees available: Certificate, associate degree

Michigan State University (East Lansing, MI)
517/432-2634
http://dmat.msu.edu/degrees/gamespecialization.html
Degrees available: Bachelor's degree, master's degree

Montgomery College-Rockville Campus (Rockville, MD)
240/567-5136
www.studygaming.com
Degrees available: Certificate, associate degree

University of Pennsylvania (Philadelphia, PA)
cggt@cis.upenn.edu
www.cis.upenn.edu/grad/cggt/cggt-overview.shtml
Degrees available: Bachelor's degree, master's degree

Rochester Institute of Technology (Rochester, NY)
585/475-6179
www.it.rit.edu/it/undergrad/bsgdd and
www.it.rit.edu/prosGrad.php
Degrees available: Bachelor's degree, master's degree, advanced certificate

For More Information:

Entertainment Software Association
www.theesa.com

International Game Developers Association
www.igda.org

Interview: Deborah Solomon

Deborah Solomon is the Program Coordinator of the Computer Gaming and Simulation Program at Montgomery College (Rockville Campus) in Rockville, Maryland. She discussed the program and the education of computer game development students with the editors of *They Teach That in College!?*

Q. Tell us about your program.

A. Computer gaming and simulation is part of a rapidly growing and exciting new industry. Gaming is not only the fastest-growing segment of the technology industry but also the fastest-growing segment of the entertainment industry. Gaming is not just about entertainment; game technology is increasingly being applied in a variety of settings, from medical and corporate training to advocacy, advertising, and emergency response simulation.

At Montgomery College, where I have been teaching for the past five years, we offer an interdepartmental A.A. degree in computer gaming and simulation. We also offer a shorter certificate that is focused on web game development. The degree has three tracks: game programming, game production and design, and game art and animation.

Our degree presents students with an introduction to the skills needed to explore this emerging technology area. Students are exposed to core game development skills and theory, gaming and computer simulation technology applications, and computer graphics technology. Information about classes, the degree and transfer opportunities for students can be found at www.studygaming.com.

Students can take classes about the game industry, level design, 2D design, 3D modeling, motion capture, computer graphics, and programming. They can even study "serious games"—games that are not just focused on entertainment, but also have a serious purpose like training, advertising, military recruitment, or crime scene reconstruction.

One of our new classes in Exergaming and Health Games covers the cutting-edge topic of health and fitness games, from movement games like Dance Dance Revolution and Kinetic to games that reduce pain for cancer patients, help kids manage diabetes, treat autism and ADHD, and educate about topics like drug addiction, AIDS prevention, immunology, and nutrition.

Another new class will teach students how to program games for cell phones and PDA's. Mobile gaming is an exciting part of the industry that is growing rapidly.

After graduating with the A.A. degree in gaming, qualified students can transfer to the University of Baltimore (UB) to complete their junior and senior years for a four-year degree in game development. UB gaming classes are taught near to Montgomery College on the Universities of Shady Grove campus, so students do not have to commute to the main campus in Baltimore.

Q. What high school subjects/activities should students focus on to be successful in this major?

A. To be successful in the game degree program, students should have experience playing a variety of games from different genres, not just their favorite genres. That is probably not too unpleasant a task for most high school students! However, they should play analytically—asking themselves what makes the game fun? What was frustrating? Were there any bugs? How is this game similar to or different from other games in the same genre? And how could they change the game design to improve the playing experience?

Students may also want to try creating mods and levels, using the free tools that ship with many major game titles. For example, level editing tools come free with Unreal, Half-Life, Crysis, Neverwinter Nights, Elder Scrolls, and many other popular game series.

Students need to take their high school education seriously. Game development is a very challenging and competitive field. Students won't succeed without solid skills. This includes basic skills like math and English, as well as "soft skills" like being able to work well on a team. Math is not just important for programmers. It is also surprisingly integral to many other tasks—from a 3D artist calculating shaders to a game quest designer balancing gameplay statistics. English skills are critical for good communication, both with other team members and with publishers, press, and online communities.

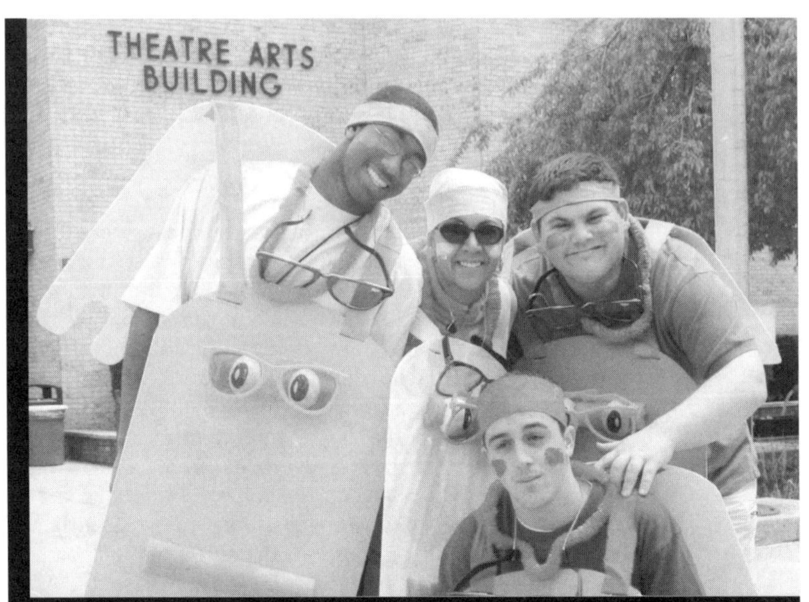

Each year, students in Montgomery College's Computer Gaming and Simulation Program translate a digital game into a life-sized format. For Pac-MC, they turned the campus into a Pac-Man-style game board. (Photo courtesy of Deborah Solomon)

Beyond the basics, specific subjects/activities to focus on depend on the student's interest. There are many different career paths in gaming, such as programming, 2D art/animation, 3D art/animation, audio, script writing, etc. For more information about these different career paths, I suggest that students take a look at the website of the International Game Developers Association, www.igda.org/breakingin.

Q. What are the most important personal and professional qualities for computer gaming students?

A. As mentioned above, game development is a challenging, rapidly evolving field. Students should be detail oriented, intelligent, able to rapidly learn new software and techniques, and most important, able to communicate and work in a team environment. Students with "left brain" and "right brain" skills, who can work both creatively and technically, are in high demand.

Q. What educational level is typically required for computer gaming graduates to land good jobs in the industry?

A. It varies. Some game professionals landed their first job based on creating a great mod, without any academic training at all. Mods and levels are still very effective as samples to have in one's portfolio. The level of skill and education required varies widely depending on the career path. For example, someone who wants to be able to program a game engine or write complex artificial intelligence algorithms might need graduate degree-level skills. On the other hand, a texture artist might be OK with a two-year or four-year degree program. My advice to students is to think about their specific career goals and to research typical education requirements for that career path in the gaming industry.

We hope to prepare students so they can go on to succeed in advanced gaming studies and entry-level game industry careers. We strongly encourage students to continue on to a four-year program because gaming skill sets are becoming more specialized as the industry matures, and having a four-year degree will give them better flexibility in their future careers.

Q. Where do computer gaming graduates find employment?

A. Maryland has been called the "East Coast hub of the gaming industry." People are often surprised to find out just how many game companies are based in Maryland, particularly in Montgomery County and Baltimore County. Take a look at the map on studygaming.com to see just how many interactive technology companies are based in Maryland (almost 100!). Because we are so close to the federal government and biotechnology industry, there are also many "serious game" and simulation companies in the neighborhood. Students graduating with game development skills can look to all of these companies for potential employment opportunities.

Students graduating with an A.A. degree could be prepared for a number of entry-level jobs after graduation—particularly in art, 2D animation, web games, web development, game testing, and basic level design. Game testers and texture artists are probably the most common entry-level positions in the industry. However, as explained above, we strongly encourage most of our students to continue on to a four-year degree program.

Some of our students have already found employment and internships, even before they have completed their A.A. degrees. For example, we have several students working at Bethesda Softworks, a well-known local developer/publisher that has created a number of major games, including the Elder Scroll series, and the upcoming Fallout 3. Some former students are working for game companies in California—one is an associate producer and another is an game artist/animator. Others are working for other local companies. The University of Baltimore has also had a lot of success in helping their gaming graduates find jobs in the industry.

We also provide opportunities for students to gain work experience for college credit. For example, I am supervising a team of gaming students that has been hired by the National Oceanic and Atmospheric Administration to work on an educational game that will teach 6th-8th graders about estuary environments. Those students can receive college credit (as well as getting paid) for their work. It is a wonderful experience for them.

In addition to opportunities in entertainment gaming and serious gaming, students may find that their technical and team-based skills open doors in other converging industries like film and cartoon production, web and software development, and database design.

Q. How will the field change in the future?

A. An interesting question. There are many possible answers, and of course, it is difficult to predict the future. But change is apparent on many different layers:

Hardware: For example, the new generation of consoles like the XBOX 360, PlayStation 3, and Nintendo Wii are changing player expectations of game appearance, functionality, quality and online services. New types of controllers like the Eyetoy camera, the Wii controller, and the guitars and drums used in Harmonix's Guitar Hero and Rock Band games are bringing new players to the marketplace and making games more immersive, as well as adding more physicality and exercise potential.

Development costs: There are a number of forces making games more expensive to produce (larger teams, more content, Hollywood voice-over talent, licensing of intellectual property, etc.). However it is still sometimes possible to achieve success with a small independent game project.

Software and content: Faced with rising development costs, game developers are looking into content and gameplay that is either generated procedurally (created dynamically during the game by the game engine) or created by users (or some combination of the two). Also, more games will likely be able to dynamically measure the player's skill level and adjust difficulty accordingly.

Serious Games: Many industries now are beginning to see how gaming technologies can be used in the workplace—to train employees, to simulate complex molecular interactions, to increase awareness of safety issues, and so on. I expect that the field of serious games will grow exponentially over the next decade.

Conflict Resolution and Peace Studies

The 20th century and the early years of the 21st century have been marked by world wars, regional conflicts, ethnic cleansing, and terrorist attacks. Many people have sought to find nonviolent solutions to the world's problems. Conflict resolution and peace studies majors explore the exciting frontiers of nonviolent alternatives to conflict—alternatives that do not tear down, but work to build positive relations between adversaries. The core requirements of this major are drawn from different departments: political science, psychology, economics, philosophy, and religion. In the modern, globalized world, conflict intervention that fosters peace between world leaders and governments is becoming increasingly vital. Yet peacebuilding and conflict resolution initiatives and activities within local, regional, statewide, and national communities are also important. Graduates are prepared to contribute to peacebuilding in conflict and post-conflict societies as well as their own local and national communities.

Typical Courses:

- International Politics
- Religions and War
- Sociology of Violence and Non-Violence
- Analysis of War and Peace
- Conflict Analysis and Resolution
- Social Movements
- Philosophy of Religion
- Cultural Anthropology
- International Economics and Law
- Cross-Cultural Psychology

Potential Employers:

- Peace research organizations
- Social service agencies
- Citizens' action organizations
- Universities and colleges
- Humanitarian nonprofit organizations
- Government agencies, the United Nations, and related agencies

Available At:

It is estimated that one-third of our nation's 221 Roman Catholic Colleges and universities offer some type of Peace Studies program or classes. Visit the website of the Association of Catholic Colleges and Universities (www.accunet.org) or www.conflict-resolution.org/sitebody/education/grad.htm for a searchable list of institutions.

American University (Washington, DC)
202/885-1600
www.american.edu/academic.depts/sis/academics/fieldofstudy/ipcr.htm
Degrees available: Master's degree

Chapman University (Orange, CA)
714/997-6620
www.chapman.edu/wcls/peacestudies
Degrees available: Bachelor's degree

Colgate University (Hamilton, NY)
315/228-7628
www.colgate.edu/DesktopDefault1.aspx?tabid=1631
Degrees available: Bachelor's degree

University of Denver (Denver, CO)
303/871-6477
www.du.edu/con-res/grad_program
Degrees available: Master's degree

Georgetown University (Washington, DC)
202/687-0513
http://conflictresolution.georgetown.edu
Degrees available: Master's degree

Kennesaw State University (Kennesaw, GA)
www.kennesaw.edu/pols/mscm
Degrees available: Master's degree

Manchester College (North Manchester, IN)
www.manchester.edu/Academics/departments/Peace_Studies
Degrees available: Bachelor's degree

University of Missouri (Columbia, MO)
galliherj@missouri.edu
www.missouri.edu/~peacewww
Degrees available: Bachelor's degree

Portland State University (Portland, OR)
503/725-9175
www.conflictresolution.pdx.edu
Degrees available: Master's degree

Salisbury University (Salisbury, MD)
410/219-2873
www.conflict-resolution.org
Degrees available: Bachelor's degree, master's degree

For More Information:

Center for Conflict Resolution
410/219-2873
www.conflict-resolution.org/sitebody/education/domestic.htm

U.S. Institute of Peace
202/457-1700
www.usip.org

Interview: John Galliher

John Galliher, professor of sociology and director of the Peace Studies Program at the University of Missouri-Columbia, discussed his program with the editors of *They Teach That in College!?*

Q. What are Peace Studies?

A. Peace Studies courses cover a myriad of disciplines. Here at MU these include sociology, religious studies, history, political science, anthropology, communications, and women and gender studies, as well as others. All of these courses involve a search for non-violent and non-coercive means to solve conflicts.

Q. Tell us about your program.

A. We offer a major in peace studies and as well as a minor. Most of our courses are cross listed with nine-to-10 other academic programs.

Q. What type of internship opportunities are provided by your program?

A. We approve of internships with any not-for-profit organization emphasizing social justice.

Q. Where do Peace Studies graduates find employment?

A. Employment opportunities are found with non-governmental organizations.

Q. What are the most important qualities for Peace Studies students?

A. Peace studies students are all those who dream of a better, more just, and more peaceful world.

Construction Management

Every building, big or small, that makes up the skyline of your town or city has been constructed under the vision and management of a few key individuals—the *construction manager* among them. Construction managers work with architects, building owners, contractors, and tradesworkers to oversee the development of a variety of projects, including residential housing, commercial construction such as stores and shopping malls, skyscrapers, transportation systems, municipal services, and utilities. College degree programs in construction management typically include many industry-specific courses, combined with business courses in operations, finance, and marketing. Degrees in construction management are available at all academic levels. Approximately 70 construction management programs are accredited by the American Council for Construction Education. Opportunities for graduates of construction management programs are good. In fact, according to the U.S. Department of Labor, employment in construction is projected to increase by 10 percent from 2006 to 2016.

Typical Courses:

- Construction Methods
- Concrete and Concrete Form Systems
- Surveying and Building Layout
- Structural Steel Systems
- Construction Estimating and Bidding
- Electrical Systems
- Soil Mechanics
- Construction Safety and Risk Management
- Heavy Civil and Highway Construction
- Field Work Experience

Potential Employers:

- General contractors
- Specialty contractors such as mechanical, plumbing, and electrical
- Architectural firms
- Engineering firms
- Government agencies

Available At:

The following list of colleges that offer degrees in construction management is not exhaustive. For a complete listing of accredited two- and four-year programs in construction management, visit the American Council for Construction Education's website at www.acce-hq.org.

Alfred State College (Alfred, NY)
607/587-4649
www.alfredstate.edu/academics/programs/construction-management-engineering-technology
Degrees available: Bachelor's degree

Auburn University (Auburn, AL)
334/844-4518
www.bsci.auburn.edu
Degrees available: Bachelor's degree, master's degree

Boise State University (Boise, ID)
210/495-6161
http://coen.boisestate.edu/cm/home.asp
Degrees available: Bachelor's degree

Central Washington University (Ellensburg, WA)
509/963-1756
www.cwu.edu/~iet/programs/cmgt/cmgt.html
Degrees available: Bachelor's degree

Edmonds Community College (Lynwood, WA)
425/640-1026
http://const.edcc.edu
Degrees available: Certificate, associate degree

Indiana State University (Terre Haute, IN)
800/742-0891
www.indstate.edu/mct/ct.htm
Degrees available: Bachelor's degree, master's degree, doctorate

John Brown University (Siloam Springs, AR)
479/524-9500
www.jbu.edu/academics/ecm
Degrees available: Bachelor's degree

Louisiana State University (Baton Rouge, LA)
225/578-5112
cm@lsu.edu
www.cm.lsu.edu
Degrees available: Bachelor's degree

New York City Technical College (Brooklyn, NY)
718/260-5575
www.citytech.cuny.edu/academics/deptsites/constructiontech
Degrees available: Associate degree

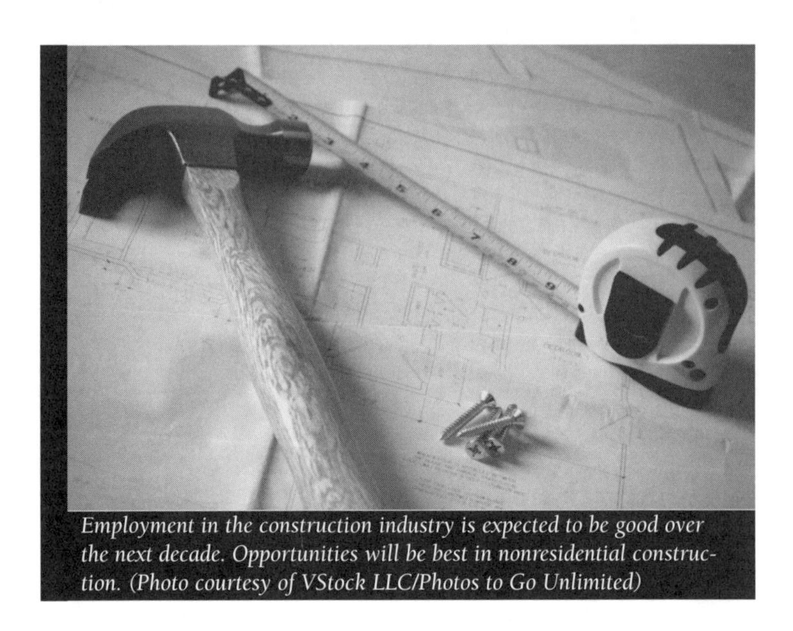

Employment in the construction industry is expected to be good over the next decade. Opportunities will be best in nonresidential construction. (Photo courtesy of VStock LLC/Photos to Go Unlimited)

University of North Florida (Jacksonville, FL)
904/620-2683
www.unf.edu/ccec/bcm
Degrees available: Bachelor's degree, master's degree

North Lake College (Irving, TX)
972/273-3000
www.northlakecollege.edu/academics/degrees.html
Degrees available: Associate degree

Northern Arizona University (Flagstaff, AZ)
928/523-4679
http://home.nau.edu/cens/cm
Degrees available: Bachelor's degree

State Fair Community College (Sedalia, MO)
660/530-5800
www.sfcc.cc.mo.us/pages/206.asp
Degrees available: Associate degree

Triton College (River Grove, IL)
708/456-0300
www.triton.edu/cgi-bin/r.cgi/
department_detail.html?SESSION=k1vDG2eZxv&ContentID=126
Degrees available: Associate degree

For More Information:

American Council for Construction Education
210/495-6161
www.acce-hq.org

Court and Real-Time Reporting

Court reporters use stenotype machines to record legal proceedings in courtrooms. *Real-time reporters* combine shorthand machine reporting with computer-aided transcription to provide real-time testimony in courtrooms and other settings. Other professionals help people with hearing or visual disabilities by creating closed captioning for television shows, radio broadcasts, and movies, as well as in classrooms and other settings. An associate degree in court reporting is required to work in the field.

Typical Courses:

> Theory
> Introduction to Computer-Aided Transcription
> Speed Development
> Realtime Reporting Punctuation and Proofreading
> Realtime Concepts
> Introduction to Transcription Preparation
> Technical Dictation
> Principles of Captioning/CART
> Captioning/CART Speed Development
> Medical Terminology and Anatomy
> Legal Terminology

Potential Employers:

> Courts
> Law firms
> Broadcasting companies
> Organizations that provide services to the deaf

Available At:

The following list of colleges that offer degrees in court reporting is not exhaustive. Visit http://ncraonline.org/EducCertification/Schools for a complete list of programs.

Academy of Court Reporting
(six campuses in Michigan, Ohio, and Pennsylvania)
www.acr.edu
Degrees available: Associate degree

Alfred State College (Alfred, NY)
800/4-ALFRED
www.alfredstate.edu
Degrees available: Associate degree

Community College of Allegheny County (Pittsburgh, PA)
412/237-4600
www.ccac.edu
Degrees available: Associate degree, advanced certificate

Alvin Community College (Alvin, TX)
281/756-3757
www.alvincollege.edu/Current/Court_Reporting.cfm
Degrees available: Associate degree

Cerritos College (Norwalk, CA)
562/865-3276
www.cerritos.edu
Degrees available: Certificate, associate degree

Did You Know?

Court reporters earn an average annual salary of more than $60,000, according to the National Court Reporters Association.

Chattanooga State Technical College (Chattanooga, TN)
423/697-2551
www.chattanoogastate.edu
Degrees available: Associate degree

Cuyahoga Community College (Parma, OH)
216/987-5112
www.tri-c.edu/ccr/Default.htm
Degrees available: Associate degree

Gadsden State Community College (Gadsden, AL)
256/549-8200
www.gadsdenstate.edu
Degrees available: Associate degree

GateWay Community College (Phoenix, AZ)
http://business.gatewaycc.edu/Programs/
RealTimeClosedCaptioning/default.htm
Degrees available: Certificate, associate degree

Green River Community College (Auburn, WA)
www.greenriver.edu/staff/divisionindex.asp
Degrees available: Associate degree

Huntington Junior College (Huntington, WV)
www.huntingtonjuniorcollege.com/Real-timeReporting.htm
Degrees available: Associate degree

Key College (Dania, FL)
www.keycollege.edu/page9.html
Degrees available: Associate degree

Las Vegas College (Henderson, NV)
http://lasvegas-college.com
Degrees available: Associate degree

Lenoir Community College (Kinston, NC)
www.lenoir.cc.nc.us/nsite/academicprogs/crt/courtreport.html
Degrees available: Associate degree

Madison Area Technical College (Madison, WI)
http://matcmadison.edu/matc/asp/programlist.asp
Degrees available: Associate degree

Miami Dade Community College (multiple campuses, Florida)
https://sisvsr.mdc.edu/ps/sheet.aspx
Degrees available: Associate degree

South Suburban College (South Holland, IL)
www.ssc.cc.il.us/acad/career/depts/legalstudies/courtreport.htm
Degrees available: Associate degree

West Kentucky Community and Technical College (Paducah, KY)
http://business.westkentucky.kctcs.edu/legal
Degrees available: Associate degree, diploma

For More Information:

American Association of Electronic Reporters and Transcribers
www.aaert.org

National Court Reporters Association
www.ncraonline.org

National Verbatim Reporters Association
www.nvra.org

Interview: Carol Adams

Carol Adams is an instructor in the Real-Time Reporting Program at Huntington Junior College in Huntington, West Virginia. She discussed the program and the education of real-time reporting students with the editors of *They Teach That in College!?*

Q. Please tell us about your program.

A. Huntington Junior College offers an associate degree in real-time reporting. Students can specialize in Judicial Reporting or Captioning/CART. Judicial Reporting focuses on the legal profession. Graduates can become official reporters, those who work in the courtroom, or freelance reporters, reporters taking pretrial testimony for attorneys. Captioning/CART graduates focus on providing text for television programming or other live events for the deaf and hard-of-hearing community.

Q. What high school subjects should students focus on to be successful in college and in their careers?

A. High school students today have such a grasp on computers, and that's important as our profession is very high-tech. Our profession is all about words: hearing them, processing them, preparing written transcripts. Vocabulary, spelling, and punctuation are extremely important subjects.

Q. What are the most important personal and professional qualities for court reporting majors?

A. Perseverance and willingness to work hard. There's a lot of homework involved in this program, as you are training to transform the spoken word into text instantaneously. Completing exercises once or twice is not enough: repetition is the key to eliminate hesitation when performing this skill. Maturity is also important: dealing with hard-to-work-with-attorneys and deadlines can be stressful!

Q. Where do real-time reporting graduates find employment?

A. Judicial reporters work in the courtroom as an official reporter or as freelance reporters for court reporting firms or on their own, taking depositions of witnesses involved in lawsuits before trial. Captioners/CART providers work for captioning companies providing text for live television, or they can be self-employed providing text for deaf and hard-of-hearing consumers at live events.

Q. How will the field change in the future?

A. This profession continues to explore and implement new technology to benefit the legal community and the deaf and hard-of-hearing community. Court reporting and captioning jobs are expected to grow. In the judicial field, a third party will always be necessary to record legal proceedings to ensure impartiality. In the captioning/CART field, captioners are in demand due to a federal mandate that all new live programming must be captioned.

Crime Analysis

The popularity of police and crime shows on television has glamorized the work of law officials and forensic specialists—it seems they can find the serial killer within the timeframe of an hour episode. Maybe so…with the invaluable help of crime analysis! *Crime analysts* collect, maintain, analyze, and disseminate important crime details for the area in which they are assigned. For example, a city is plagued with house burglaries. Crime analysts gather all details about each crime and study them. They systematically find similarities and patterns of each crime in order to find a trend. Questions such as the type of house targeted, method of entry, items stolen, and the time of day in which the crime took place are noted. Their findings are then circulated to all area police stations in hopes of keeping other burglaries from taking place, and finally to the arrest of the criminals. Crime analysts use many different methods of data mining and crime mapping including computerized information programs, statistics, and their own critical thinking. Many crime analysts make formal presentations of their findings to local police officials, federal agencies, and any company officials that hire their services.

Typical Courses:

> Fundamentals of Crime Analysis
> Crime Mapping and Analysis
> Writing and Speaking for Professionals
> Introduction to Geographical Information Systems
> Abnormal Psychology
> Crime Prevention/Environmental Design

Potential Employers:

> State and local law enforcement agencies
> Federal agencies such as the Federal Bureau of Investigation Department of Justice, Department of Homeland Security, Central Intelligence Agency, and Customs & Border Protection
> Private security companies

Available At:

Indiana Institute of Technology (Fort Wayne, IN)
260/422-5561
www.indianatech.edu/GeneralStudies/
BS-CriminalJusticeCrimeAnalysis.aspx
Degrees available: Bachelor's degree

University of New Haven (West Haven, CT)
www.newhaven.edu/show.asp?durki=249
Degrees available: Bachelor's degree

St. Joseph's University (Philadelphia, PA)
610/660-1000
www.sju.edu/academic_programs/grad_art_science/crime_just/pages/degree.html
master's concentration
Degrees available: Master's degree

Tiffin University (Tiffin, OH)
800/968-6446, ext 3401.
www.tiffin.edu/mcsjcrimeanalysis
Degrees available: Master's degree

For More Information:

American Society of Criminology
614/292-9207
www.asc41.com

International Association of Crime Analysts
800/609-3419
www.iaca.net

International Association of Law Enforcement Intelligence Analysts
www.ialeia.org

Dance Therapy

Dance therapists, sometimes called *movement therapists,* create and conduct dance sessions to assist physically, emotionally, and mentally ill people. Dance therapists also use these sessions to help doctors and rehabilitation specialists determine an individual's progress in rehabilitation. Students become dance therapists by completing a master's degree program in dance therapy—some of which are approved by the American Dance Therapy Association (ADTA). Others receive dance therapy training to supplement a master's degree in dance or in a mental health field. Undergraduate coursework in dance therapy is also available.

Typical Classes:

- Neuroanatomy/Neurophysiology
- Anatomy and Kinesiology
- Developmental Body Movement
- Introduction to Dance/Movement
- Movement Observation
- Dance/Movement Therapy Clinical Practicum
- Family Dance/Movement Therapy
- Applied Ethics for the Creative Arts Therapies
- Theories in Psychotherapy
- Medical Dance/Movement Therapy
- The Kestenberg Movement Profile
- Laban Movement Analysis

Potential Employers:

- Adult day care centers
- After-school programs
- Hospitals
- Mental health facilities
- Nursing homes
- Private practice
- Schools
- Substance abuse treatment centers
- Community centers
- Rehabilitation facilities

Available At:

The following schools are approved by the American Dance Therapy Association (ADTA).

Antioch New England Graduate School (Keene, NH)
admissions@antiochne.edu
800/553-8920
http://apdept.antiochne.edu/ap/dmt
Degrees available: Master's degree

Columbia College Chicago (Chicago, IL)
312/344-7697
www.colum.edu/graduate/04-05/graddance.html
Degrees available: Master's degree, advanced certificate

Drexel University (Philadelphia, PA)
215/762-8288
www.drexel.edu/cnhp/graduate_programs.asp
Degrees available: Master's degree

Lesley University (Cambridge, MA)
800/999-1959
www.lesley.edu/offcampus/term/nmagss_express_dance.html
Degrees available: Master's degree

Naropa University-Paramita Campus (Boulder, CO)
800/772-6951
www.naropa.edu/somatic/index.html
Degrees available: Master's degree

Pratt Institute (Brooklyn, NY)
718/636-3428
www.pratt.edu/ad/ather
Degrees available: Master's degree

For a list of alternative training opportunities, visit the ADTA's website, www.adta.org/resources/education.cfm.

For More Information:

American Dance Therapy Association
410/997-4040
info@adta.org
www.adta.org

Digital Media

Turn on your television and you will be unable to escape a barrage of advertisements for the latest cellular phone—and it probably shoots videos, sends email, and more. This is just one example of emerging digital media. Ten years ago there would have been those among us who had never used the Internet, and the idea of digital radios, televisions, or cameras was just a dream. Today, digital media is commonplace in today's modern world. As a result, colleges across the country have been developing degree programs in this emerging field. After all, someone needs to be skilled in producing the content for all forms of existing and emerging digital media! Prospective students should have a desire for a truly multidisciplinary course of study. Courses housed in the departments of art, communications, engineering, and computer science are required. If developing digital media for DVDs, CD-ROMs, and the Internet; creating video projects; and capturing and manipulating video, image, and audio files sounds fun to you, then a degree in digital media studies will be the first step into this fast-growing field. Degrees in digital media are offered at all academic levels.

Typical Courses:

- Digital Video Art
- Interactive Art and Design
- Digital Design Concepts
- Field Production and Editing
- Web Building and Site Management
- Web Application Development
- Telecommunication and Internet Law
- Technical Foundations of Digital Media
- Digital Animation
- 2D and 3D Design

Potential Employers:

- Advertising agencies
- Graphic design firms
- Film and television companies
- Game design firms
- Book and publishing companies
- Corporate art and graphic design departments

Available At:

The following programs are just a sampling of the opportunities that are available to students interested in digital media. Visit the websites of schools in your area to see if they offer study options in the field.

Borough of Manhattan Community College-City University of New York (New York, NY)
212/220-1476
www.bmcc.cuny.edu/computer/multimedia/MMP.html
Degrees available: Associate degree

Community College of Baltimore County
(offered at multiple campuses, Maryland)
410/918-4045
www.ccbcmd.edu/sait/programs/immt.html
Degrees available: Certificates, associate degrees

Broward Community College-South Campus
(Pembroke Pines, FL)
www.broward.edu/ext/ProgramOverview.jsp?A018
Degrees available: Associate degree

Canisius College (Buffalo, NY)
www.canisius.edu/comm_stud/dma
Degrees available: Bachelor's degree

Columbus State Community College (Columbus, OH)
www.cscc.edu/DOCS/intermediacurr.htm
Degrees available: Certificates, associate degree

Delaware Technical and Community College-Terry Campus
(Dover, DE)
302/857-1312
www.dtcc.edu/terry/program_pdfs/multimedia_design.pdf
Degrees available: Associate degree

University of Denver (Denver, CO)
303/871-2088
http://soc.du.edu
Degrees available: Bachelor's degree

Florida Community College (Jacksonville, FL)
tajohnso@fccj.edu
www.fccj.edu/prospective/programs/data07_08/2152.html
Degrees available: Associate degree

Gibbs College (Norwalk, CT)
888/309-8444
www.gibbsnorwalk.edu/digfilm.asp
Degrees available: Associate degree

Marist College (Poughkeepsie, NY)
845/575-3000
www.marist.edu/commarts/comm/multimedia.html
Degrees available: Bachelor's degree

Otis College of Art and Design (Los Angeles, CA)
310/665-6987
www.otis.edu
Degrees available: Bachelor's degree

Portland Community College-Cascade Campus (Portland, OR)
503/978-5398
www.pcc.edu/pcc/pro/progs/mm
Degrees available: Certificate, associate degree

Seminole Community College (Sanford, FL)
407/708-4505
www.scc-fl.edu/digitalmedia
Degrees available: Certificates, associate degree

Southern Maine Community College (South Portland, ME)
207/741-5500
www.smccme.edu
Degrees available: Associate degree

Valencia Community College (Orlando, FL)
407/582-2361
www.valenciacc.edu/asdegrees
Degrees available: Certificate, associate degree

West Georgia Technical College (LaGrange, GA)
706/837-4231
www.westgatech.edu/academics/DigitalMedia/DigitalMedia.htm
Degrees available: Certificate, associate degree

For More Information:

International Digital and Media Arts Association
765/285-1889
www.idmaa.org

Interview: Troy Johnson

Troy Johnson is the Instructional Program Manager for the Digital Media Arts program at Florida Community College in Jacksonville, Florida. He discussed the school's program and the education of students in this field with the editors of *They Teach That in College!?*

Q. Please tell us about your Program?

A. At Florida Community College we offer a two-year associate of science degree that teaches all the skills and knowledge needed to gain entry-level employment in digital media design or digital production industry. We offer a core of courses and concentrations in areas of graphic design, web design, motion graphic/3-D animation, and television video production. Students will all complete an internship and portfolio prior to graduation. We stress quality portfolio development for the portfolio is the key essential with the degree to gain employment. The degree opens the door and the portfolio lands you the job. The portfolio will demonstrate both your technical proficiencies and creative ability.

Q. What is digital media?

A. Digital media is the production of everything you see—from entertainment, games, broadcasting, and advertising, to corporate presentations and 3-D animations. Digital media is part of our everyday experience and will continue to become an increasing part of our everyday lives. Through the continued convergence of technology there will an ever-increasing need for digital production.

Q. What high school subjects/activities should students focus on to be successful in this major?

A. Art, television production and computer science courses tend to be the most common high school courses offered today.

Q. What are the most important personal and professional qualities for digital media students?

A. Students should consider themselves artistic, self-motivated, and patient.

Q. Where do digital media graduates find employment?

A. Students find employment in all sorts of settings and industries-medical, corporate, broadcasting, game design, advertising and marketing, digital production houses, and more.

Q. How will the field of digital media change in the future?

A. Digital media is an ever-evolving field of technology. Through the ever-increasing convergence of technology, digital media has already entered our lives from television, cable, broadcasting, and radio to computers, cell phones, PDAs, and other forms of mobile media such as mp3 players and iPod pod casting. Digital media is everywhere, and in the future as the Internet, telecommunications (telephones, cell phones), cable, and broadcasting technology and services continue to merge, the science fiction of today's movies will be tomorrow's digital media

Drama Therapy

According to the National Association for Drama Therapy (NADT), drama therapy is "the intentional use of drama and/or theater processes to achieve therapeutic goals." Therapy methods used include pantomime, role-playing, puppetry, theater games, storytelling, improvisation, and original scripted dramatization. Students become drama therapists by attending drama therapy master's or doctoral degree programs that are approved by the NADT. There are only two such programs in the United States and one in Canada. Others who have advanced degrees in theater or mental health fields prepare for the field by receiving drama therapy training via the NADT's alternative training program.

Typical Courses:

- Introduction to Drama Therapy
- Drama Therapy Process and Technique
- Drama Therapy Practice
- Creative Dramatics
- Psychodrama
- Drama Therapy with Special Populations
- Theater Lab: Advanced Improvisation and Group Process
- Special Methods in Drama Therapy
- Theories of Individual and Family Therapy

Potential Employers:

- Adult day care centers
- After-school programs
- Corporations
- Correctional facilities
- Hospitals
- Mental health facilities
- Nursing homes
- Private practice
- Schools
- Substance abuse treatment centers
- Theaters

Available At:

California Institute of Integral Studies (San Francisco, CA)
415/575-6100
www.ciis.edu/academics/pdt.html
Degrees available: Master's degree

Concordia University (Montreal, QB Canada)
514/848-2424, ext. 5214
infodt@alcor.concordia.ca
http://art-therapy.concordia.ca/dr_index.htm
Degrees available: Master's degree

New York University (New York, NY)
212/998-5402
nyudramatherapy@yahoo.com
http://steinhardt.nyu.edu/music
Degrees available: Master's degree

For a list of alternative training opportunities, visit the National Association for Drama Therapy's website, www.nadt.org/alttrainopptys.html.

For More Information:

National Association for Drama Therapy
585/381-5618
www.nadt.org

Ecotourism

If your idea of a great vacation is seeing the natural beauty of an exotic destination, or perhaps wildlife and fauna of your own city, then a career in ecotourism might be for you! Growing travel trends include green trips—vacations based on environmental and cultural awareness of the local area and people. *Ecoguides* lead visitors on city or geographical tours highlighting the topography and customs of the local area. Planned activities include walking tours, hiking, rock climbing, or wildlife viewing. They may also schedule participation in local customs such as harvests, cultural or religious ceremonies, or other activities that would not interfere with the lifestyle of the locals. Ecoguides spend a great deal of time familiarizing themselves with the environment and local customs before leading a tour of that area. For example, an ecoguide conducting a tour of Costa Rica would include a tour to view the diverse array of flowers and plants found only within a rain forest. They may point out wildlife such as macaws, sloths, and monkeys, or schedule a hike alongside the rim of a volcano. Each activity is planned to create the least amount of environmental disturbance. Interested students should be passionate about world travel, as well as sensitive to conservation and the rights and concerns of local indigenous peoples. Only a handful of schools offer degrees in ecotourism.

Typical Courses:

- Introduction to Ecotourism
- Environmental Issues
- Outdoor Leadership
- Wilderness Travel Skills
- Geography
- Natural History
- Cultural Interpretation
- Resource & Business Management
- Ecotourism Travel Plan Development

Potential Employers:

- Tour companies
- Self-employed

Available At:

Central Lakes College-Brainerd Campus (Brainerd, MN)
800/933-0346

Travel to the deserts of the American Southwest is one popular ecotourism destination. Visitors learn about the flora and fauna of the desert, as well as the cultures of its Native American inhabitants. (Photo courtesy of Andrew Morkes)

dkeran@clcmn.edu
www.clcmn.edu/academicprograms/new/ecotourism/ecotourism.htm
Degrees available: Associate degree

Hocking College (Nelsonville, Ohio)
877/462-5464
www.hocking.edu/academics/schools/natural_resources/ecotourism_and_adventure_travel/index.htm
Degrees available: Associate degree

Medicine Hat College (Medicine Hat, AB Canada)
403/529-3898
www.mhc.ab.ca/etol/Expedition/fourth.html
Degrees available: Bachelor's degree

For More Information:

Ecoclub.com
www.ecoclub.com

International Ecotourism Society
202-347-9203
www.ecotourism.org

National Tour Association
www.ntaonline.com

Outdoor Industry Association
www.outdoorindustry.org

Interview: Doug Keran

Dr. Doug Keran is the Lead Professor in the Ecotourism Program at Central Lakes College in Brainerd, Minnesota. The College is one of the few schools in the United States that awards a degree in ecotourism. Dr. Keran discussed the school's program and the education of students in this field with the editors of *They Teach That in College!?*

Q. Please tell us about your program

A. Our program consists of a 64-credit A.A.S. degree. There are 48 credits of required course work, and electives that are broken into areas of emphasis. The emphasis areas are: Nature Viewing, Cultural, Business, and Miscellaneous. Students do not have to follow a specific emphasis, but depending on their interests, can be directed to specific courses that meet their individual needs.

Q. What high school subjects/activities should students focus on to be successful in this major?

A. High school students should take the following subjects: biological sciences, earth sciences, speech and related courses, social sciences (especially geography and society and cultures); and environmental science and related courses.

Q. What are the most important personal and professional qualities for ecotourism majors?

A. They should have a sensitivity and understanding of ecological and cultural issues and concerns, have good oral communications skills, and have an ability to deal with travelers.

Q. What is the employment outlook for the field of ecotourism?

A. Ecotourism is responsible travel to natural areas that conserves the environment and sustains the well being of local people. It is growing at approximately 39 percent annually. The area where most people do not think about when hearing or talking about ecotourism is here in North America. More and more people from other countries are coming here and want to participate in a green trip.

Electronic Commerce

Online retailing has become big business—an essential component to every retailer's sales plan. What critics once thought would never catch on—has. Consumers around the world have gotten over their fear of giving out their personal information electronically and continue to make the Internet an ever-expanding marketplace. There is hardly anything that you CAN'T purchase online today. Purchasing items while sitting at your computer, in the comfort of your own home, is indeed a phenomenon that marketers, retailers, and business owners have to study. As a result, programs focused on this new e-commerce phenomenon have sprung up, attracting more and more students into this new field. While all programs combine core courses in business and technology, students with a particular interest in one or the other should be aware that some programs are more business-based, that is, they focus on how to attract online customers and expand online sales, while others are technological-based, focusing on the engineering fundamentals that make it possible to buy a car at the click a mouse button. Degrees in electronic commerce and related fields are available at all academic levels.

Typical Courses:

- E-Commerce Website Engineering
- Data Communications
- Object Oriented Modeling
- Technical Fundamentals of Distributed Information
- Intranets and Portals
- Internet Supply Chain Management
- Secure Electronic Commerce
- Internet Marketing
- Software Project Development and Management
- Java Programming

Potential Employers:

- Internet-based or communications-related businesses
- Traditional product/service companies using electronic commerce
- Consulting companies in the virtual or actual marketplace

Available At:

The following programs are just a sampling of the opportunities that are available to students interested in electronic commerce. Visit the websites of schools in your area to see if they offer study options in the field.

Carnegie Mellon University (Pittsburgh, PA)
412/268-8525
www.tepper.cmu.edu/
master-in-computational-finance/index.aspx
Degrees available: Master's degree

Clarkson University (Potsdam, NY)
315/268-6400
www.clarkson.edu/programs_of_study/programs/ebusiness.html
Degrees available: Bachelor's degree

DePaul University (Chicago, IL)
312/362-8381
cti@cti.depaul.edu
www.cti.depaul.edu/programs
Degrees available: Bachelor's degree, master's degree

Did You Know?

According to NetRatings, the top 10 Internet advertisers by industry in 2007 were Financial Services, Web Media, Telecommunications, Retail Goods & Services, Hardware & Electronics, Consumer Goods, Entertainment, Public Services, and Travel.

Milwaukee Area Technical College (four campuses in Wisconsin)
http://matc.edu/student/offerings/degrees.html
Degrees available: Certificate, associate degree

Pellissippi State Technical Community College (Knoxville, TN)
www.pstcc.edu/community_relations/catalog/ctp/programs/
emarke.html
Degrees available: Associate degree

University of Scranton (Scranton, PA)
http://matrix.scranton.edu/academics/
ac_factsheet_electronic_commerce.shtml
Degrees available: Bachelor's degree

Sheridan College (Sheridan, WY)
www.sheridan.edu/programs/ecommerce.asp
Degrees available: Associate degree

For More Information:

Information Technology Association of America
www.itaa.org

Enology and Viticulture

Harvesting grapes, trucking them to the winery, loading them into the crushers, and supervising the aging, racking, and blending of wine is what students studying viticulture and enology experience as part of their hands-on internship experience. A select few colleges in the United States offer programs in the specialized fields of viticulture, the science of wine-grape growing, and enology, the science of wine-making. Students in these disciplines study the scientific principles that are involved in growing grapes and manufacturing wine. Degrees are available at all academic levels.

Typical Courses:

- Organic Chemistry
- Plant Propagation
- Viticulture and Small Fruits
- Chemistry and Biochemistry of Fruit and Wine
- Vineyard and Winery Systems
- Advanced Horticultural Crop Physiology
- Viticulture-Enology Interface
- Varietal wines (international and domestic)
- Winery production practices
- Must and wine analysis

Potential Employers:

- Wineries
- Distribution and retail businesses

Available At:

University of California-Davis
530/752-0380
http://wineserver.ucdavis.edu/content.php?category=Academics
Degrees available: Bachelor's degree, master's degree

University of California-Fresno
559/278-2089
http://cast.csufresno.edu/ve/index.htm
Degrees available: Certificate, bachelor's degree, master's degree

Shawnee Community College (Ullin, IL)
618/634-3216
www.shawneecc.edu/courses/viticulture.asp
www.shawneecc.edu/courses/enology_asst.asp

Degrees available: Certificate (one-year program in viticulture and one-year program in enology)

Viticulture and Enology Science and Technology Alliance
Missouri State University-Mountain Grove
417/836-5053
http://vesta-usa.org
Degrees available: Certificate, associate degree
This is a partnership between Missouri State University, Northeast Iowa Community College, Shawnee Community College in Illinois, and the Mid-America Viticulture and Enology Center, along with state agricultural agencies, to create a collaborative program of study in the fields of viticulture and enology.

Did You Know?

There are more than 3,000 wineries in all 50 states, according to the American Wine Society. Approximately 556,000 people work in wine-related careers in the United States.

Walla Walla Community College (Walla Walla, WA)
Walla Walla Institute for Enology and Viticulture
509/522-2500
www.wwcc.edu/CMSX/main.php?module=departmentlist
Degrees available: Certificate, associate degree

University of Washington (Pullman, WA)
509/335-4561
www.wineducation.wsu.edu
Degrees available: Certificate (non-credit, two-year programs), bachelor's degree, master's degree

For More Information:

American Society for Enology and Viticulture
530/753-3142
www.asev.org

American Wine Society
678/377-7070
www.americanwinesociety.com

Entertainment Engineering

Heart-pounding roller coaster rides. Death-defying magic shows. Awe-inspiring stage productions in which actors seem to fly through the air or walk on water. Captivated by the spectacle of Las Vegas and Broadway shows, few people stop to think about the professionals who are responsible for creating and engineering these exciting extravaganzas. But as high-tech entertainment has grown in popularity, colleges have begun to focus on training students in the new field of entertainment engineering, which combines training in engineering and theater.

Typical Courses:

> Introduction to Engineering
> Mechanical Engineering
> Electrical Engineering
> Mathematics
> Physics
> Introduction to Stage Production

Potential Employers

> Entertainment design companies (especially in Las Vegas and Los Angeles)
> Amusement parks
> Motion picture industry
> Theaters

Available At:

University of Nevada-Las Vegas
www.eed.egr.unlv.edu
Degrees available: Undergraduate minor currently available; bachelor's degree available in 2008

New York City Technical College (Brooklyn, NY)
718/260-5588
www.citytech.cuny.edu/academics/deptsites/enttech/index.html
Degrees available: Certificates, bachelor's degree

Valencia Community College (Orlando, FL)
407/582-2372
www.valenciacc.edu/asdegrees
Degrees available: Certificate, associate degree

Roller coasters are just one of the many high-tech entertainment technologies designed by entertainment engineers. (Photo courtesy of FogStock LLC/Photos to Go Unlimited)

For More Information:

American Society for Engineering Education
202/331-3500
www.asee.org

Junior Engineering Technical Society
703/548-5387
info@jets.org
www.jets.org

Entrepreneurship

To own one's own business and work for oneself is for many people a significant step towards achieving their version of the American Dream. Whether the goal is to start a small, modest company that will provide enough income to live on comfortably or a company for which the goal is to become the next Wal-Mart of its industry—the dominant presence in the marketplace—becoming an entrepreneur requires a certain amount of business savvy, book smarts, and risk taking. It also requires high levels of independence and responsibility, along with the realization that the traditional work week will probably exceed 40 hours. After all, the success of your business comes from what you put into it. Most businesses, particularly in the early stages of start-up, require a significant time commitment. If your American Dream is such that through hard work you will attain a level of independent financial prosperity while pursuing a passion that is all your own, becoming your own boss—an entrepreneur—might be the right direction for you.

Typical Courses:

- Introduction to Entrepreneurship
- Accounting/Finance
- Marketing and Advertising
- Business Communications
- Business Law
- Business Management
- Business Planning
- International Trade and Exports
- Macroeconomics and Microeconomics

Potential Employers:

- Self-employment

Available At:

The following list of entrepreneurship programs is not exhaustive. Check with academic institutions near you to determine if majors, minors, certificates, or concentrations are available in entrepreneurship. The Princeton Review and *Entrepreneur* magazine also compile a list of the best undergraduate and graduate programs in entrepreneurship. Visit www.entrepreneur.com for the latest list.

University of Arizona (Tucson, AZ)
520/621-5078
http://entrepreneurship.eller.arizona.edu
Degrees available: Certificate, bachelor's degree, master's degree

Babson College (Babson Park, MA)
781-235-1200
www3.babson.edu/ESHIP/default.cfm
Degrees available: Bachelor's degree, master's degree

Borough of Manhattan Community College-City University of New York (New York, NY)
212/220-8205
www.bmcc.cuny.edu/business/SBE/sbe.html
Degrees available: Associate degree

Bristol Community College (Fall River, MA)
508/678-2811
www.bristolcc.edu/catalog/degree/dp_entrepreneurship.cfm
Degrees available: Associate degree

Did You Know?

Entrepreneurs report the highest levels of job and career satisfaction. Although only 20 percent of people in the United States are self-employed, they make up more than two-thirds of U.S. millionaires.

Chapman University (Orange, CA)
714/997-6815
www.chapman.edu/argyros/asbecenters/leatherby
Degrees available: Bachelor's degree, master's degree

DePaul University (Chicago, IL)
312/362-8783
http://ent.depaul.edu
Degrees available: Bachelor's degree, master's degree

University of Dayton (Dayton, OH)
937/229-3127
http://sba.udayton.edu/entrepreneur
Degrees available: Bachelor's degree

Delaware County Community College-Marple Campus (Media, PA)
www.dccc.edu/catalog/career_programs.html#small_business
Degrees available: Certificate, associate degree

Housatonic Community College (Bridgeport, CT)
203/332-5200
www.hcc.commnet.edu/academics/programs/dynamic/progDetail.asp?keyCode=EA89
Degrees available: Associate degree

University of Houston (Houston, TX)
713/743-4555
www.bauer.uh.edu/marketing/index.asp
Degrees available: Bachelor's degree

Loyola Marymount University (Los Angeles, CA)
800/568-4636
www.lmu.edu/Page20647.aspx
Degrees available: Bachelor's degree, master's degree

New Hampshire Community Technical College-Nashua (Nashua, NH)
603/882-6923
www.nashua.nhctc.edu/nhctc_test/academic_programs/academic_programs.htm
Degrees available: Certificate, associate degree

University of North Dakota (Grand Forks, ND)
701/777-2463
http://business.und.edu/entr
Degrees available: Bachelor's degree

Northeast Community College (Norfolk, NE)
402/371-2020
www.northeastcollege.com/PS/PDF/Degree_Offerings/BM_Entrepreneurship_AAS.pdf
Degrees available: Associate degree

Spokane Falls Community College (Spokane, WA)
888-509/7944
http://tech.spokanefalls.edu/SmallBus/default.asp?page=Outline
Degrees available: Associate degree

Syracuse University (Syracuse, NY)
315/443-3164
http://whitman.syr.edu/eee
Degrees available: Bachelor's degree, master's degree, doctorate

Temple University (Philadelphia, PA)
215/204-3082
http://sbm.temple.edu/iei
Degrees available: Bachelor's degree, master's degree

Williston State College (Williston, ND)
www.wsc.nodak.edu/academics/programs.htm
Degrees available: Certificate, associate degree

For More Information:

International Franchise Association
www.franchise.org

Students in Free Enterprise
www.sife.org

U.S. Small Business Administration
www.sba.gov

Interview: Michael Morris

Dr. Michael Morris is the Executive Director of Entrepreneurship and Emerging Enterprises in the Martin J. Whitman School of Management at Syracuse University in Syracuse, New York. He was recently named one of the top professors of entrepreneurship in the United States by *Fortune Small Business.* Dr. Morris discussed his school's program with the editors of *They Teach That in College!?*

Q. Please tell us about your program.

A. We teach 26 dedicated entrepreneurship courses, and a total of 60 sections per year. They range from more typical courses such as Entrepreneurial Finance and Entrepreneurial Marketing to courses in Imagination, Entrepreneurial Dilemmas and Debates, and Discovering the Entrepreneur Within. Just over 2,000 students on the Syracuse campus take entrepreneurship courses each year. We offer an undergraduate major in entrepreneurship, an undergraduate minor in entrepreneurship, an M.B.A. concentration in entrepreneurship, a master's of science in entrepreneurship, and one of the few Ph.D. programs in entrepreneurship. As one of the only academic departments of entrepreneurship in the U.S., we are better able to define and create new innovations in curriculum, research initiatives, and outreach.

Q. What makes your program an appealing option for students?

A. Our program appeals on multiple levels. First, we are teaching entrepreneurship as a life philosophy, not as the mechanics of starting and running a small business. Second, we adopt a total immersion principle, where students have the ability to be immersed in multiple facets of entrepreneurship both inside and outside the classroom. We have a model of the ways in which they can be immersed from first semester of freshman year through last semester of graduate school. This is epitomized in our Entrepreneurship Dormitory, which we call the Creativity, Innovation and Entrepreneurship Learning Community—where students eat, sleep, and breathe entrepreneurship. These efforts are coupled with a very strong commitment to experiential learning. Every course has a substantive experiential learning component, and the curriculum is coupled by a strong mix of outside the classroom learning opportunities. Students are expected to put together an Entrepreneurial Portfolio, to be reviewed when they are graduating. The portfolio could include completed business plans, feasibility studies, small business consulting projects, marketing inventions, entrepreneurial audits, interviews of entrepreneurs, entrepreneurial internship reports, apprenticeship in incubators, reports from working in our South Africa entrepreneurship initiative or our inner city entrepreneurship initiative, and so forth. We get students involved in active leadership of outreach projects as well, such as helping to run our microcredit fund, to organize our annual Bootcamps, and leading our Women Igniting the Spirit of Entrepreneurship initiative. All of this is supported by an aggressive program of entrepreneurial outreach.

Q. Tell us about your Student Entrepreneurship Incubator?

A. We actually have two incubator opportunities for students. One is the Couri Hatchery on campus, where students can get office space, computers, telephone, fax access, a conference room, and more. They are part of structured interventions to set measurable goals and help them work towards those goals. Students can also locate in our South Side Innovation Center, which is an incubator we have opened in the inner city. There, they are surrounded by other start ups that are often further along than the ones in the Couri Hatchery. They enjoy full use of all the services, training programs, and the intervention model we employ—which is an even more aggressive intervention approach.

Q. What high school subjects/activities should students focus on to be successful in this major?

A. I think students in high school do not need to focus on particular subjects. They should focus on working hard, getting good grades, and being broadly exposed to as many opportunities as they can in high school. They should get involved in leadership positions and in starting new things in high school. They should focus on developing their abilities to recognize and evaluate opportunities, manage risks, and leverage resources.

Q. What is the future of entrepreneurial education at the postsecondary level? Is it growing in popularity?

A. It has an explosive future. I see a significant growth in cross-campus entrepreneurship programs, where entrepreneurship is integrated into majors and disciplines across the campus. I see much more in-depth experiential engagement in terms of entrepreneurship-related projects. Another important future trend is an emphasis on metrics to gauge the impact of entrepreneurship programs. For instance, how much are we affecting the 'opportunity recognition' or 'guerrilla' capabilities of students? There will also be a growth in master's programs and Ph.D. programs in entrepreneurship.

Equestrian Studies

According to a study by the American Horse Council, the equine industry adds $102 billion to our economy and offers more than 1.4 million full-time jobs. Colleges have responded to our love of all things equine by creating a variety of equestrian studies programs. Majors may include equine administration or equine business, which offer training for people who are interested in becoming instructors, trainers, equine managers, riders, equine insurance adjusters, bloodstock agents, race track administrators, farm managers, and equine product salespersons, and Equestrian Science, which offers training to those interested in becoming trainers, equine managers, instructors, and riders.

Typical Courses:

> Horse Industry Overview
> Techniques of Horse Management
> Anatomy, Movement, and Farrier Methods
> Equine Nutrition
> Stable Management
> Equine Care
> Equine Health and First Aid
> Horse Show and Event Management
> Principles of Management

Potential Employers:

> Racetracks
> Stables
> Breeding and racing organizations
> Sales industry
> Insurance industry

Available At:

The following list of schools offering programs in equestrian studies is not exhaustive. For a complete list of programs, visit www.horseschools.com.

Ellsworth Community College (Iowa Falls, IA)
641/752-4645
www.iavalley.cc.ia.us/Catalog05-06/VocTech/VTEquineManagement.htm
Degrees available: Associate degree

University of Louisville (Louisville, KY)
502/852-6440
http://cbpa.louisville.edu/eip
Degrees available: Bachelor's degree, advanced certificate

Morehead State University (Morehead, KY)
800/585-6781
www.moreheadstate.edu/ahs/index.aspx?id=2772
Degrees available: Bachelor's degree

State University of New York (Morrisville, NY)
315/684-6083
admissions@morrisville.edu
www.morrisville.edu/Academics/Ag_NRC/Equine_Science
Degrees available: Associate degree, bachelor's degree

Northeastern Junior College (Sterling, CO)
800/626-4637
www.njc.edu/agriculture/equine.html
Degrees available: Associate degree

Sul Ross State University (Alpine, TX)
432/837-8200
www.sulross.edu/pages/3232.asp
Degrees available: Bachelor's degree, master's degree

Truman State University (Kirksville, MO)
660/785-4584
http://agriculture.truman.edu/areas_study/equine.asp
Degrees available: Bachelor's degree

William Woods University (Fulton, MO)
573/592-4397
www.williamwoods.edu/category.asp?271
Degrees available: Bachelor's degree

For More Information:

American Horse Council
202/296-4031
AHC@horsecouncil.org
www.horsecouncil.org

American Riding Instructors Association
239/948-3232
aria@riding-instructor.com
www.riding-instructor.com

American Youth Horse Council
800/879-2942
info@ayhc.com
www.ayhc.com

Exercise Physiology/Science

Combine your interest in physical fitness and people skills with a career in exercise physiology. *Exercise physiologists* use different methods of physical activity to help patients recuperate from illnesses such as heart disease, diabetes, and arthritis. They first assess the patient's condition and abilities, then prescribe a routine of exercise and therapy. For example, they help patients suffering from lung disease using low-intensity exercises such as arm cycles to increase lung capacity. Or they may use weights and elastic bands to improve an arthritic patient's flexibility. Exercise physiologists use equipment often found at regular gyms such as treadmills, free weights, and Bosu balls, but also use modified equipment and machines. Hospitals often employ exercise physiologists to conduct cardiac and pulmonary tests. Exercise physiologists are also in demand by individual athletes, sport teams, health clubs, and schools to help with their athletic programs. In this capacity, exercise physiologists design and implement exercise routines to improve athletic ability and strength. Students who think they might want to pursue a career in exercise science should not only have an interest in physical fitness, but a desire to help people achieve maximum health.

Typical Courses:

- Introduction to Exercise Science/Physiology
- Chemistry
- Kinesiology
- Biology
- Strength and Conditioning
- Nutrition/Health
- Medical Ethics

Potential Employers:

- Clinics
- Colleges and universities
- Fitness centers and health clubs
- High schools
- Hospitals
- Nursing homes
- Professional sports teams
- Rehabilitation centers

Available At:

Two- and four-year programs in exercise physiology are located throughout the United States, but only five are accredited by the American Society of Exercise Physiology.

Bloomsburg University (Bloomsburg, PA)
570/389-4049
www.bloomu.edu/admin/acad/hpe
Degrees available: Bachelor's degree, master's degree

Marquette University (Marquette, WI)
414/288-6175
christopher.simenz@marquette.edu
www.marquette.edu/chs/exercise
Degrees available: Bachelor's degrees

University of New Mexico-Albuquerque
505/277-4136
www.unm.edu
Degrees available: Bachelor's degree, master's degree, doctorate

The College of St. Scholastica (Duluth, MN)
218/723-6000
www.css.edu/x1464.xml
Degrees available: Bachelor's degree, master's degree

Slippery Rock University (Slippery Rock, PA)
724/738-4864
http://academics.sru.edu/ers/webpage/Exercise_science-home.htm
Degrees available: Bachelor's degree

For More Information:

American College of Sports Medicine
317/637-9200
www.acsm.org

American Council on Exercise
800/825-3636
support@acefitness.org
www.acefitness.org

American Physiological Society
301/634-7164
www.the-aps.org

American Society of Exercise Physiologists
218/723-6297
www.asep.org

The Center for Exercise Physiology
www.exercisephysiologists.com

Interview: Christopher Simenz

Dr. Christopher Simenz is a Clinical Assistant Professor and Practicum Coordinator in Exercise Science at Marquette University in Milwaukee, Wisconsin. It is only one of five exercise science programs in the United States that is accredited by the American Society of Exercise Physiologists. Dr. Simenz discussed his school's program and the education of students in this field with the editors of *They Teach That in College!?*

Q. Please tell us about your program.

A. The programs in exercise science and athletic training exist within the Department of Physical Therapy at Marquette University. Our program provides a strong basic science foundation as well as applied coursework in the areas of athletic training, exercise physiology, fitness, health and wellness. Our students are prepared through coursework and internship experiences for a broad spectrum of jobs in the athletic, wellness, and healthcare industries as well as for graduate or professional study in the healthcare field.

The Exercise Science Program offers a bachelor of science degree (B.S.) in exercise science and a bachelor of science degree in athletic training. Many of our students also enter college as members of the Direct Admit Physical Therapy program, engaging in a curriculum that combines three-plus years of undergraduate coursework in exercise science or athletic training combined with two-plus years of graduate physical therapy coursework for a combined total of six years. These students earn both a B.S. degree and a doctor of physical therapy degree upon graduation.

Q. What makes your program an appealing option for students interested in exercise science/physiology?

A. Our program appeals to students interested in exercise physiology and exercise science for a number of reasons. Primary amongst these is the unique focus of our program on preparation for physical therapy and other graduate programming. Our basic science-heavy curriculum and strong applied anatomy and physiology components leave students well prepared to matriculate to one of a number of graduate schooling options including medical school, physician's assistant programs, and more traditional graduate programs in science such as physiology, kinesiology, or exercise physiology. Additionally, Marquette's program in exercise science offers incredible access to our faculty and staff for students. Our faculty members work with undergraduate students in both classroom and laboratory settings in the production of scholarly research and teaching materials. Students truly get a hands-on education. Finally, our students gain access to a web of more than 400 potential internship sites across the country and abroad, offering a clinical/professional experience that is second to none.

Q. Can you tell us more about your internship program?

A. Exercise science and athletic training students are required to enroll in two internship courses as undergraduates. The first, a junior practicum, provides a window into the fields of exercise science and athletic training and allows students to acclimate to the professional environment. Sites are chosen by students from a strong pool of local clubs, corporations, schools, and healthcare settings. The senior practicum offers students a semester-long, full-time experience in preparation for either a first job or graduate school. Among our senior internship sites are professional sports teams, world-class exercise research facilities and hospitals, community health programs, private clubs, and others. At these sites, our students apply information learned in coursework within the professional environment.

Q. What are the most important personal and professional qualities for exercise science/physiology majors?

A. Essential personal qualities for Marquette Exercise Science and Athletic Training students include a strong sense of empathy, a hard-working nature, personal responsibility, and a willingness to learn. Professionally, we expect our students to exhibit strong communication skills including active listening, the ability to utilize analytical reasoning, and problem solving.

Q. What is the employment outlook for the field of exercise science/physiology?

A. The employment outlook for exercise science and athletic training is bright. With an obesity epidemic facing the nation, the demand for professionals trained in preventative wellness and fitness will only continue to grow. Athletic training enjoys a similar job outlook, with many facilities now looking to hire athletic trainers to treat both athletic and working populations.

Fashion Design

Are you obsessed with the latest fashions? Do you have a creative side that manifests itself in the unique clothes you wear? If so, perhaps a career in the fast-paced world of fashion design would be a perfect fit. But, don't be fooled into thinking fashion design is all glamour and no work. The recent Tyra Banks-hosted fashion reality television show, *America's Next Top Model*, proved how cutthroat the world of fashion design can be. However, there is plenty of room for professionals in the industry who don't attain pop star-like fame by creating their own lines of clothing. A degree in fashion design prepares students to work as designers, pattern makers, illustrators, fabric buyers, sewers, and sample makers, and each of these positions plays a vital role in the developmental process of creating a line of clothing. Individuals well suited for careers in fashion design are those who thrive under pressure, are resourceful, original thinkers, and enjoy some level of risk taking. Degrees in fashion design are available at all academic levels.

Typical Courses:

- Concept Development
- Drawing Fundamentals
- 3D Design
- Fashion History, Culture, and Society
- Fashion Drawing
- Computer-Aided Design
- Shoe Design
- Studio Methods
- Current Issues in the Global Fashion Industry
- Flat Pattern/Draping

Potential Employers:

- Fashion studio owners
- Textile and apparel manufacturers
- Retailers
- Department stores
- Fashion magazines and other publications
- Fashion houses

Available At:

The following schools are endorsed by the American Apparel & Footwear Association Education Foundation:

Buffalo State College (Buffalo, NY)
716/878-5803
www.buffalostate.edu/technology/x536.xml?bpid=72
Degrees available: Bachelor's degree

Fashion Institute of Design and Merchandising (Los Angeles,CA)
800/624-1200
www.fidm.com/academics/majors
Degrees available: Associate degree

Fashion Institute of Technology (New York, NY)
212/217-7667
www.fitnyc.edu
Degrees available: Associate degree, bachelor's degree

George Brown College (Toronto, ON Canada)
800/265-2002
www.georgebrown.ca/fashionstudies/programs.aspx
Degrees available: Diploma

Iowa State University (Ames, IA)
515/294-2695
www.aeshm.hs.iastate.edu/tc
Degrees available: Bachelor's degree, master's degree

North Carolina State University (Raleigh, NC)
www.ncsudesign.org
Degrees available: Bachelor's degree

Philadelphia University (Philadelphia, PA)
215/951-2785
www.philau.edu/FashionDesign
Degrees available: Certificate, bachelor's degree

University of North Carolina (Greensboro, NC)
336/334-5250
http://www.uncg.edu/tdm
Degrees available: Bachelor's degree

University of Wisconsin-Stout (Menomonie, WI)
715/232-1106
www.uwstout.edu/programs/ugrad.shtml
Degrees available: Bachelor's degree

The following schools also offer programs in fashion design. Many have nationally and internationally acclaimed programs. For a complete list of programs, visit the following website, http://fashionschools.com.

Ball State University (Muncie, IN)
765/289-1241
www.bsu.edu/fcs/undergrad
Degrees available: Bachelor's degree, master's degree

Houston Community College-Central College (Houston, TX)
713/718-2000
www.hccs.edu
Degrees available: Certificate, associate degree

Kent State University (Kent, OH)
330/672-3010
www.fashionschool.kent.edu/majors.htm
Degrees available: Bachelor's degree

Oregon State University (Corvallis, OR)
541/737-3220
www.hhs.oregonstate.edu/dhe/undergraduate/apparel-design.html
Degrees available: Bachelor's degree, master's degree

Otis College of Art and Design (Los Angeles, CA)
310/665-6875
www.otis.edu
Degrees available: Bachelor's degree

Parsons The New School for Design (New York, NY)
212/229-8989
Degrees available: Associate degree, bachelor's degree

Santa Ana College (Santa Ana, CA)
714/564-6000
www.sac.edu/degrees/sac/Fashion_Design_and_Custom_Clothing.htm
Degrees available: Certificate, associate degree

Santa Monica College (Santa Monica, CA)
310/434-4000
http://homepage.smc.edu/mobasheri_fereshteh/fm
Degrees available: Certificate, associate degree

Southern Illinois University (Carbondale, IL)
618/453-3734
www.siu.edu/~arc_id/fashion.htm
Degrees available: Bachelor's degree

Stephens College (Columbia, MO)
800/876-7207
www.stephens.edu/academics/programs/fashion
Degrees available: Bachelor's degree

For More Information:

American Apparel and Footwear Association
www.apparelandfootwear.org

Careerthreads.com
www.careerthreads.com

Council of Fashion Designers of America
www.cfda.com

International Association of Clothing Designers and Executives
www.iacde.com

National Association of Schools of Art and Design
http://nasad.arts-accredit.org

Interview: Jane Workman

Dr. Jane Workman, Professor and Program Representative for Fashion Design and Merchandising at Southern Illinois University in Carbondale, Illinois, discussed her program and the education of fashion students with the editors of *They Teach That in College!?* (Note: This interview covers both fashion design and fashion merchandising; for more information on fashion merchandising see the chapter, "Fashion Merchandising, Marketing, and Management.")

Q. Please provide an overview of your program.

A. Students who successfully complete the Fashion Design and Merchandising major at Southern Illinois University-Carbondale will receive a bachelor of science degree. The program is a four-year baccalaureate degree with two specializations: fashion design and fashion merchandising. In addition to the core curriculum required by the university, all students in the Fashion Design and Merchandising major take foundation classes that contain information pertinent to both specializations. Examples of these classes are: Careers in Fashion, Textiles, Fashion Product Analysis, Basic Principles of Clothing Design, Fashion History, and Fashion Motivation.

There are courses tailored to each specialization. For example, the Fashion Design specialization includes courses in fashion production, fashion illustration, flat pattern making, draping, computer-aided design, mass-market apparel design, and experimental design. The Fashion Merchandising specialization includes courses in fashion promotional strategies, fashion merchandising mathematics, and personnel issues in fashion retailing. Students in the Fashion Merchandising specialization earn a minor in business with courses in marketing and management.

Q. What makes your program an appealing option for students interested in fashion design and merchandising?

A. In the program at Southern Illinois University, a student will receive a solid foundation of skills on which to build a career. The courses are sequenced so that advanced level skills are taught only after basic level skills have been attained. Southern Illinois University is a public university, which makes the cost of an education more affordable than at private universities. Our graduates find jobs with top apparel companies, such as The Gap, Neiman Marcus, JC Penney, Bridal Originals, Saks Fifth Avenue, Limited Brands, American Eagle Outfitters, Dillard's, Macy*s, Kohl's, New York and Company, and Ann Taylor Loft.

Q. What type of internship opportunities are provided by your program?

A. An internship is required for the Fashion Merchandising specialization and is encouraged for the Fashion Design specialization. Students are responsible for arranging their own internship positions. There are also opportunities for short-term work experiences called "externships" whereby students can shadow an alumnus for one week during spring break.

Q. What high school subjects/activities should students focus on to be successful in these majors?

A. During high school, students interested in fashion design should take classes in art, computers, drafting, family and consumer sciences, mathematics (especially geometry), psychology, and speech. Activities that will allow students to develop their visual spatial and fine motor skills are recommended, for example, sewing, knitting, crocheting, photography, and sketching.

Students interested in fashion merchandising should take classes in accounting, art, business, computers, family and consumer sciences, mathematics, psychology, and speech. Activities that will allow students to develop their sense of business and marketing are recommended, for example, yearbook, student council, newspaper, and class or organization officer.

Q. How will the fields of fashion design and merchandising change in the future?

A. As in most fields, computers will change the field of fashion. Computer-aided design is used for such fashion design tasks as sketching, pattern making, grading (making patterns in all sizes needed), and marker making (laying out of patterns for cutting). Computers are essential for fashion merchandising tasks such as store layouts, fashion promotion, fashion buying, and fashion distribution. The global nature of fashion and the growth of the Internet are factors that will change both design and merchandising of fashion.

Fashion Merchandising, Marketing, and Management

If last winter's hottest trend was tucking your jeans into colorful, furry boots, no doubt this winter it will be a fashion no-no. Yet, 10 years from now, the look may reappear—with a new twist. Black is in. Brown is out. Flats are in, heels are out. The world of fashion is indeed one of constant, evolutionary change. The "business" behind the "trends" is no different. Those who enter the field are generally those who strive to always stay a step ahead of the crowd with the latest styles. They have an aptitude for business and people, and a sincere dedication to a career that promises to never become stagnant! Students' studies will focus on the areas of retailing, merchandising, marketing, and management. They'll explore topics such as consumer influence, global economics, and emerging technology, as they relate to the business of fashion. Professionals with fashion-related degrees may become managers of stores, departments or areas within stores, or groups of stores. Others go on to manage special events such as fashion shows, create marketing campaigns, design store window displays, or purchase lines of clothing for department stores. Entrepreneurial minded students open their own boutiques. Degrees are available at all academic levels.

Typical Courses:

- Clothing Adornment and Human Behavior
- Textile and Apparel Economics
- Textile Science
- Merchandising Promotion
- Merchandising Systems
- Social-Psychological Aspects of Clothing
- Historic Textiles
- Retail Sales and Customer Strategies

Potential Employers:

- Retailers
- Wholesalers

Available At:

The following schools are endorsed by the American Apparel & Footwear Association Education Foundation:

Buffalo State College (Buffalo, NY)
716/878-5803
www.buffalostate.edu/technology/x536.xml?bpid=72
Degrees available: Bachelor's degree

California State Polytechnic University (Pomona, CA)
909/869-4772
www.csupomona.edu/~amm
Degrees available: Bachelor's degree

Fashion Institute of Design and Merchandising
(Los Angeles, CA)
800/624-1200
www.fidm.com/academics/majors
Degrees available: Associate degrees

Fashion Institute of Technology (New York, NY)
212/217-7667
www.fitnyc.edu
Degrees available: Associate degree, bachelor's degree

George Brown College (Toronto, ON Canada)
800/265-2002
www.georgebrown.ca/fashionstudies/programs.aspx
Degrees available: Diploma

Iowa State University (Ames, IA)
515/294-2695
www.aeshm.hs.iastate.edu/tc
Degrees available: Bachelor's degree, master's degree

North Carolina State University (Raleigh, NC)
919/515-3442
www.tx.ncsu.edu/departments/tatm/
textile_and_apparel_management.html
Degrees available: Bachelor's degree

University of Missouri-Columbia
573/882-6425
http://web.missouri.edu/~umchestamwww
Degrees available: Bachelor's degree, master's degree, doctorate

University of North Carolina (Greensboro, NC)
336/334-5250
http://www.uncg.edu/tdm
Degrees available: Bachelor's degree, master's degree, doctorate

Philadelphia University (Philadelphia, PA)
215/951-2827
www.philau.edu/sba/undergradmajors/Fash_Merch
Degrees available: Bachelor's degree

University of Wisconsin-Stout (Menomonie, WI)
715/232-1106
www.uwstout.edu/programs/ugrad.shtml
Degrees available: Bachelor's degree

The following schools also offer programs in fashion design. Many have nationally and internationally acclaimed programs. For a complete list of programs, visit the following website, http://fashionschools.com.

Ball State University (Muncie, IN)
765/289-1241
www.bsu.edu/fcs/undergrad
Degrees available: Bachelor's degree, master's degree

Houston Community College-Central College (Houston, TX)
713/718-2000
www.hccs.edu
Degrees available: Certificate, associate degree

Kent State University (Kent, OH)
330/672-3010
erhodes1@kent.edu
www.fashionschool.kent.edu/majors.htm
Degrees available: Bachelor's degree, master's degree

Oregon State University (Corvallis, OR)
541/737-3220
hhs@oregonstate.edu
www.hhs.oregonstate.edu/dhe/undergraduate/merchandising.html
Degrees available: Bachelor's degree, master's degree

Parsons The New School for Design (New York, NY)
212/229-8989
studentinfo@newschool.edu
www.parsons.edu/departments
Degrees available: Associate degree

University of Rhode Island (Kingston, RI)
401/874-4574
www.uri.edu/hss/tmd
Degrees available: Bachelor's degree, master's degree, advanced certificate

Sam Houston State University (Huntsville, TX)
936/294-1242
www.shsu.edu/catalog/degrees.html
Degrees available: Bachelor's degree

Santa Ana College (Santa Ana, CA)
714/564-6000
www.sac.edu/degrees/sac/Fashion_Merchandising.htm
Degrees available: Certificate, associate degree

Santa Monica College (Santa Monica, CA)
310/434-4000
http://homepage.smc.edu/mobasheri_fereshteh/fm
Degrees available: Associate degree

Stephens College (Columbia, MO)
800/876-7207
www.stephens.edu/academics/programs/fashion
Degrees available: Bachelor's degree

For More Information:

American Apparel and Footwear Association
www.apparelandfootwear.org

American Purchasing Society
630/859-0250
www.american-purchasing.com

Careerthreads.com
www.careerthreads.com

The Fashion Group International
212/302-5511
www.fgi.org

International Association of Clothing Designers and Executives
405/602-8037
newyorkiacde@cox.net
www.iacde.com

National Retail Federation
800/673-4692
www.nrf.com

Interview: Jean Gipe

Professor Jean Gipe is the Professor Emeritus and the co-creator of the Apparel Merchandising and Management degree of the Apparel Merchandising & Management Department at California State Polytechnic University in Pomona, California. She discussed her program and the education of fashion students with the editors of *They Teach That in College!?*

Q. Please provide a brief overview of your program.

A. The Apparel Merchandising and Management (AMM) degree prepares students for professional positions in the apparel and textile complex. AMM students learn about the business of fashion (and related sewn products), which includes manufacturing, wholesaling, and retailing. Students take courses in fashion, business, and engineering to be prepared for supervisory and management-level positions.

Q. What high school subjects/activities should students focus on to be successful in this major?

A. Students who complete a college preparatory program with strong math skills and computer skills will be best prepared. Art courses are recommended for those interested in the creative side of the business.

Q. What are the most important personal and professional qualities for fashion merchandising/management majors?

A. We recommend students look for a career that they have a passion for, and most of our AMM students really enjoy everything about fashion. The fashion industry is high energy, fast paced, all about change, and "beating the clock." The environment is all about delivering great product to a target customer and making money in the process.

Some of the positions in the industry are very analytical, requiring excellent management/organizational skills. Other positions are more creative, requiring an eye for design and style and an understanding of what would appeal to the customer.

Q. How will the field of fashion merchandising/management change in the future?

A. Technology will continue to change the industry. Time is money and technology continues to remove wasted time from the process of doing business. While the apparel industry has always been a global industry, enhanced technology will require stronger management skills to do an ever increasing volume of business at a distance.

Forensic Accounting

Do you want a career that combines your keen sense of numbers with your interest in detective work? If so, then pursue a career in forensic accounting—the fastest growing accounting specialty today. *Forensic accountants* use their knowledge of accounting, auditing, and investigative skills to find evidence of financial discrepancies and assist in legal matters. Their specialties include investigations in cases of crime, fraud, partnership disputes, royalties, business losses, or personal injury. Since 9/11, the works of forensic accountants have been instrumental in finding terrorists and following their money trails throughout the world. Some forensic accountants may work on civil cases—for example searching for hidden assets in cases of divorce of partnership dissolution. Others may work for the government to investigate cases of embezzlement or financial crimes. In these cases, forensic accountants may often be called under oath to provide expert testimony. Only a few colleges and universities in the United States offer certificates and degrees in forensic accounting.

Typical Courses:

- Principles of Accounting
- Advanced Accounting
- Auditing
- Criminology and Ethics
- Fraud Investigation Techniques
- Fraud Examination
- Principles of Economics
- Statistics
- Written & Oral Communication
- Computer SCience

Potential Employers:

- Accounting companies that are involved in litigation support for law firms, accounting firms, and other organizations
- Federal, state, and local governments

Available At:

Carlow University (Philadelphia, PA)
800/333-2275
www.carlow.edu/schools/sch-mgmt/forens-accting-major.html
Degrees available: Certificate, bachelor's degree

Franklin University (Columbus, OH)
877-341-6300
www.franklin.edu
Degrees available: Associate, bachelor's degree

Mount Marty College (Yankton, SD)
800/658-4552
www.mtmc.edu/academics/majors/forensic_accounting/index.aspx
Degrees available: Bachelor's degree

Myers University (Cleveland, OH)
877/366-9377
www.myers.edu/admissions/Majors/Forensic%20Acctg/Forensic%20Acctg.pdf
Degrees available: Bachelor's degree

Waynesburg College (Waynesburg, PA)
724/627-8191
www.waynesburg.edu
Degrees available: Bachelor's degree

West Virginia University (Morgantown, WV)
304/293-7845
www.wvu.edu/~forensic/forensic_accounting.html
Degrees available: Advanced certificate

For More Information:

National Association of Forensic Accountants
800/523-3680
mail@nafanet.com
www.nafanet.com

Forensic Science

If the terms DNA, body decay, blood splatter, and rigor mortis fascinate rather than repulse you, you might have a future in the forensic sciences. Popularized by television shows such as *CSI: Crime Scene Investigation*, *Crossing Jordan*, and *The X Files*, the forensic sciences are enjoying remarkable popularity on college campuses. Degrees (at all academic levels) are available in the following concentrations: Forensic Science, Forensic Accounting, Forensic Psychology, Forensic and Toxicological Chemistry, Forensic and Investigative Science, Forensic DNA Profiling, Forensic Anthropology, Forensic Biology, Forensic Pathology, and Forensic Accounting. No formal accreditation system exists for these programs. The National Institute of Justice, a branch of the Justice Department, is working to develop standards that may eventually result in a voluntary accreditation system. In the meanwhile, those interested in forensic science should be sure to carefully investigate programs of interest before enrolling.

Typical Courses:

- Crime Scene Investigation
- Forensic Anthropology
- Survey of Forensic Science
- Death Investigation
- Firearms Evidence
- Forensic Entomology
- Medical Terminology
- Human Physiology
- Laboratory Measurements and Techniques
- Organic Chemistry
- Forensic Chemistry
- Biochemistry
- Statistics for Biomedical Sciences
- Criminology

Potential Employers:

- State and local law enforcement agencies
- Hospitals
- Medical schools
- Medical examiners

> Government agencies (i.e., the Drug Enforcement Administration; the Bureau of Alcohol, Tobacco, Firearms, and Explosives; the Federal Bureau of Investigation; the U.S. Postal Service; the Secret Service; the Central Intelligence Agency; and the U.S. Fish and Wildlife Services)

Available At:

The following list of colleges that offer degrees in forensic science is not exhaustive. Visit the websites of the American Academy of Forensic Sciences (www.aafs.org) and the Council on Forensic Science Education (www.criminology.fsu.edu/COFSE/default.html) for more colleges and universities that offer programs in forensic science. (Note: degrees/certificates are in forensic science unless otherwise indicated.)

Anne Arundel Community College (Arnold, MD)
410/777-2222
www.aacc.edu/criminaljustice/ForensicScience.cfm
Degrees available: Associate degree

Baylor University (Waco, TX)
800/BAYLOR-U
www.baylor.edu/forensic_science
Degrees available: Bachelor's degree

University of California-Davis (Davis, CA)
530/754-4013
www.extension.ucdavis.edu/forensics
Degrees available: Master's degree

Chaminade University of Honolulu (Honolulu, HI)
808/735-4711
www.chaminade.edu
Degrees available: Bachelor's degree, master's degree

George Washington University (Washington, DC)
202/994-7319
forsc@gwu.edu
www.gwu.edu/~forensic
Degrees available: Master's degree

Grossmont Community College (El Cajon, CA)
619/644-7000
www.grossmont.edu/aoj/forensic.asp
Degrees available: Associate degree

John Jay College of Criminal Justice (New York, NY)
212/237-8000
www.jjay.cuny.edu
Degrees available: Bachelor's degree (forensic science, forensic psychology), master's degree (forensic science, forensic computing, forensic psychology), doctorate (forensic psychology)

Michigan State University (East Lansing, MI)
517/353-7133
forsci@msu.edu
www.forensic.msu.edu
Degrees available: Master's degree

University of North Dakota (Grand Forks, ND)
701/777-3008
forensic@und.nodak.edu
www.und.edu/dept/forensic
Degrees available: Bachelor's degree

Oklahoma State University (Tulsa, OK)
918/582-1972
www.healthsciences.okstate.edu/forensic/index.htm
Degrees available: Master's degrees (forensic science, forensic sciences administration), advanced certificate (forensic examination of questioned documents)

West Virginia University (Morgantown, WV)
304/293-2453
forensicinfo@mail.wvu.edu
www.wvu.edu/~forensic
Degrees available: Bachelor's degree, master's degree (forensic science, biology/forensic biology, forensic chemistry/toxicology), doctorate (biology/forensic biology, forensic chemistry/toxicology), advanced certificate (forensic accounting)

For More Information:

American Academy of Forensic Sciences
719/636-1100
www.aafs.org

American Board of Criminalistics
www.criminalistics.com

Council on Forensic Science Education
www.criminology.fsu.edu/COFSE/default.html

Society of Forensic Toxicologists
888-866-7638
office@soft-tox.org
www.soft-tox.org

Interview: Phoebe Stubblefield

Dr. Phoebe Stubblefield, Assistant Professor and Director of the Forensic Science Program at the University of North Dakota, in Grand Forks, North Dakota, discussed her school's program and the education of forensic science students with the editors of *They Teach That in College!?*

Q. Tell us about your program.

A. Our program offers the bachelor of science degree in forensic science. Students may take one of two tracks depending on their career interests. We offer the Evidence Technician track for those planning on entering law enforcement for a career as a scene technician. The Evidence Analyst track requires more upper division biology in support of those interested in a career in a forensic laboratory.

Q. What makes your program an appealing option for students interested in forensic science?

A. We have forensic professionals involved in the program—the program director is a forensic anthropologist and one of the advisors is a forensic psychologist. The program mission includes providing science education for criminal justice students, not just those interested in a laboratory career. Our program has an interdisciplinary composition in order to increase exposure to the various fields of the forensic sciences. We have strong academic advising to increase student awareness of forensic fields outside of anthropology, criminalistics, chemistry, and biology, and to advertise internship and job opportunities. The program supports an active student club which, through student leadership, encourages students to participate in science outreach to the general public, and to advance in their careers by participation in the Academy of Forensic Sciences.

Q. What type of internship opportunities are provided by your program? Where do students work?

A. Most students in our program seek internships with the Bureau of Criminal Apprehension labs in Minnesota. We encourage students to seek and compete for internship opportunities wherever possible, but we do not offer an exclusive opportunity for our students. We do place a limited number of students with the state forensic laboratory in Bismarck. The limited number of positions means students really must search broadly to find an internship. The program director advises students as they search for internship positions beginning in their junior year.

The program funds one to two student assistant positions for students each year, which usually go to seniors in the program. These students assist in class preparation for the evidence analysis lab course, and assist the director with her research.

Q. What educational level is typically required for forensic science graduates to land good jobs?

A. The education level depends on the science involved. Crime scene technicians can still get to their position by working and training after entering a police academy with a high school diploma (but police academies increasingly prefer a four-year degree from applicants). Entry-level laboratory positions, such as "forensic scientist I" or "criminalist I", can be accessed with a B.S. in biology, chemistry, or forensic science, although there is increasing competition for these positions from applicants with a master's degree. Expert status in some fields—such as forensic pathology, forensic nursing, forensic odontology, or forensic accounting—requires a professional degree. Other fields (e.g., forensic anthropology, forensic botany, forensic entomology, and more obscure fields such as forensic geology) require the Ph.D. for expert status. Students should decide, hopefully by the end of their sophomore year, what their area of interest is in the forensic sciences, or their priority for a forensic career. If a high salary is their priority, chemistry (with a B.S. or M.S.) or pathology (M.D.) are top areas. If a certain science is the priority, then students should prepare for whatever terminal degree is necessary.

Q. How the field change in the future?

A. Since the "CSI Effect" has had a great impact on interest in forensic science careers and spurred a proliferation of forensic science education programs, I think an additional change will be increased public desire for forensic services for defendants and not just the prosecution. This demand may take the form of state legislation as is developing in Great Britain, or have a more commercial bent as more at-home kits become available. I think forensic science will become an aspect of individual safety training, in the same way that individuals learn to lock doors and protect credit cards, they'll learn to collect and preserve evidence in order to protect their own legal interests.

Gallery Management

The *gallery manager* serves a vital role in the success of an art show or popularity of a special museum exhibit. An associate degree in gallery management will prepare you for a career in this exciting field. Your coursework will include exhibition design, proper handling of art pieces, and correct lighting and display, as well as the publicity and marketing of an exhibit. You will also learn Web-based applications for art media such as digital photography. Santa Fe Community College offers this degree as well as the chance for its students to get hands-on experience working within the confines of its onsite visual arts gallery.

Typical Courses:

> Art Criticism
> Connoisseurship/Art Collection Management
> Gallery Practices
> Introduction to Web Design
> Sales: The Art of the Deal
> Professional Framing/Matting
> Contemporary Art
> Digital Photography
> Photoshop
> Office Information Management

Potential Employers:

> Art galleries
> Museums

Available At:

Santa Fe Community College (Santa Fe, NM)
505/428-1501
www.sfccnm.edu/sfcc/pages/1296.html
Degrees available: Associate degree

For More Information:

Art Dealers Association of America
212/488-5550
www.artdealers.org

Fine Art Dealers Association
www.fada.com

Gaming Industry

Casinos are found not just in Las Vegas and Atlantic City anymore; they are popping up throughout the United States. Whether you love or hate casinos, it is clear that the gaming industry is playing an increasing role in the health of local economies across the United States. In addition to gambling entities on Native American reservations, commercial casinos can be found in Colorado, Illinois, Indiana, Iowa, Louisiana, Michigan, Mississippi, Missouri, Nevada, New Jersey, and South Dakota. Although educational requirements vary by casino, our nation's colleges are beginning to recognize the demand for training in "gambling-ology." Certificates and degrees are available in casino management, tribal gaming, and other areas.

Typical Courses:

> Introduction to Gaming Management
> Gaming Device Management
> Surveillance and Security
> Casino Industry Regulation
> Casino Resort Management Food and Beverage
> Marketing
> Mathematics and Statistics
> Introduction to Indian Gaming

Potential Employers:

> Commercial casinos
> Native American casinos

Available At:

Grossmont College (El Cajon, CA)
619/644-7000
www.grossmont.edu
Degrees available: Certificate, associate degree

Mohave Community College (Kingman, AZ)
866/664-2832
www.mohave.edu/pages/262.asp
Degrees available: Certificates

University of Nevada-Las Vegas (Las Vegas, NV)
Gamadviz@unlv.edu
http://hotel.unlv.edu/departGameMgt.html
Degrees available: Bachelor's degree

Did You Know?

More than 354,000 people worked in casinos in 2005, according to the American Gaming Association.

Northeast Wisconsin Technical College (Green Bay, WI)
800/442-NWTC, ext. 5444
www.nwtc.tec.wi.us
Degrees available: Associate degree

San Diego State University (San Diego, CA)
619/594-5489.
www.ces.sdsu.edu/casino.html
Degrees available: Certificate

Tulane University (New Orleans, LA)
www.tulane.edu/~choose/new_page_8.htm
Degrees available: Associate degree, advanced certificate

For More Information:

American Gaming Association
202/552-2675
www.americangaming.org

National Indian Gaming Association
202/546-7711
www.indiangaming.org

Geographic Information Systems

Geographic information systems technology is a computer-based system that allows users to gather any type of information about the Earth that has a spatial component. This information is used in planning and carrying out of countless tasks, from implementing precision farming; setting up branches or ATMs for banks; creating routes for emergency response teams; designing, building, and operating a public transportation system; assessing the environmental impact of a major construction project; mapping the outbreak of an infectious disease; assessing climate change; designing a cellular phone network; and managing entire cities. Students who are successful in this field have an interest in geography, computer science, statistics, and computers.

Typical Courses:

- Introduction to Geographic Information Systems
- Geography
- Computer Information Systems
- Mathematics
- Statistics
- Acquiring Geographic Information Systems Data
- Elements of Cartography
- Elements of Photogrammetry
- Geographic Information Systems Software
- Advanced Geographic Information Systems Applications

Potential Employers:

- Government agencies (such as the U.S. Geological Survey, Centers for Disease Control, and the U.S. Forest Service)
- Construction industry
- Banking industry
- Health care industry
- Transportation industry
- Insurance industry
- Energy industries
- Marketing research firms
- Telecommunications companies
- Environmental organizations

> Map and database publishers
> Timber companies
> Utilities

Available At:

The following list of geographic information systems programs is not exhaustive. Visit the Urban and Regional Information Systems Association's website, www.urisa.org/career_center, for more programs.

Bismarck State College (Bismarck, ND)
701/224-2448
www.bismarckstate.edu/faculty/GIS.pdf
Degrees available: Certificates, associate degree

Cayuga Community College (Auburn, NY)
315/255-1743, ext. 2310
www.cayuga-cc.edu/academics/programs/index.php
Degrees available: Associate degree

Central Michigan University (Mount Pleasant, MI)
www.cmich.edu
Degrees available: Bachelor's degree, master's degree

Fort Hays State University (Hays, KS)
www.fhsu.edu/geo/geography
Degrees available: Certificate, bachelor's degree

Hinds Community College (Jackson, MS)
601/987-8111
http://hindscc.edu/Departments/geographic_information/default.aspx
Degrees available: Certificate, associate degree

University of Illinois-Urbana-Champaign
217/333-1880
www.geog.uiuc.edu
Degrees available: Bachelor's degree, master's degree

Indiana University-Bloomington
812/855-6303
www.indiana.edu/~geog/programs/gis.htm
Degrees available: Bachelor's degree, master's degree, doctorate

Michigan State University (East Lansing, MI)
517/355-4649
www.geo.msu.edu
Degrees available: Bachelor's degree

University of Minnesota-Twin Cities (Minneapolis, MN)
www.geog.umn.edu/umucgis
Degrees available: Bachelor's degree, master's degree, doctorate

Moorpark College (Moorpark, CA)
805/378-1459
www.moorparkcollege.edu/catalog
Degrees available: Associate degree

University of Nebraska-Kearney
www.unk.edu/acad/geography/index.php?id=1611
Degrees available: Bachelor's degree

New Hampshire Community Technical College-Berlin
603/752-1113, ext. 2002
www.berlin.nhctc.edu/courses/gis.html
Degrees available: Associate degree

The Ohio State University (Columbus, OH)
www.geography.ohio-state.edu
Degrees available: Bachelor's degree, master's degree, doctorate

San Jacinto College-Central Campus (Pasadena, TX)
281/476-1813
www.sjcd.edu/program/geographic_info.html
Degrees available: Certificate, associate degree

South Dakota State University (Brookings, SD)
605/688-4840
www3.sdstate.edu/Academics/CollegeOfArtsAndSciences/Geography
Degrees available: Bachelor's degree

Southern Utah University (Cedar City, UT)
435/586-7700
www.suu.edu/sci/physci/gis
Degrees available: Certificate, bachelor's degree

Texas State Technical College-Waco
254/867-4815
www.waco.tstc.edu/gis
Degrees available: Certificate, associate degrees

University of Wisconsin-Madison
www.geography.wisc.edu
Degrees available: Bachelor's degree, master's degree, advanced certificate

For More Information:

American Society for Photogrammetry and Remote Sensing
www.asprs.org/career

Association of American Geographers
www.aag.org

GIS.com
www.gis.com

University Consortium for Geographic Information Science
www.ucgis.org

Urban and Regional Information Systems Association
www.urisa.org

Golf Course Management

The work of golf course managers is not all fun and games. These key professionals in the golf industry must be expert marketers, merchandisers, accountants, managers, and event planners, as well able to handle the more technical aspects of the career such as golf course maintenance and golf club repair. Degree programs in professional golf management offer interdisciplinary curriculums in business, general studies, recreation and tourism management, and golf that prepare graduates for successful careers. The Professional Golfers' Association of America (PGA) Professional Golf Management University Program, a four-and-a-half-year college curriculum for aspiring PGA professionals, is offered at 19 PGA-accredited colleges and universities nationwide. (Note: Other schools offer programs in golf course management that are not accredited by the PGA. Visit the websites of schools in your area to see if they offer study options in the field.)

Typical Courses:

- Tournament Operations and the Rules of Golf
- Facility Operations
- Turfgrass Management
- Fundamentals of Golf Instruction
- Managerial Accounting
- Principles of Marketing
- Economics
- Business Information Systems
- Small Business Management
- Golf Internships

Potential Employers:

- Golf courses
- Golf equipment manufacturers
- Colleges and universities
- Resorts

Available At:

The following schools are accredited by the Professional Golfers' Association of America:

Arizona State University (Mesa, AZ)
480/727-1180
www.east.asu.edu/msabr/pgm
Degrees available: Bachelor's degree

Campbell University (Buies Creek, NC)
800/334-4111, ext. 1395
http://web.campbell.edu/business/pgm
Degrees available: Bachelor's degree

University of Central Oklahoma (Edmond, OK)
405/974-5247
pgm@ucok.edu
www.busn.ucok.edu/pgm
Degrees available: Bachelor's degree

Clemson University (Clemson, SC)
864/656-0112
pgmc@clemson.edu
www.clemson.edu/hehd/prtm/pgm
Degrees available: Bachelor's degree

Coastal Carolina University (Conway, SC)
843/349-2639
Cthrash@coastal.edu
www.coastal.edu/business
Degrees available: Bachelor's degree

University of Colorado-Colorado Springs
719/262-3609
dwert@uccs.edu
http://business.uccs.edu/pgm
Degrees available: Bachelor's degree

Eastern Kentucky University (Richmond, KY)
859/622 4976
kim.kincer@eku.edu
www.pgm.eku.edu
Degrees available: Bachelor's degree

Ferris State University (Big Rapids, MI)
231/591-2380
PGM@ferris.edu
www.ferris.edu/htmls/colleges/business/pgm
Degrees available: Bachelor's degree

Florida Gulf Coast University (Fort Myers, FL)
239/590-7719
http://cps.fgcu.edu/pgm
Degrees available: Bachelor's degree

Florida State University (Tallahassee, FL)
850/644-4787
www.cob.fsu.edu/dsh/pgm_major.cfm
Degrees available: Bachelor's degree

University of Idaho (Moscow, ID)
208/885-4746
www.cbehome.uidaho.edu/pgm
Degrees available: Bachelor's degree

Methodist University (Fayetteville, NC)
800/488-7110, ext. 7278
www.methodist.edu/pgm
Degrees available: Bachelor's degree

Mississippi State University (Mississippi State, MS)
662/325-1990
www.msupgm.com
Degrees available: Bachelor's degree

University of Nebraska-Lincoln (Lincoln, NE)
800/742-8800, ext. 2541
pgm@unl.edu
www.pgm.unl.edu
Degrees available: Bachelor's degree

University of Nevada-Las Vegas (Las Vegas, NV)
702/895-2932
http://hotel.unlv.edu/PGM.htm
Degrees available: Bachelor's degree

New Mexico State University (Las Cruces, NM)
505/646-2814
http://pgapgm.nmsu.edu
Degrees available: Bachelor's degree

North Carolina State University (Raleigh, NC)
919/515-8792
http://cnr.ncsu.edu/pgm
Degrees available: Bachelor's degree

Pennsylvania State University (University Park, PA)
814/865-7034
www.hhdev.psu.edu/rptm/pgm
Degrees available: Bachelor's degree

Sam Houston State University (Huntsville, TX)
936/294-4810
www.shsu.edu/~coba/pgm
Degrees available: Bachelor's degree

For More Information:

Golf Course Superintendents Association of America
800/472-7878
www.gcsaa.org

Hair Care Salon Management

Who doesn't love a great haircut or style? *Hair care salon managers* must be knowledgeable of current trends in cuts and styles, as well as treatments such as coloring, glazes, permanents, or straightening techniques. They advise clients on proper hair tools and products for their hair type, or new appliances on the market such as irons, blow dryers, or hair accessories. Hair care salon managers must also be knowledgeable about running their own business. Salons must be stocked with hair care products and supplies including scissors, rollers, combs, and brushes. Managers also purchase or maintain equipment such as chairs, floor dryers, wax pots, or hair tools. Managers hire, train, and supervise staff including stylists, estheticians, nail technicians, makeup artists, and receptionists. Students interested in this career should have an interest in hair care, including styling and grooming. They must enjoy working with and managing people and take genuine interest in helping people look and feel their best.

Typical Courses:

- Introduction to Business
- Principles of Marketing
- Principles of Management
- Applied Accounting
- Basic Mathematics
- Business Law

Potential Employers:

- Hair care salons
- Department stores with salons
- Spas
- Cruise ships

Available At:

Mott Community College (Flint, MI)
810/762-0429
www.mcc.edu/programs_courses/programs.php
Degrees available: Associate degree

For More Information:

American Association of Cosmetology Schools
www.beautyschools.org

Historic Preservation

Throughout the world, countless buildings, parks, and other resources are culturally and historically significant. Protecting these links to our past, as well as dealing with current issues such as suburban sprawl and development, are key responsibilities of historic preservationists. Students with a love of history and architecture will prosper in this interesting field. Historic preservation students typically participate in internships at some of our nation's most interesting parks and museums, as well as at local and regional establishments. This combination of coursework and internships prepares students for a career in a variety of fields in public, private, and not-for-profit sectors.

Typical Courses:

> Introduction to Historic Preservation
> Historic Preservation Technology
> Design and Presentation Techniques
> Legal and Economic Principles of Historic Preservation
> Archives and Special Collections Studies
> Historic Site Administration
> Problems in Archives and Special Collections Management
> Problems in Applied Museum Studies
> Problems in Historic Site Administration
> Museum Studies

Potential Employers:

> Local and state planning commissions and other preservation-related organizations
> Museums and cultural centers
> Historical sites and historical societies
> National Park Service (including National Register of Historic Places, the National Historic Landmarks Program, and the Historic American Buildings Survey)
> Preservation agencies

Available At:

The following programs are just a sampling of the opportunities that are available to students interested in historic preservation. Visit the National Council for Preservation Education's website, www.ncpe.us, for more programs in historic preservation.

Did You Know?

The National Trust for Historic Preservation reported that the most endangered historic places in the United States in 2007 were: Brooklyn's Industrial Waterfront (New York, NY), El Camino Real de Tierra Adentro National Historic Trail (NM), H.H. Richardson House (Brookline, MA), Hialeah Park Race Course (Hialeah, FL), Historic Places in Transmission Line Corridors (seven states), Historic Route 66 Motels (IL to CA), Historic Structures in Mark Twain National Forest (29 counties in MO), Minidoka Internment National Monument (Hunt, ID), Philip Simmons' Workshop and Home (Charleston, SC), Pinon Canyon (CO), and Stewart's Point Rancheria (Sonoma County, CA). Visit www.nationaltrust.org for the latest list.

The School of the Art Institute of Chicago (Chicago, IL)
312/629-6680
www.saic.edu
Degrees available: Master's degree

Ball State University (Muncie, IN)
765/285-1920
www.bsu.edu/preservation
Degrees available: Master's degree

Eastern Michigan University (Ypsilanti, MI)
734/487-0232
www.emich.edu/public/geo/HP/HP.html
Degrees available: Master's degree, advanced certificate

University of Georgia (Athens, GA)
706/542-1816
www.sed.uga.edu
Degrees available: Master's degree, advanced certificate

University of Mary Washington (Fredericksburg, VA)
540/654-1041
www.umw.edu/cas/historicpreservation/default.php
Degrees available: Bachelor's degree

Northwest State Community College (Archbold, OH)
419/267-5511
www.northweststate.edu
Degrees available: Associate degree

Pratt Institute (New York, NY)
718/399-4314
www.pratt.edu/historic_preservation
Degrees available: Master's degree

Roger Williams University (Bristol, RI)
www.rwu.edu/academics/departments/historicpreservation.htm
Degrees available: Bachelor's degree

Savannah College of Art & Design (Savannah, GA)
www.scad.edu/historic-preservation
Degrees available: Bachelor's degree. master's degree, advanced certificate

Southeast Missouri State University (Cape Girardeau, MO)
www.semo.edu/study/history
Degrees available: Bachelor's degree, master's degree (concentration)

Ursuline College (Pepper Pike, OH)
www.ursuline.edu/academics
Degrees available: Bachelor's degree, master's degree, advanced certificate

For More Information:

National Council for Preservation Education
www.ncpe.us

National Park Service
www.nps.gov

National Preservation Institute
www.npi.org

National Trust for Historic Preservation
www.nationaltrust.org

Interview: Steven Hoffman

Dr. Steven Hoffman, Professor of History and Coordinator of the Historic Preservation Program at Southeast Missouri State University in Cape Girardeau, Missouri, discussed his program and the education of historic preservation students with the editors of *They Teach That in College!?*

Q. Tell us about your program.

A. Southeast Missouri State University offers a bachelor of science in historic preservation degree and a master of arts in history with an emphasis in historic preservation. Students take courses in the history and theory of preservation; conduct hands-on local history research; write National Register of Historic Places nominations; learn about architectural history, tax credits, and the legal foundation of preservation; and prepare to work in archives, museums, and historic sites.

Q. What type of internship opportunities are provided by your program?

A. The undergraduate B.S. in historic preservation degree requires students to complete a nine credit hour internship. Each internship must involve at least 400 hours of work at an appropriate facility. Students in the graduate program are encouraged to take a three credit hour internship comprised of at least 150 hours of work. The work done must be sufficiently varied and challenging to provide a significant learning experience. Students are responsible for obtaining their own internships, although the program has relationships with institutions that routinely accept our interns. Students have interned with a wide variety of institutions, including the National Holocaust Museum, Washington, D.C.; The Luther Center, Wittenberg, Germany; Eisenhower National Historic Site, Gettysburg, Pennsylvania; Missouri State Archives, Jefferson City, Missouri; Scott Joplin House State Historic Site, St. Louis, Missouri; South Dakota State Historical Society, Pierre, South Dakota; Sagamore, Historic Adirondack Great Camp, Raquette Lake, New York; Minnesota Historical Society, St. Paul, Minnesota; Andersonville National Historic Site, Andersonville, Georgia; Central Park Conservancy, New York, New York; and Shiloh National Military Park, Shiloh, Tennessee.

Q. What high school subjects/activities should students focus on to prepare for study in this major?

A. To best prepare for study in this major, students should seek out opportunities to volunteer at local historic sites, museums, and archives. Having a variety of experiences in the field will provide a solid foundation for further study. In addition, advanced course work in American history is probably advantageous.

Q. Where do historic preservation graduates find employment? Are there employment areas that might surprise the typical student? If so, please detail.

A. Historic preservation graduates find employment in a wide variety of areas, including the National Park Service, state and local historic sites and museums, archives, major federal and state agencies such as departments of transportation, and private consulting firms. Students might be surprised that every state has a state historic preservation office, leading to employment performing historic resource surveys, evaluating tax credit projects, and working on National Register of Historic Places nominations. People and institu-

San Xavier del Bac Mission in Tucson, Arizona, a mission church built by the Spanish in 1797. The Patronato of San Xavier was formed in 1978 to preserve this beautiful and historical building. But efforts to protect this cultural resource began even earlier than that when it was declared a National Historic Landmark in 1960. (Photo courtesy of Andrew Morkes)

tions throughout society, from developers and property owners to government agencies and law firms, will pay individuals trained in historic preservation and public history, providing a diverse range of opportunities to make a living in the history industry.

Q. How will the field change in the future?

A. The field of historic preservation certainly faces changes in the future. Preserving the recent past is quickly becoming an issue for preservationists as the icons of modernism and post-World War II suburbanization become 50 years old and require preservation. The relationship of preservation to development, principally in the area of combating sprawl, will become increasingly important, particularly as it affects relationships with potential allies in the environmental and affordable housing movements. At the same time, however, preservation of the past becomes increasingly important in a society that embraces the future, and so the market for historic preservationists should continue to be strong.

Homeland Security/Emergency Management

Since the terrorist attacks of September 11, 2001, the U.S. government has had the daunting task of protecting our nation from future attacks—whether on infrastructure such as bridges, power plants, and dams; our food and water supply; civilians; or other targets. In November 2002, Congress created the Department of Homeland Security (DHS) to protect our nation from terrorist threats. In response, two- and four-year colleges have developed or expanded curriculum that aims to educate and train students to work for the DHS; other government agencies at the federal, state, and local level; and private security companies. Students in homeland security programs often have the opportunity to pursue a variety of tracks, including aviation safety and security, emergency medical services management, computer security, forensic sciences, public health and emergency management, telecommunication and national security, information security management, and computer fraud investigations. Students in each track take common core courses as well as general studies courses. Degrees in homeland security are available at the certificate, associate, baccalaureate, and master degree level.

Typical Courses:

- Aviation Security
- Airline Transport Security
- Risk Management
- Terrorism, Counter Terrorism, and Terrorism Response
- Disaster Preparedness and Emergency Systems
- Emergency Response to Terrorism
- Cyberterrorism

Potential Employers:

- State and local government agencies
- Federal government agencies (such as the Department of Homeland Security; the Bureau of Alcohol, Tobacco, Firearms, and Explosives; and the Federal Bureau of Investigation)
- Private security companies
- Hospitals

> Airports
> Amusement parks
> Cruise industry
> Rail transportation industry

Available At:

Many colleges and universities are in the process of developing programs in homeland security. Some schools offer a concentration in homeland security, usually within their criminal justice departments. Check with institutions near you to determine if majors, minors, or concentrations are available in homeland security. Additionally, visit the National Academic Consortium for Homeland Security's website, http://homelandsecurity.osu.edu/NACHS, for a list of member schools.

Corinthian Colleges
888/741-4271
www.cci.edu
Degrees available: Associate degree, bachelor's degree
Corinthian Colleges, Inc., one of the largest postsecondary education companies in North America, operating 94 colleges in 24 states in the U.S. and 32 colleges in seven provinces in Canada, offers degrees in Homeland Security at many of its campuses. Visit the organization's website for further information.

George Washington University (Washington, DC)
202/994-0986
www.homelandsecurity.gwu.edu
Degrees available: Certificate, associate degree, bachelor's degree, master's degree

The Ohio State University (Columbus, OH)
614/292-9657
http://psweb.sbs.ohio-state.edu/International/majors/security_intelligence.html
Degrees available: Bachelor's degree (in international studies with a specialization in security and intelligence)

Pierpont Community and Technical College (Fairmont, WV)
304/367-4678
www.fairmontstate.edu/academics/CTC_HomelandSecurity
Degrees available: Associate degree

San Diego State University (San Diego, CA)
http://homelandsecurity.sdsu.edu
Degrees available: Master's degree

Virginia Commonwealth University (Richmond, VA)
804/828-2292
www.pubapps.vcu.edu/gov
Degrees available: Bachelor's degree, master's degree, advanced certificate

Many graduates of homeland security programs find employment with U.S. Customs and Border Protection, an agency of the U.S. Department of Homeland Security. Above, U.S. Customs and Border Protection agents use sophisticated x-ray equipment to detect contraband in packages and luggage. (Photo courtesy of James R. Tourtellotte, U.S. Customs and Border Protection)

For More Information:

National Academic Consortium for Homeland Security
Program for International and Homeland Security
http://homelandsecurity.osu.edu/NACHS

U.S. Department of Homeland Security
www.dhs.gov/dhspublic

Interview: Les Boggess

Pierpont Community and Technical College in Fairmont, West Virginia, created one of the first associate degree programs in homeland security in the United States. The editors of *They Teach That in College!?* discussed the program with Les Boggess, Associate Professor of Criminal Justice and Program Coordinator.

Q. Please briefly describe your program.

A. Our program is a multitrack degree program. A student can choose to follow either criminal justice, aviation, safety, or emergency medical services tracks. There are common core classes as well as specific courses for the track, as well as general studies courses. At present, we are offering a two-year associate degree.

Q. What types of students enter your program? What are their career goals and interests?

A. Frequently, students who enroll in this program are also enrolled in the four year criminal justice program. They can count the associate degree as their minor for criminal justice. Other students are planning a career strictly in homeland security, and major only in that field.

Q. What types of careers will students be able to work in upon completion of his or her degree?

A. There are all sorts of employment opportunities opening up at the federal level, but also in the private sector and among city, local, and county government agencies.

Q. What personal qualities should a student have to be successful in your program and in their post-college career?

A. Motivation, a desire to help others and be part of a team, academic discipline, and a clean police record. They must also possess integrity, be a U.S. citizen, and be able to pass a background check.

Q. Does your school have any type of relationship with the Department of Homeland Security (DHS)?

A. Yes. I attended seminars this summer with the Department of Homeland Security and maintain close contact with representatives of the DHS. Our program is listed on the website maintained at www.training.fema.gov/EMIWeb/edu/collegelist/dhsassociate.

Q. Is the DHS a logical career path for graduates of your program?

A. Yes. There will be many jobs created in the next few years that do not currently exist. Although it is unfortunate that these jobs are necessary, political reality suggests that we must of necessity become a more careful society, guarding against attacks both from outside and from within.

Horticultural Therapy

For hundreds, if not thousands, of years, people have enjoyed the calming effect of a walk in a garden or other natural setting; others find the act of gardening to be relaxing. Horticultural therapy focuses on the therapeutic value provided by tending to flowers, plants, trees, and other gardening-related acts, as well as simply enjoying serene garden surroundings. Most horticultural therapy programs embrace a multi-disciplinary approach that includes not only the study of horticulture, but also education, gerontology, psychology, and sociology. Horticultural therapy programs instruct students on how to design and implement a therapeutic horticulture program and how to make horticulture accessible to people with various needs, such as adapting tools so they can be used by someone with limited flexibility or strength, or constructing raised flower beds so they can be used by someone who is wheelchair-bound. In addition, some programs provide training on the business-related aspects of horticultural therapy, such as funding and administration. Only a few colleges and universities offer degrees in horticultural therapy.

Typical Courses:

- Introduction to Horticultural Science
- Horticulture For Special Populations
- Case Management
- Field Techniques
- Field Experiences
- Human Issues in Horticultural Therapy
- General Chemistry
- Psychology

Potential Employers:

- Hospitals
- Rehabilitation centers
- Government social service agencies
- Correctional facilities
- Schools
- Botanical centers
- Nursing homes

Available At:

Only a few horticultural therapy programs in the United States are accredited by the American Horticultural Therapy Association; these include:

Kansas State University (Manhattan, KS)
785/532-1420
rmattson@oznet.ksu.edu
www.oznet.ksu.edu/horttherapy
Degrees available: Bachelor's degree, master's degree, doctorate

University of Maine-Orono (Orono, ME)
207/581-2948
william_mitchell@umit.maine.edu
www.umaine.edu/lhc/ugrad_therapy.htm
Degrees available: Bachelor's degree (concentration in horticultural therapy)

Rutgers University (New Brunswick, NJ)
732/932-9711
flagler@aesop.rutgers.edu
www.aesop.rutgers.edu/~horttherapy
Degrees available: Certificate, bachelor's degree

For More Information:

American Horticultural Therapy Association
800/634-1603
info@ahta.org
www.ahta.org

Interview: Richard Mattson

Dr. Richard Mattson is the Director of the undergraduate and distance learning component of the Horticultural Therapy Program at Kansas State University in Manhattan, Kansas. It is one of the few programs in the United States that is accredited by the American Horticultural Therapy Association. Dr. Mattson discussed his school's program and the education of students in this field with the editors of *They Teach That in College!?*

Q. Please tell us about your program.

A. Horticultural therapy was first offered as a B.S. curriculum in 1971 at Kansas State University in cooperation with Menningers, a private psychiatric hospital, where students completed six-month clinical internships. In 1975, the master of science specialization was first offered, followed by the Ph.D. specialization in 1979. Kansas State University was the first and remains the only university to offer all three degrees. In addition, we offer distance education courses in horticultural therapy, but no certificate program exists at the present time.

Q. What type of internship opportunities are provided by your program?

A. Internships are available in six areas, including mental health, geriatrics, vocational rehabilitation, corrections, special and public education, and community-based programs. Internships are available throughout the United States and abroad.

Q. What high school subjects/activities should students focus on to be successful in this major?

A. Horticultural therapy is a multi-disciplinary field, so high school subject areas might include chemistry, math, social sciences, biological sciences, statistics, English, and another modern language. High school activities that promote leadership skills, creative arts, community service, etc. would be useful.

Q. What are the most important personal and professional qualities for horticultural therapy students?

A. Personal skills should include compassion to help others, effective communication skills, a love of nature and horticulture, resourcefulness, an ability to motivate others, and a commitment to work with people to improve the quality of human life and environments.

Q. What is the employment outlook for horticultural therapy? How will the field change in the future?

A. Employment opportunities are excellent, but few of our graduates are hired with the title of horticultural therapist. Most institutional programs, medical centers, correctional facilities, etc. use titles such as activity therapist, vocational rehabilitation trainer, horticultural instructor, horticultural extension specialist, or Peace Corps volunteer to name a few. Horticultural therapy program consultants are in demand and most charge between $75 to $100 per hour for their advice and services. Current research in the areas of biofeedback, psycho-physiological responses, pain reduction, sensory stimulation effects, and healing garden landscapes will lead to more jobs in the future.

Interview: Joel Flagler

Professor Joel Flagler is the coordinator of the Horticultural Therapy program at Rutgers University in New Brunswick, New Jersey. Rutgers offers one of the few degree programs in the United States that is accredited by the American Horticultural Therapy Association (AHTA). Also, its certificate program is fully accredited by the AHTA. Professor Flagler discussed his school's program and the education of students in this field with the editors of *They Teach That in College!?*

Q. Please tell us about your program.

A. Rutgers offer a B.S. degree program in horticultural therapy and a certificate as well. Visit our website, www.aesop.rutgers.edu/~hortherapy, for more information.

Q. What is one thing that young people may not know about horticultural therapy?

A. Young people may not know that horticultural therapy is a combination of plant sciences and people sciences. It brings together the "People-Plant Connection" and is all about improving lives and health using plants, gardens, and greenhouses as "tools."

Q. What type of internship opportunities are provided by your program?

A. Internships are available at a wide range of facilities and agencies and schools that serve individuals with special needs. Students choose their internship site and must do 40 hours at the site under supervision of a registered horticultural therapist

Q. What types of students pursue study in your program?

A. All sorts of students pursue horticultural therapy. There are no prerequisites. All that one needs is desire to help others, especially those with disabilities, and the 'green thumb' skills to manage gardens, greenhouses, and plants.

Q. Where do your graduates find employment?

A. Graduates are working at hospitals, nursing homes, schools, botanical gardens, arboreta, mental health clinics, prisons, and many other facilities that serve people with special needs. Many go on to consult—designing programs, securing grants and funding, evaluating and documenting existing programs, etc.

Q. What is the employment outlook for horticultural therapy?

A. The outlook is very bright for horticultural therapy graduates. They are in great demand at so many facilities and institutions. Since there are few schools offering degrees and certificates, the need is greater than the supply for good, trained horticultural therapists who can facilitate these innovative and highly effective programs. The field will grow as more facilities come to recognize the benefits for participants on many levels: mental, psycho-emotional, physical, social, vocational, etc.

Hospice Education

Hospice workers care for people who are approaching death, helping patients—and their friends and families—live each day to the fullest. They may also assist family and friends with bereavement counseling after the patient has died. Since the first hospice program was established in 1974, the field has bloomed: in 2005, there were more than 3,000 Medicare-certified hospice programs in the United States. Due to an aging population and an increasing concern about end-of-life care, hospice remains a fast-growing field, attracting students who are empathetic and who like to help people. Madonna University offers the only university-based hospice education program in the United States, with certificates, associate, bachelor, and master degrees available. Students who complete one of the programs are able to apply what they have learned in a variety of fields, including bereavement counseling, social work, nursing, and gerontology. Some students opt to combine their hospice degree/certificate with degrees in another field, such as social work or nursing.

Typical Courses:

- Introduction to Hospice Care Concepts
- Management of the Bereavement Process
- Psychosocial Components of Hospice Care
- Spiritual and Ethical Considerations in Hospice Care
- Comfort and Care for the Hospice Client
- Managing Hospice Services
- Hospice Field Experience
- Emerging Issues in Interdisciplinary Hospice Care
- Life/Death Issues
- Empathy Listening Skills

Potential Employers:

- Hospice care organizations
- Hospitals

Available At:

Madonna University (Livonia, MI)
734/432-5716
www.madonna.edu/pages/hospiceeducation.cfm

Degrees available: Certificate, associate degree, bachelor's degree, master's degree, advanced certificates (bereavement, hospice education)

For More Information:

Hospice Education Institute
www.hospiceworld.org

National Association for Home Care and Hospice
www.nahc.org

National Hospice and Palliative Care Organization
www.nhpco.org

Interview: Kelly Rhoades

Dr. Kelly Rhoades is the Chair of the Hospice Education Department at Madonna University in Livonia, Michigan. The school offers the only university-based hospice education program in the United States, with certificates, associate, bachelor, and master degrees available. Dr. Rhoades discussed her program with the editors of *They Teach That in College!?*

Q. What activities should high school students focus on to be successful in this major?

A. Any service learning or volunteer opportunities would be most helpful in preparing for a career in the hospice and palliative care field. Many hospices offer volunteer training programs that target young adults. It is an experience that benefits students at a personal and professional level.

Q. What type of internship opportunities are provided by your program?

A. Internships are required at both the undergraduate and graduate levels. Placements are made within hospices, hospice residences, or hospice and palliative care programs within larger health care settings (i.e., in hospitals). The internships range form 90 to 125 hours of actual field time, and 15 hours of seminar. Students design their experiences by choosing a site and creating their personal objectives.

Did You Know?

More than 1.3 million people received hospice care in 2006, according to the National Hospice and Palliative Care Organization.

Q. What type of individuals make good hospice workers?

A. People who pursue this field often have had a significant life experience that has been life-altering, and changed their perspective on what is important. It often leads them toward a search for meaning, that includes opportunities to give of themselves. So it takes sensitivity, compassion, and a commitment toward caring for people at what is often the most difficult time of their lives. One has to be comfortable with discussion about life and death issues.

Q. Why is hospice care such a good option for those who are terminally ill?

A. The most valuable aspect of hospice care is that it addresses the needs of both the patient and the family at a very stressful and confusing time in life. Curative care is not an appropriate model when someone has a life-threatening illness, yet we see health care professionals, hence families, resisting hospice care because they think of it as "giving up." Nothing is further from the truth. Hospice care is about living life fully until death, thus opportunities for relationships at end of life that could be overlooked are enhanced within the interdisciplinary model of hospice. End of life care delivery is a growing field, and one that is in need of continued education within university health care programs and the communities that surround them.

Integrated Marketing Communications

Integrated marketing communications programs teach students how to examine the natural connections between what were once seen as separate disciplines—public relations, marketing, business, communications, advertising, sales promotion, and electronic marketing. Attracting the attention of today's consumers—especially in a world of podcasts, cable television, the 24-hour newscycle, and the Internet—is increasingly difficult, yet key if businesses are to be successful. Students in integrated marketing communications programs gain fun and practical experience developing and presenting communications strategies for real companies and work at such diverse internship placements as all four major American television networks, Capitol Records, Comedy Central, DDB Worldwide, and National Public Radio.

Typical Courses:

- Advertising
- Public Relations
- Marketing
- Consumer Behavior
- Research Methods
- Quantitative Mass Media Research Methods
- Media Writing
- Statistics
- Consumer Behavior
- Marketing on the Internet

Potential Employers:

- Advertising agencies
- Public relations firms
- Governmental agencies
- Nonprofit organizations
- Media outlets
- Corporations

Available At:

The following programs are just a sampling of the opportunities that are available to students interested in integrated marketing communications. Visit the websites of schools in your area to see if they offer study options in the field.

Emerson College (Boston, MA)
617/824-8354
www.emerson.edu/marketing_communication/index.cfm
Degrees available: Master's degree

Golden Gate University (San Francisco, CA)
800/448-4968
www.ggu.edu/academic_programs
Degrees available: Master's degree, advanced certificate

Ithaca College (Ithaca, NY)
607/274-1021
www.ithaca.edu/rhp/programs/imc
Degrees available: Bachelor's degree

Loyola University Chicago (Chicago, IL)
312/915-6501
www.luc.edu/scps/managmentimc_curriculum.shtml
Degrees available: Bachelor's degree

Manhattanville College (Purchase, NY)
914/694-2200
www.manhattanville.edu/AcademicsandResearch/GraduateStudies/BusinessandManagement/IntegratedMarketingCommunications/Default.aspx
Degrees available: Master's degree

Roosevelt University (Chicago, IL)
312/341-3500
www.roosevelt.edu/cas/comm/imc.htm
Degrees available: Master's degree

For More Information:

Advertising Educational Foundation
212/986-8060
www.aef.com/industry/careers

American Advertising Federation
800/999-2231
www.aaf.org

Public Relations Society of America
212/460-1400
www.prsa.org

International Rescue and Relief

During times of natural or man-made disaster, specially trained professionals are key in providing rescue, survival or humanitarian relief. Working with federal agencies or privately run organizations, international rescue and relief workers travel to affected areas to try to bring order where there is chaos. For example, workers may travel to areas of conflict such as Darfur, Sudan. Workers set up camps and clinics to dispense badly needed healthcare, nutrition intervention, and education. They may also teach residents how to better manage crops and resources. Others may travel to areas ravaged by natural disasters. They provide medical assistance and counseling as well as the physical help needed to rebuild homes and businesses. Interested students should prepare for hard work, rough and sometimes dangerous living conditions, and travel to often remote areas of the world. Their work may take them to politically and culturally volatile regions. The payback is great, however. Rescue and relief workers make a major impact in the lives of those less fortunate, and are many times the difference between life and death.

Typical Courses:

- EMT Basic
- Emergency Care
- Travel/Tropical Medicine
- Basic Survival and Jungle, Coastal, Ocean Survival
- Swift Water Technician or Rope Rescue Technician
- Critical Incident Stress Management

Potential Employers:

- Private humanitarian organizations, such as the Red Cross, Doctors Without Borders, and International Rescue Committee
- Federal government agencies

Available At:

Union College (Lincoln, NE)
402/486-2980
miduehrs@ucollege.edu
www.ucollege.edu
Degrees available: Bachelor's degree

For More Information:

American Red Cross
www.redcross.org

Landscape Architecture

If you've ever admired a well-designed and beautiful park, playground, garden, college or high school campus, country club, shopping center, zoo, or even skate park, then you've seen the work of a landscape architect first-hand. Landscape architects analyze, plan, design, and manage outdoor spaces. They use computer-aided design software, computer mapping systems, and other tools to design outdoor spaces that not only serve practical needs, but also protect the environment. You will need a bachelor's or master's degree in landscape architecture to work in this field. Employment prospects for landscape architects are excellent. The U.S. Department of Labor predicts that the career of landscape architect will grow about as fast as the average for all occupations through 2016. Approximately 28,000 landscape architects are employed in the United States.

Typical Courses:

- Landscape Design Methods
- Plans and Design
- Landscape Graphics
- Regional Landscape History
- Landscape Construction
- The Urban Landscape
- World Gardens
- Landscape Architectural Practice
- Drawing the Landscape

Potential Employers:

- Consulting firms
- Public agencies
- Landscape construction and nursery companies
- Government agencies such as the National Park Service, U.S. Forest Service, Bureau of Land Management
- Self-employment

Available At:

Approximately 65 colleges and universities offer undergraduate and.or graduate programs that are accredited by the Landscape Architectural Accreditation Board. A portion are listed below. Visit www.asla.org for a complete list of programs.

Arizona State University (Tempe, AZ)
480/965-3536
http://design.asu.edu/sala/index.shtml
Degrees available: Bachelor's degree

California State Polytechnic University (Pomona, CA)
909/869-2673
www.csupomona.edu/~la
Degrees available: Bachelor's degree, master's degree

Colorado State University (Fort Collins, CO)
www.colostate.edu/Depts/LArch
Degrees available: Bachelor's degree

University of Connecticut (Storrs, CT)
www.canr.uconn.edu/plsci/la/index.html
Degrees available: Bachelor's degree

University of Florida (Gainesville, FL)
352/392-6098 (ext. 321, undergraduate), (ext. 326, graduate)
www.dcp.ufl.edu/landscape
Degrees available: Bachelor's degree, master's degree

University of Georgia (Athens, GA)
706/542-1816
www.sed.uga.edu
Degrees available: Bachelor's degree, master's degree

University of Idaho (Moscow, ID)
www.caa.uidaho.edu/larch
Degrees available: Bachelor's degree, master's degree

University of Illinois-Champaign-Urbana
217/333-0176
LADept@uiuc.edu
www.landarch.uiuc.edu
Degrees available: Bachelor's degree, master's degree, doctorate

University of Kentucky (Lexington, KY)
859/257-7295
www.uky.edu/Agriculture/LA
Degrees available: Bachelor's degree

Louisiana State University (Baton Rouge, LA)
225/578-1434
www.design.lsu.edu
Degrees available: Bachelor's degree, master's degree

University of Maryland (College Park, MD)
301/405-4359
www.larch.umd.edu
Degrees available: Bachelor's degree

North Dakota State University (Fargo, ND)
www.ndsu.edu/ndsu/landarch
Degrees available: Bachelor's degree

University of Oregon (Eugene, OR)
541/346-3634
http://landarch.uoregon.edu
Degrees available: Bachelor's degree, master's degree

Purdue University (West Lafayette, IN)
765/494-4600
www.hort.purdue.edu/hort/landarch/landarch.shtml
Degrees available: Bachelor's degree

Texas A&M University (College Station, TX)
979/845-1046
http://archone.tamu.edu/LAUP
Degrees available: Bachelor's degree, master's degree

For More Information:

American Society of Landscape Architects
www.asla.org

LAprofession.org
www.laprofession.org

Interview: Gary B. Kesler and James Wescoat Jr.

Gary Kesler and James Wescoat, faculty in the Department of Landscape Architecture at the University of Illinois at Urbana-Champaign, discussed their program and the education of landscape architecture students with the editors of *They Teach That in College!?*

Q. Tell us about your program.

A. The Department of Landscape Architecture offers bachelor's, master's, and doctoral degrees. The undergraduate program leads to a professionally accredited bachelor of landscape architecture, which enables students to work with professional landscape architecture design firms, design-build firms, multidisciplinary planning firms, public park districts, and related environmental fields. The professional B.L.A. and M.L.A. degrees also meet the educational requirement for taking the Landscape Architectural Registration Examination offered in all but a few states. The Department trains students broadly in the fields of environmental design and planning. We also have specializations in 1) Ecological Landscape Design; 2) Community-Based Urban Landscape Design; and 3) Cultural Heritage Landscape Design. In 2006, the Department initiated a new specialization, The

Business of Landscape Architecture, which helps students who envision business leadership as well as professional practice.

Q. What makes your program an appealing option for students interested in the field?

A. Students are drawn to landscape architecture for its combination of artistic creativity, intellectual stimulation, and professional opportunities to harmonize environmental and human well-being. Students can look forward to making a physical difference in the places where people live, work, and recreate. In addition, our "design studio" method of teaching ensures strong bonding among students and close student-faculty relationships—all set within the large context of a large research university. It combines the best aspects of the small college and large university.

Q. What type of internship opportunities are provided by your program?

A. Historically, we have helped arrange summer internship opportunities for undergraduate and graduate students with landscape architecture firms, design-build firms, and public agencies. This year, we are organizing a new program of full-year internships to increase student professional experience; and in the near future, it is our goal for all students to participate in a full-year internship (or combination internship-study abroad year). In addition to internships, the Department has many scholarships, including prestigious international and domestic traveling fellowships.

Q. What high school subjects/activities should students focus on to be successful in this major?

A. Students come to landscape architecture with a wide range of environmental, technical, and artistic interests. It is helpful if they have some prior computer-aided design, freehand drawing, graphic design, and/or general art classes. But most important is their passion to help to make the world a better place for human and natural communities, which may be expressed in community service projects, environmental projects, gardening, and a host of other activities.

Q. How will the field change in the future?

A. Landscape architecture ranges from small-scale residential garden design to urban design and large-scale river basin

Third-year BLA student Sam Zimbovsky, a student at the University of Illinois at Urbana-Champaign, receives comments from Department Head James Wescoat on his final design project. (Photo courtesy of the University of Illinois at Urbana-Champaign)

planning. In the future, landscape architects will increasingly be involved in "sustainable ecological design" and "green building" to conserve scarce resources and protect and restore natural ecosystems. Landscape architects will work on increasingly complex community design and cultural heritage projects. And they will do so in an increasingly dynamic context of globalization and global environmental change.

Q. What is the employment outlook for landscape architects?

A. The future is very bright for new landscape architects. The U.S. Department of Labor predicts landscape architecture to experience faster than average growth (18-26 percent) for all occupations through 2014. There are more jobs than students, both within the Midwest and nationwide; and entry-level salaries are increasing. In large measure, these trends reflect landscape architects ability to work on pressing problems, to draw upon different branches of knowledge to help solve those problems, and to envision hopeful futures for the next generation.

Legal Nurse Consulting

If you are interested in both nursing and the law, then you might be interested in learning more about the career of *legal nurse consultant.* Legal nurse consultants are registered nurses who have considerable experience and knowledge of the health care and legal industries. They use this knowledge to assist lawyers in health care-related cases. According to the American Association of Legal Nurse Consultants, the leading professional organization for the profession, legal nurse consultants offer support to the law profession in the following practice areas: personal injury, product liability, medical malpractice, workers' compensation, toxic torts, risk management, medical licensure investigation, criminal law, elder law, and fraud and abuse compliance. To enter legal nurse consulting programs, applicants must typically have a bachelor of science in nursing and/or have nursing experience.

Typical Courses:

- Legal Nurse Consulting: Principles and Practice
- Fundamentals of Law
- Legal Research and Writing
- Computer Assisted Legal Research
- Paralegalism and Legal Procedure
- Elder Law
- Health Law
- Rules of Evidence
- Personal Injury and Product Liability
- Medical Ethics

Potential Employers:

- Law firms
- Insurance companies
- Corporations—such as pharmaceutical companies and medical equipment manufacturers—that deal with health-related products or services
- Government agencies
- Hospitals (in risk management departments)
- Forensic environments
- Consulting firms
- Health management organizations

Available At:

Bergen Community College (Paramus, NJ)
201/447-7100
www.bergen.edu/ecatalog/
programview.asp?program.cbn=15&semester.rm=1
Degrees available: Associate degree

Elgin Community College (Elgin, IL)
847/697-1000
www.elgin.edu
Degrees available: Advanced certificate

Johnson County Community College (Overland Park, KS)
913/469-8500
www.jccc.net
Degrees available: Advanced certificates (legal nurse consultant, legal nurse consultant entrepreneurship)

Kent State University (Kent, OH)
330/672-3000
www.kent.edu
Degrees available: Advanced certificate

Madonna University (Livonia, MI)
800/852-4951
www.madonna.edu/pages/npcertificate.cfm
Degrees available: Advanced certificate

Roger Williams University (Bristol, RI)
www.rwu.edu/academics/departments
Degrees available: Advanced certificate

University of Toledo (Toledo, OH)
419/530-4636
www.utoledo.edu/hshs/paralegal/index.html
Degrees available: Advanced certificate

For More Information:

American Association of Legal Nurse Consultants
877/402-2562
www.aalnc.org/becomeLnc

Mechatronic Systems Engineering

Mechatronic systems engineering is an interdisciplinary field that encompasses mechanical engineering, electrical and computer engineering, math, and computer science. It's goal is to seamlessly integrate the se disciplines to design complex systems that can used to perform tasks. Students of mechatronic system engineering programs focus on the analytical skills and the principles of mechanical design. The field of mechatronics is growing rapidly because it offers consistency, profitability, reliability, and overall quality control in many areas of production that can be used in many different environments. *Mechatronic systems engineers* are found in a variety of settings, working with vehicle assembly, food and medicine processing, defense systems, computer chip production, robotics, to name a few examples. The demand for graduates of mechatronic system engineering programs is expected to grow as mechatronics are used in an increasing number of applications.

Typical Courses:

> Analytical and Adaptive Dynamics in Mechatronic Systems
> Mechanical Design of Mechatronic Systems/Robots
> Modern Control in Mechatronic Systems
> Adaptive Control in Mechatronic Systems
> Optimization in Mechatronic Systems
> Intelligent Control
> Mechatronic Systems Implementation

Potential Employers:

> Automotive
> Aerospace
> Robotics and Manufacturing
> Military
> Federal government
> Biomedical Engineering
> Transportation
> Agriculture
> Communication Systems and Media
> Businesses of all sizes

Available At:

University of Denver (Denver, CO)
303/871-2102
www.du.edu/grad/bulletins/engineering
Degrees available: Master's degree

Lawrence Technological University (Southfield, MI)
248/204-2577
vantsevich@ltu.edu
www.ltu.edu/engineering/mechanical/mechatronics.asp
Degrees available: Master's degree

Simon Fraser University (Burnaby, BC Canada)
778/782-4371
www.ensc.sfu.ca/undergraduates/mechatronics
Degrees available: Bachelor's degree

For More Information:

American Society of Mechanical Engineers
800/843-2763
www.asme.org and http://divisions.asme.org/dscd

International Network of Mechatronics Universities
www.mechatronics-net.de/international

Mechatronics Education Center
www.mechatronics-mec.org

Interview: Vladimir Vantsevich

Dr. Vladimir Vantsevich is a Professor and Director of the Mechatronic Systems Engineering Program at Lawrence Technological University in Southfield, Michigan. He discussed his school's program and the education of students in this field with the editors of *They Teach That in College!?*

Q. What is mechatronics systems engineering?

A. In general, mechatronic systems engineering (MSE) is an interdisciplinary, high technology field in engineering. MSE synergizes the knowledge outcome by integrating the specific areas of mechanical engineering, electrical and computer engineering, and math and computer science.

The major objective of MSE is the design and implementation of mechatronic systems as a new type of system in which mechanical, electro, and electronic subsystems are naturally designed into a whole system.

As an interdisciplinary field, mechatronic systems engineering interfaces with other engineering fields and natural and technical sciences. This has lead to novel areas in research and engineering such as biology-inspired systems, optomechatronics, biomedical engineering, and innovative material-based systems.

Q. Please tell us about your program.

A. This program is unique in the United States and offers the degree of master of science in mechatronic systems engineering (MSMSE). Graduates will:

1. Learn the principles in mechanical design for mechatronic systems
2. Develop strong analytical and application skills in the analytical and adaptive dynamics of mechatronic systems
3. Obtain expert knowledge in the areas of logic design of mechatronic systems, the classical and modern intelligent/robust control algorithm development, and the design of mechanical systems in conjunction with their control systems
4. Develop analytical skills in the optimization of mechatronic systems
5. Learn principles of design and will be capable to implement control algorithms in hardware-mechatronic systems.

The MSMSE program relates to various types of systems. Emphasis is placed on mechatronic systems engineering for land vehicles and industrial robots, and the program will provide a skill set much in demand. Land vehicles include (i) autonomous (unmanned, mobile robotic) vehicles for various applications and (ii) conventional vehicles such as trucks, cars, and tractors.

The MSMSE program and its new laboratory of mechatronic systems offers deep analytical product-oriented courses and hand-on laboratory work. Balanced sets of lectures and hands-on labs on pneumatically and hydraulically controlled mechatronic systems, industrial robotic manipulators, and measurement and data acquisition systems are included in the program. Software products such as MATLAB and Simulink, LabVIEW, MSC.ADAMS, and dSPACE are in use. A special feature of the MSMSE program is the unique 4x4 vehicle chassis dynamometer with independent wheel control. Professionals can get the training in classes that are conveniently scheduled in the evenings. More details about the program and scholarship are available at www.ltu.edu/engineering/mechanical/mechatronics.asp.

Q. What type of internship opportunities are provided by your program?

A. Multiple branches in the industry seek mechatronic systems engineers. The International Industry Advisory Board of the MSMSE Program is comprised of engineers, executives, and other working professionals from 20 companies, governmental research agencies, and professional societies. The Board provides input on the needs of industry, advice on curriculum, course, and laboratory development. The Board also recommends potential research topics and assists in program assessment. Human resources departments from various industries have established relations with the University's office of career service and offer attractive internships and co-ops.

Q. What are the most important personal and professional qualities for mechatronics engineering students?

A. Admission to the program is competitive. Applicants with strong analytical and creative engineering skills must:

✔ Hold a bachelor of science degree in mechanical engineering, electrical, or computer engineering or an equivalent degree from an Accreditation Board for Engineering Technology-accredited college or university. Individuals with a bachelor of science in mathematics or computer science, or an equivalent degree from an accredited college or university, and three to five years of experience working in mechatronic systems engineering, may apply.

✔ Have a minimum undergraduate overall GPA of 3.0.

The diversity of the MSMSE program and student population provides professional growth and a competitive advantage for stable employment opportunities in today's and future job markets. The ages of the student population ranges from under 30 to over 50. All students are practicing engineers, with a range of graduate and undergraduate degrees, including one student who holds a Ph.D. degree in materials.

Q. What is the employment outlook in mechatronics engineering? How will the field change in the future?

A. Mechatronic systems engineers combine sets of engineering skills, bridging mechanical engineering and electronic/computer engineering, and are attractive to employers because they are so versatile. 25 percent of the MSMSE current students have been promoted or obtained better jobs after the program started in September 2006. Such engineers can find positions and work in many fields, including:

- ✔ Aerospace and Automotive
- ✔ Robotic Industry and Manufacturing
- ✔ Military Vehicle and Autonomous Vehicle Engineering
- ✔ Defense Systems Engineering
- ✔ Biomedical Engineering
- ✔ Truck and Agricultural Tractor Engineering
- ✔ Climate Control Systems Engineering
- ✔ Material Processing
- ✔ Machine Test Systems Engineering
- ✔ Communication Systems and Media
- ✔ Big and small business companies in countless fields of human activities.

The way that the MSMSE program was designed provides high-level expertise and skills for a stable and multiple-year professional career. Emerging research trends in biomechanics and chemistry, bio-materials, and biology in general will bring new horizons in mechatronic systems engineering.

Medical Illustration

Are you a talented artist with a fascination for medicine, biology, and related fields? If so, you may have a career as a medical illustrator in your future. Medical illustrators, according to the Association of Medical Illustrators, are "professional artists . . . who create visual material to help record and disseminate medical, biological, and related knowledge." They illustrate medical and surgical procedures and techniques and biological and anatomical structures (such as the human heart, the bones of the foot, and arteries and veins) and processes. They may also create work in three dimensions, such as models for simulated medical procedures and anatomical teaching models. A master's degree in medical illustration is required for most positions in medical illustration. Four colleges in the United States and one in Canada offer accredited graduate programs in medical illustration.

Typical Courses:

> Digital Illustration
> Reference Photography
> Two- and three-dimensional design
> Head, Hands, and Facial Expressions
> Figures in Motion
> General and Human Biology
> Human Gross Anatomy
> Zoological and Botanical Illustration
> 3-D Model Design
> Anatomical Visualization

Potential Employers:

> Hospitals
> Medical centers
> Specialty clinics
> Medical organizations
> Medical journals
> Colleges and universities
> Private companies
> Book and magazine publishers
> Advertising agencies
> Pharmaceutical and medical product companies
> Law firms

Available At:

The following graduate medical illustration programs are accredited by the Commission on Accreditation of Allied Health Education Programs:

University of Illinois-Chicago (Chicago, IL)
312/996-7337
www.ahs.uic.edu/bhis/programs/bvis.php
Degrees available: Master's degree

John Hopkins University (Baltimore, MD)
410/955-3213
medart-info@jhmi.edu
www.med.jhu.edu/medart
Degrees available: Master's degree

Medical College of Georgia (Augusta, GA)
706/721-3266
medart@mcg.edu
www.mcg.edu/medart
Degrees available: Master's degree

University of Texas (Dallas, TX)
214/648-4699
biocomm@utsouthwestern.edu
www.utsouthwestern.edu/biomedcom
Degrees available: Master's degree

University of Toronto (Toronto, ON Canada)
416/978-2659
www.bmc.med.utoronto.ca/bmc
Degrees available: Master's degree

For More Information:

Association of Medical Illustrators
866/393-4264
hq@ami.org
http://medical-illustrators.org

BioCommunications Association, Inc.
919/245-0906
office@bca.org
www.bca.org

Health and Science Communications Association
860/376-5915
www.hesca.org

Interview: Steven Harrison

Steven Harrison is the Chairman of the Department of Medical Illustration at the Medical College of Georgia, which is located in Augusta, Georgia. He discussed his program and the education of medical illustration students with the editors of *They Teach That in College!?*

Q. Please provide an overview of your medical illustration program.

A. Medical illustrators are specially trained artists who communicate complex scientific ideas in a meaningful, aesthetic, and understandable manner. They create visuals for a variety of audiences and media, including art for print (textbooks, journals, magazines, and posters), and projection (animation and still art for television, classroom, and interactive multimedia presentations). Medical illustrators are employed in medical schools, urban medical centers, large hospitals, and specialty clinics. They may work in single-artist studios or large production departments. Advertising agencies, publishers, and pharmaceutical and medical product companies use the services of private-practice medical illustrators. Attorneys may commission medical illustrators to produce artwork to be used as demonstrative evidence in the courtroom.

The Medical Illustration Graduate Program at the Medical College of Georgia has been in existence since 1949 and offers a two-year (five semesters, 21 months) curriculum leading to a Master of Science degree in Medical Illustration. The curriculum combines coursework in the basic medical sciences (human gross anatomy, cell biology, histology, pathology), mostly taken with medical students, and instruction in illustration techniques in traditional and digital media. Problem solving assignments stress clarity and accuracy of scientific content and storytelling directed to specific audiences and education levels (professional, patient, and/or lay public). Students spend considerable time drawing from the human cadaver and other references, as well as observing and sketching in the operating room.

Admission to the program is competitive and based on academic performance, a portfolio of artwork demonstrating advanced drawing and painting ability, and a personal interview. A baccalaureate degree is required, as are prerequisite courses in human physiology and comparative vertebrate anatomy/morphology.

Q. What are the most important personal and professional qualities for medical illustration majors?

A. Medical illustration majors should have advanced drawing and painting skills, as demonstrated by a comprehensive portfolio of artwork. We prefer to see artwork that is drawn from life and not from photographic reference. Even though professional illustrators may use some photographic references, medical illustrators often draw what cannot be seen, and thus must have strong conceptualization abilities when direct reference materials are unavailable. Prospective students should also have a keen interest in science. The ability to conceptualize complex subject matter and reconstruct information into a visual story is most important. Creativity and problem solving skills are invaluable to any successful illustrator. It is important to be able to produce high quality work under tight deadline schedules.

Many prospective medical illustration students have undergraduate majors in art (usually drawing and painting). However, perhaps a third of our applicants major in the biological sciences with a minor in art. Realistic rendering skills and attention to detail are hallmarks of the profession.

Q. What advice would you offer MI majors as they graduate and look for jobs?

A. Job placement in the field of medical illustration is quite good for recent graduates. It may be necessary to relocate to different geographic locations to secure employment, so the graduating student must be flexible in this regard. A professional quality portfolio and resume are essential to gaining employment. Additional skills in digital media (e.g., animation and Web design), graphic design, and writing make the individual more valuable to an employer.

Q. What educational level is typically required for medical illustration graduates to land good jobs in the industry?

A. All medical illustration programs accredited by the Association of Medical Illustrators and the Commission on Accreditation of Allied Health Education Programs must be at the graduate (master's degree) level. Professional certification is available to graduates of accredited programs or individuals who have practiced in the field for five or more years. Certification examination and credentials are administered by the Board of Certification for Medical Illustrators.

Q. How will the field of medical illustration change in the future?

A. The future of the profession of medical illustration has been, and will continue to be, influenced by developing technologies in communication and computer graphics. Knowledge of these technologies and visual graphics software is becoming a necessity for the practicing illustrator, although strong drawing and conceptualization skills remain key. I am often asked if the computer is going to replace the medical illustrator. The computer is merely one of the many artistic tools with which we work, and new technologies have created an even greater need for the trained and knowledgeable medical illustrator. The growing mass of scientific and medical knowledge, and the increasing need to communicate such and educate more audiences, will provide a greater need for medical illustrators. For example, in the last few years, I have seen an increase in the use of, and jobs in, medical animation and 3-D modeling.

Motorsport Engineering

Are you a fan of auto racing? Do you like designing and building things? If so, the Motorsport Engineer Program at Colorado State University may help you put the pedal to the metal when it comes to preparing for a career in motorsport engineering. The graduate-level (master's and Ph.D.) program seeks to train motorsport engineers in vehicle design, vehicle setup, and race preparation. Graduates work as *motorsport design engineers,* who design and analyze competitive race vehicles, and *motorsport team engineers,* who work as a member of a race team to improve the competitiveness of the vehicle and driver. To be eligible for graduate programs, students must have a bachelor's degree in an engineering field. Program facilities include state-of-the-art computational facilities, testing areas, and laboratories.

Typical Courses:

- Vehicle Dynamics
- Computational Fluid Dynamics
- Internal Combustion Engines
- Advanced Mechanical Systems
- Advanced Mechanics of Materials
- Fundamentals of Vibrations
- Finite Element Method
- Mathematical Analysis

Potential Employers:

- Racing teams
- Automobile manufacturers

Available At:

Colorado State University (Fort Collins, CO)
970/491-6909
www.engr.colostate.edu/me/motorsport
Degrees available: Master's degree, doctorate degree

For More Information:

American Society for Engineering Education
www.asee.org

Junior Engineering Technical Society
www.jets.org

Society of Manufacturing Engineers
www.sme.org

Multicultural Marketing

The United States is becoming an increasingly diverse place to live. The number of Asian Americans, Hispanic Americans, and people from other countries who do not speak English as their first language continues to increase. Hispanics are the fastest-growing ethnic group in the United States, and the U.S. Census Bureau predicts that they will account for more than 15.5 percent of the U.S. population by 2010. As a result, businesses of all types are beginning to focus on marketing to Hispanics and other diverse—and highly lucrative—demographics. Only two schools—Florida State University and DePaul University—offer training in this field, but expect more to add classes, concentrations, and majors as the United States becomes a more diverse nation.

Typical Courses:

- Intro to Marketing Research
- Quantitative Methods in Marketing
- Strategic Tools for Marketers
- Advanced Marketing Management
- Integrated Marketing Communications for Multicultural Markets
- Marketing Across Cultures
- Marketing Internship with a Multicultural Marketer

Potential Employers:

- Any company that seeks to market its services or products toHispanics or other ethnic groups

Available At:

DePaul University (Chicago, IL)
312/362-8788
market@depaul.edu
www.marketing.depaul.edu/multicultural
Degrees available: Bachelor's degree (concentration in multicultural marketing)

Florida State University (Tallahassee, FL)
850/644-8766
HMC@comm.fsu.edu
http://hmc.comm.fsu.edu
Degrees available: Master's degree (with emphasis in hispanic marketing communication), advanced certificate (hispanic marketing communication)

For More Information:

American Advertising Federation
800/999-2231
aaf@aaf.org
www.aaf.org

American Marketing Association
800/262-1150
www.marketingpower.com

Marketing Research Association
860/682-1000
email@mra-net.org
www.mra-net.org

Interview

The editors of *They Teach That in College* discussed the field of multicultural marketing with three educators at DePaul University: Steven Kelly, Associate Professor and Director of the Multicultural Marketing Program; Luis Larrea, Director of Partner Relations and faculty member; and Loida Rosario, Marketing Executive-in-Residence faculty member.

Q. Please tell us about your program.

A. Both the major and minor address the unique needs of an increasingly diverse society. By 2013, 35 percent of the U.S. population will be of a diverse ethnic heritage; by 2050 that number rises to about 50 percent. These are big numbers. We are starting with emphasis on the Hispanic marketplace and are already integrating African American and multiple Asian groups into our courses. Students study a combination of cultural awareness, marketing disciplines, and practical applications. Graduates could pursue careers in marketing, advertising, sales, and communications.

Multicultural Marketing majors follow the standard course curriculum with some specific course requirements for electives. Required courses include: MKT 202 Quantitative Methods in Marketing, MKT 315 Strategic Tools for Marketers, MKT 305 Intro to Marketing Research, and MKT 359 Advanced Marketing Management.

Students in this concentration must complete MKT 341 Integrated Marketing Communications for Hispanic Markets, MKT 340 Marketing Across Cultures: A Cultural Perspective on Latin Markets, and MKT 393 Marketing Internship with a Hispanic Marketer.

It is also highly recommended, but not required, that students in this concentration take the following electives to broaden their backgrounds: SPN 320 Commercial Spanish and/or demonstrate proficiency in Spanish through that department's classes or testing procedures, and MKT 376 Effective Business Communications. Commerce students have a communications requirement, which can be fulfilled by CMN 212 [Small Group Communication] or CMN 220 [Public Speaking], but MKT 376 is the Marketing Department's recommendation for this concentration, and any courses that might fit into the student's IP requirement in studying history or culture of Spanish-speaking countries.

Q. What types of students enter your program? What are their career goals and interests?

A. Students who take this concentration are undergraduates who either are marketing majors or students from liberal arts, such as communications or Spanish majors, who want to minor in marketing with a concentration in Multicultural Marketing-Hispanic Marketplace. Generally these students enter the marketing program during their junior year but don't take their internship and MKT 340 and 341 until senior year. The majority of the students are of Hispanic culture, but not all.

Q. What personal qualities should students have to be successful in your program and in their post-college careers?

A. Ideally, students who know a second language or are interested in working in multicultural markets in the U.S. or abroad. (We do not limit our students if they have an interest/background even if they are not fully bilingual.) Students should also have the ability to work in unfamiliar surroundings; be adaptable to change; have inquisitiveness, because it is new ground; respect for all cultures, since you cannot understand or connect with people from different cultures without respecting them; a desire to become a sophisticated marketer, because the field brings more complexity to the basic principles of marketing; and innovativeness, because many processes, metrics, and media are in developing stages.

Q. Who are the major employers of graduates of your program?

A. Even though we don't have students recruited yet, we have received enthusiastic responses from companies when they hear about the program. We do know that the companies asking for the development of the program are from all business areas. We have had suggestions from banking, retailing, insurance, advertising, and marketing research. This is a reflection of the types of industries our typical student goes to for employment.

Q. What is the future of your program?

A. Our Hispanic program is just the beginning. Our vision is to develop a multicultural marketing program at both the undergraduate and graduate level. These programs will develop expertise in dealing with not only the Hispanic, but also the African American, Asian, and Gay, Lesbian, Bisexual, and Transgender markets.

Museum Studies

Art, archaeology, anthropology, sociology, science, history . . . just some of the many subjects that museums everywhere focus on. For people who have an interest in a certain subject and want to share their knowledge with others, a career working in a museum or museum-like setting can be quite rewarding. Museum studies programs prepare students by exposing them to the different aspects needed to keep a museum functioning, such as how to obtain items for display, approaches in public education, how to manage collections (and staff), conservation and archival techniques, and how to design exhibits. Students who participate in museum studies programs gain the knowledge and experience they need to be successful through a variety of coursework and internships. They can expect to find employment options in the public or private sectors, working as an archivist, curator, manager, exhibit designer, or other related careers.

Typical Courses:

- Introduction to Museum Studies
- Curatorial Methods and Practices
- Special Topics in Museum Studies
- Museum Exhibitions: Theory and Development
- Museums and Technology
- Collections Care and Management
- Museum Management
- Principles and Practices of Museum Collection Management
- Museum Internship

Potential Employers:

- Museums and cultural centers
- Historical societies
- Local, state and federal parks and monuments
- Zoos and botanical gardens
- Libraries and archives

Available At:

University of the Arts (Philadelphia, PA)
http://prod.uarts.edu/graduate/ms/chome.html
http://prod.uarts.edu/graduate/ms/ehome.html
Degrees available: Master's degrees (museum communications, museum education)

Chadron State College (Chadron, NE)
www.csc.edu/sandoz/apphist.htm
Degrees available: Bachelor's degree

University of Denver (Denver, CO)
720/913-0153
www.du.edu/art/graduate/MAmuseum.htm
Degrees available: Master's degree

Indiana University-Purdue University Indianapolis
www.iupui.edu/~iuihome/
degree_info.php?degree=museum%20studies
Degrees available: Master's degree, advanced certificates (undergraduate, graduate)

University of Kansas (Lawrence, KS)
www2.ku.edu/~museumst
Degrees available: Master's degree

University of Michigan-Dearborn
313/593-5000
www.casl.umd.umich.edu/humanities/arthistorymain.html
Degrees available: Bachelor's degree

Michigan State University (East Lansing, MI)
517/353-1943
www.msu.edu/~msumsp
Degrees available: Bachelor's degree, advanced certificate

New York University (New York, NY)
212/998-8080
www.nyu.edu/fas/program/museumstudies
Degrees available: Master's degree, advanced certificate

San Francisco State University (San Francisco, CA)
415/405-0599
www.sfsu.edu
Degrees available: Master's degree

Seton Hall University (South Orange, NJ)
973/761-9022
www.shu.edu/academics/artsci/ma-museum-professions/index.cfm
Degrees available: Master's degree

Texas Tech University (Lubbock, TX)
806/742.2011
www.depts.ttu.edu/museumttu/msp.html
Degrees available: Master's degree

For More Information:

American Association of Museums
www.aam-us.org

Association of Art Museum Directors
www.aamd.org

Music Business

The music business is much more than just the performers we hear on the radio and see in concert or in videos on TV. Who works behind the scenes to make the stars look good? Who engineers the recording of a hit song? Who promotes the band and its merchandise? Who books shows and plans entire concert tours? People with a love for music and a head for business work behind-the scenes in this demanding, yet rewarding, industry. They handle all of the tasks mentioned above and more. Several schools across the United States now offer degrees that address the business side of music, preparing students for careers as music executives, sales representatives, music producers, music distributors, talent managers, recording engineers, sound technicians, booking agents, concert venue managers, music retailers, and more. Degrees in music business and related fields are available at all academic levels.

Typical Courses:

- Music Theory
- Music History
- Music Merchandising
- Accounting
- Principal Instrument/Voice
- Artist Management
- Music Copyright and Publishing
- Marketing and Advertising
- Basic or Choral Conducting
- Record Industry Operations
- Consumer Behavior
- Arts Administration and Venue Management

Potential Employers:

- Artist management agencies
- Music distributors
- Music production companies
- Music promoters
- Music publishers
- Music retailers
- Postsecondary institutions
- Professional symphonies and opera companies
- Recording studios

Available At:

The following list of schools offering programs in music business is not exhaustive. For more programs, visit the Music and Entertainment Industry Educators Association's website, www.meiea.org.

Belmont University (Nashville, TN)
615/460-6000
www.belmont.edu/mb
Degrees available: Bachelor's degree

Eastern Kentucky University (Richmond, KY)
859/622-3266
www.music.eku.edu
Degrees available: Bachelor's degree

Lewis University (Romeoville, IL)
815/836-5619
music@lewisu.edu
www2.lewisu.edu/%7Emcferrmi
Degrees available: Bachelor's degree

University of Massachusetts-Lowell (Lowell, MA)
978/934-3850
www.uml.edu/degrees.html
Degrees available: Bachelor's degree

University of Miami (Coral Gables, FL)
305/284-2241
www.music.miami.edu
Degrees available: Bachelor's degree, master's degree

Miami Dade Community College (multiple campuses, Florida)
305/237-8888
mdccinfo@mdc.edu
https://sisvsr.mdc.edu/ps/sheet.aspx
Degrees available: Associate degree

University of Southern California (Los Angeles, CA)
213/740-3224
www.usc.edu/schools/music/programs
Degrees available: Bachelor's degree

Valparaiso University (Valparaiso, IN)
219/464-5362
Marcia.Lewis@valpo.edu
www.valpo.edu/music/BAMusIndustry.html
Degrees available: Bachelor's degree

University of Wisconsin-Oshkosh (Oshkosh, WI)
920/424-4224
music@uwosh.edu
www.uwosh.edu/departments/music
Degrees available: Bachelor's degree

For More Information:

American Marketing Association
800/262-1150
info@ama.org

American Society of Composers, Authors, and Publishers
212/621-6000
www.ascap.org

National Association of Schools of Music
703/437-0700
info@arts-accredit.org
http://nasm.arts-accredit.org

Recording Industry Association of America
202/775-0101
www.riaa.com

Interview: Marcia Lewis

Valparaiso University in Valparaiso, Indiana, offers an interdisciplinary program in music and business that leads to a bachelor of arts degree in music (music industry option). The editors of *They Teach That in College!?* discussed this interesting program with Marcia Lewis, Associate Professor of Music.

Q. Please tell us about your program.

A. Music Enterprises is an innovative, four-year interdisciplinary program in music and business designed to prepare students for management positions in arts administration and the manufacturing, publishing, distribution, and retailing aspects of the music industry. Students take 40 credits of music, including three specialized music business courses (survey, legal aspects, and current issues) as well as an internship. The 31-credit business minor includes courses in math, accounting, economics, business law, statistics, management, marketing, and finance.

Q. What high school subjects/activities should students focus on to be successful in this major?

A. I think students need a solid background in mathematics and computer technology. They also need to take speech and writing courses. Economics is also beneficial to this major. Their activities should include work in management and production, if possible.

Q. What are the most important personal and professional qualities for majors in this field?

A. Individuals in this major need to have an outgoing personality, good writing and verbal skills, entrepreneurial and organizational abilities, and be creative people with a passion for music.

Q. What advice would you offer students as they graduate and look for jobs?

A. Be persistent and realistic in your search for an entry-level position in the music industry. Your ultimate goal may be to be a producer, but this is not where you start. You have to network and go to trade shows and conferences to get into the industry. You must be aggressive in your search for a job.

Q. What educational level is typically required for graduates to land good jobs in the industry?

A. A bachelor's degree is most common to land your first job. A master's degree (probably in business) may be required to advance professionally. This is presently the terminal degree in the music industry.

Q. Where do music merchandising graduates find employment?

A. Entry-level jobs are available in the music products fields and arts administration. It's presently very difficult to find entry-level jobs in the recording industry because this sector of the industry is laying off rather than hiring personnel.

Q. How will the field of music merchandising change in the future?

A. The field of music merchandising will continue to become more entrepreneurship- and technology-based in the future. Changes in the industry have always been fast-paced, but presently the business model is completely changing and charging forward at a rather overwhelming pace. The future is wide open.

Music Therapy

Although music has been used informally for centuries to achieve therapeutic goals, it was not until World War I, when professional and amateur musicians visited veteran's hospitals to play music for injured veterans, that the medical community realized the healing power of music and began to incorporate this philosophy into health care regimens. Music therapy involves the use of music to accomplish a variety of therapeutic aims, including the restoration, maintenance, and improvement of mental and physical health. A music therapist may work with individuals of all ages who require treatment due to behavioral, social, learning, or physical disabilities. In essence, music is used as a tool to help people maintain or improve upon important life skills. Music therapy can be a satisfying career for individuals with strong musical backgrounds who are also interested in a health care profession. A bachelor's degree in music therapy is required to become a music therapist.

Typical Courses:

> Sociology
> Abnormal Psychology
> Music in Recreation
> Piano
> Percussion Methods
> Guitar Methods
> Studio Instruction
> Music Theory
> Music and Culture
> Music Therapy Techniques

Potential Employers:

> Hospitals
> Schools
> Rehabilitation centers
> Nursing homes
> Health care facilities

Available At:

More than 70 degree programs in 30 states, the District of Columbia, and Canada are approved by the American Music Therapy

Association. For a complete list of schools, visit the following website, www.musictherapy.org/handbook/schools.html.

Arizona State University (Tempe, AZ)
480/965-6563
http://music.asu.edu/musictherapy
Degrees available: Bachelor's degree

California State University-Northridge (Northridge, CA)
818/677-3174
www.csun.edu/~hcmus006/MusicTherapy.html
Degrees available: Bachelor's degree

University of Georgia (Athens, GA)
706/542-3737
www.music.uga.edu/degree_programs/undergrad/#BM-Therapy
Degrees available: Bachelor's degree, master's degree

Illinois State University (Normal, IL)
309/438-8198
www.cfa.ilstu.edu/music/undergraduate/music_therapy.shtml
Degrees available: Bachelor's degree, master's degree

University of Iowa (Iowa City, IA)
319/335-1657
www.uiowa.edu/~music/current/therapy_undergrad.htm
Degrees available: Bachelor's degree, master's degree

University of Kansas (Lawrence, KS)
785/864-4784
www2.ku.edu/~memt
Degrees available: Bachelor's degree, master's degree, doctorate

University of Miami (Coral Gables, FL)
305/284-2241
www.music.miami.edu/music_ed_music_th.html
Degrees available: Bachelor's degree, master's degree

University of Missouri-Kansas City (Kansas City, MO)
816/235-1000
http://conservatory.umkc.edu/musiceducationtherapy.asp
Degrees available: Bachelor's degree, master's degree, doctorate

Temple University (Philadelphia, PA)
215/204-8310
www.temple.edu/boyer/music/programs.htm
Degrees available: Bachelor's degree, master's degree, doctorate

West Texas A&M University (Canyon, TX)
800/99WTAMU
www.wtamu.edu/academic/fah/mus/prospective/bmmt.html
Degrees available: Bachelor's degree

University of Wisconsin-Eau Claire (Eau Claire, WI)
715/836-4260
www.uwec.edu/mus-the/degrees/Music_Therapy.htm
Degrees available: Bachelor's degree

For More Information:

American Music Therapy Association
301/589-3300
info@musictherapy.org
www.musictherapy.org

Interview: Cynthia Colwell

Dr. Cynthia Colwell, Associate Professor and Clinic Director of the Music Therapy Program at the University of Kansas in Lawrence, Kansas, discussed her program and the education of music therapy students with the editors of *They Teach That in College!?*

Q. Tell us about your program.

A. Music therapy is an exciting field where students combine their love of and dedication to music with their desire to work in human service-related fields. Music is a powerful medium that resonates with most on a personal level, making it an idea tool for facilitating therapeutic change. Our approach to music therapy is from a behavioral perspective with an effort to create an awareness of other approaches found within our profession. We offer degrees at the undergraduate and graduate level with both master's and Ph.D. programs.

Our undergraduate degree program has four years of coursework followed by the six-month internship. Students take the core music courses expected of all music majors, behavioral science courses, standard general education requirements, as well as a series of music therapy theory and practice courses. Internal to the coursework years are four clinical practicum experiences in diverse settings with varied populations. Students begin their freshman year with Introduction to Music Therapy and are enrolled each semester in a course internal to the Music Education and Music Therapy division designed to promote their professional growth as a music therapist.

At the graduate level, we offer an equivalency program for students who have an undergraduate degree not in music therapy but perhaps in a related field (i.e., music education or psychology). This is intended to provide the coursework that would have been obtained in the undergraduate program. This equivalency program is typically combined with a master's degree in which the student would also take additional graduate coursework and complete either a thesis or project as a culminating experience.

The doctoral program is a research-focused degree for those clinicians who desire to go on to more advanced clinical experiences or most frequently to college teaching and research. Doctoral students typically choose a minor outside of the music department in an area of clinical/research interest. These students are provided extensive opportunities to team teach with the faculty as well as have primary responsibility for teaching a class in addition to completing rigorous research competencies prior to completing a dissertation. The dissertation is the capstone for the Ph.D.

For detailed information on these programs, please see the following website: www2.ku.edu/~memt.

Q. What makes your program an appealing option for students interested in music therapy?

A. The University of Kansas had one of the first music therapy programs in the country and has a tradition of excellence in training therapists and researchers in the field. Many of the leading music therapy researchers and faculty members around the country have their training from KU. In addition, we are fortunate at The University of Kansas to have three full-time music therapy faculty who have diverse areas of clinical and research productivity. We collectively have experience with early intervention programs, school settings, hospitals, a variety of settings for elderly clients, and hospice programs. We are all working in clinical settings on a weekly basis where students can have immediate hands-on experience as observers or providers. The ongoing clinical work also adds to teaching through cutting-edge practice. The faculty are all active researchers who are involved at the regional, national, and international levels in the growth of our profession through our professional organization, the American Music Therapy Association (AMTA).

Q. What type of internship opportunities are provided by your program?

A. Students participate in a minimum of four semester-long practica with diverse populations under the supervision of board certified-music therapists while still enrolled in coursework at the University of Kansas. Following academic courses, students complete a six-month internship. Our national association, AMTA, has a list of national roster internship sites from around the country. These are approved through AMTA with each having an internship director who is committed to training interns for a full-time, six-month internship. In addition to the national roster, we have university-affiliated internships at a few sites within our immediate area of Kansas City. After completion of the internship, students are eligible to sit for the board certification exam through the Certification Board for Music Therapists (CBMT). The CBMT is the credentialing body for music therapists (MTs) nationwide and provides quality assurance for MTs as well as the many people that we serve.

Did You Know?

According to the American Music Therapy Association, music therapy can help children and adults who have developmental and learning disabilities, mental health needs, Alzheimer's disease and other aging-related conditions, brain injuries, physical disabilities, substance abuse problems, and acute and chronic pain.

Q. What high school subjects/activities should students focus on to be successful in this major?

A. To prepare for an undergraduate degree in music therapy, high school students should focus on becoming competent musicians. As music therapists, our music skills must become second nature so that our primary focus can be on the clients in our sessions. Functional skills in voice, piano, and guitar should be promoted and, although addressed at the college level, can be initially developed at the high school level. If available, classes in behavioral sciences as well as human anatomy and physiology can help prepare the future music therapist for coursework at the college level. Due to the professional documentation aspect of our field, good writing skills are essential and could be addressed through a variety of English courses. Volunteer/work experiences in the human services can also be an asset to individuals planning a career in music therapy-volunteering at the local hospital, participating in a school tutoring program, or being part of a "grandchild" program at a local nursing home.

Q. Where do music therapy graduates find employment?

A. The answer to this question is very broad. Music therapists can work with individuals before birth (labor and delivery) through death (hospice and bereavement). They work with individuals who have mental, physical, and cognitive disabilities as well as those in wellness programs. That being said, you can find music therapists working in hospitals, nursing homes, psychiatric facilities, counseling clinics, prisons and correctional facilities, rehabilitation centers, hospice programs, wellness centers, early intervention centers, school districts, and private practice.

Q. How will the field of music therapy change in the future?

A. The field will be impacted by a variety of factors. As the field grows, there is a growing interest in advanced levels of practice and advanced competencies appropriate for therapists in specific areas of clinical practice. Reimbursement remains a focus of the profession as we strive to be recognized as a therapist comparable to physical therapy, speech therapy, and occupational therapy that are all currently reimbursed through medical plans. Legislative issues are a new challenge as state task forces are being called on to advocate for appropriate language in legislation that may impact the practicing music therapist. Our national organization, the American Music Therapy Association, has kicked off a new initiative as part of our long-term strategic plan. This initiative is focused on outcomes-based research and how therapists in the field can participate in research within their current clinical settings to provide evidenced-based outcomes to support the efficacy of music therapy in a variety of venues.

Musical Instrument Repair

Behind every top-performing professional symphony orchestra, high school band, and amateur musician lies the integral work of the music instrument repair technician. Although the musical instrument repair industry is small—nearly 5,000 U.S. workers in 2005—employment prospects are good for aspiring repairers willing to receive training via an apprenticeship or a formal music instrument repair program. Only five postsecondary institutions in the United States and Canada offer training in music instrument repair.

Typical Courses:

> Introduction to Music
> Introduction to Band Instrument Repair
> Shop Practices and Safety for Band Instrument Repair
> Dent Removal Techniques
> Soldering and Brazing Techniques
> Brass Techniques
> Woodwind Techniques
> The Percussion Instruments
> Mathematics for Band Instrument Repair
> Human Relations for Band Instrument Repair

Potential Employers:

> Musical instrument repair shops
> Manufacturers
> Colleges and universities

Available At:

Badger State Repair School (Elkhorn, WI)
262/723-4062
MrStregs@aol.com
Degrees available: None (the School offers a 48-week course in brass and woodwind instrument repair)

Keyano College-Clearwater Campus (McMurray, AB Canada)
780/791-8979
mir@keyano.ca
www.keyano.ca/prospective_students/programs/index.htm
Degrees available: Diploma

The repair of stringed musical instruments is just one of several study areas for musical instrument repair majors. (Photo courtesy of Keith Levit Photography/Photos To Go Unlimited)

Minnesota State College-SE Technical (Red Wing, MN)
877/853-8324
http://it.southeastmn.edu/programs/index.asp
Degrees available: Certificate (musical string instrument construction), diplomas (band instrument repair, musical string instrument repair-guitar, musical string instrument repair-violin)

Renton Technical College (Renton, WA)
425/235-2453
www.rtc.edu/Programs/TrainingPrograms/BIRT
Degrees available: Certificate, associate degree (both in band instrument repair technology)

Western Iowa Tech Community College (Sioux City, IA)
800/352-4649
www.witcc.com/programs/index.cfm
Degrees available: Certificate (electronic musical instrument repair), associate degree (band instrument repair technology)

For More Information:

Guild of American Luthiers
www.luth.org

National Association of Professional Band Instrument Repair Technicians
www.napbirt.org

Piano Technicians Guild
www.ptg.org

Musical Theatre Writing

Students who enjoy writing for musical theatre and opera may be interested in learning more about the Graduate Musical Theatre Writing Program at New York University. What are the major criteria for admission to this program? According to the Program's website, "talent, originality, and an ability to work well in collaboration." Students in the program participate in writing workshops that help them develop their creative voice, collaborate with others, and learn about genres and storytelling techniques. They also attend integrated craft and history seminars, which provide an overview of music in theatre through the years, as well as participate in fieldwork opportunities in New York City, the capital of the U.S. theatre industry. Students complete the program by writing a full-length theatrical work.

Typical Courses:

> Musical Theater Structures
> Joint Playwriting Tutorial
> Seminar: Critique
> Musical Theater History
> Tutorials, Seminars, and Labs (covering various topics)
> Creative Producing
> Seminar: Collaboration

Potential Employers:

> Theatrical production companies

Available At:

New York University (New York, NY)
212/998-1830
musical.theatre@nyu.edu
http://gmtw.tisch.nyu.edu/page/home
Degrees available: Master's degree

For More Information:

National Association of Schools of Theater
http://nast.arts-accredit.org

Theater Communications Group
212/609-5900
www.tcg.org

Nanoscience/Nanotechnology

Advances in the past century have led to a new branch of science: nanotechnology/nanoscience. This emerging science studies the composition, structure, properties, and behavior of material at an extremely small scale, the nanometer range. A nanometer is one-billionth of a meter—an extremely small unit of measurement, to say the least! To put it into perspective, the page you are reading right now is six inches in width, nine inches in length, and about *100,000 nanometers* in thickness.

According to scientists, at the nanometer range, the properties of materials differ in important and valuable ways from the properties of materials at a larger scale. These differences have opened up a world of exciting new options. Nanotechnology has already been used to create materials used in products ranging from computer disk drives to tires, as well as being used in the manufacture of such items as water filtration systems and sunscreen products. In the future, it is expected that nanotechnology will play an important role in enhancing technology already used in such areas as the production of solar power and the development of medicine.

Typical Courses:

- Fundamentals of Nanoscience
- Laboratory Instrumentation
- Semiconductor Fabrication
- Manufacturing Quality Assurance
- Nanobiotech/Agriculture
- Nanomaterials/Coatings
- Thin Film Technology
- Surface and Thin Film Analysis Techniques

Potential Employers:

- Biomedicine/biotechnology industry
- Microelectronics/microfabrication industry
- Materials/coatings/polymers industry.
- Agriculture production/food processing industry
- Bio-remediation and energy industry

Available At:

Fewer than 15 colleges and universities offer degree programs in nanotechnology, including the following programs. Visit www.nano.gov/html/edu/eduunder.html for additional programs.

Dakota County Technical College (Rosemount, MN)
651/423-8328
www.dctc.edu/prospStudents/programs/nanoTech.cfm
Degrees available: Associate degree

Louisiana Tech University (Ruston, LA)
318/257-4647
www.latech.edu/coes
Degrees available: Bachelor's degree, master's degree, doctorate

Minnesota State Community and Technical College-Moorhead
(a collaborative effort with North Dakota State College of Science)
800/426-5603, ext. 6512
www.minnesota.edu/programs_majors/nanoscience_technology
Degrees available: Associate degree

North Dakota State College of Science (Wahpeton, ND)
(a collaborative effort with Minnesota State Community and Technical College-Moorhead)
800/342-4325
www.ndscs.nodak.edu/departments/nanoscience/index.jsp
Degrees available: Associate degree

North Seattle Community College (Seattle, WA)
206/527-3746
plortz@sccd.ctc.edu
www.northseattle.edu/nanotech
Degrees available: Certificate, associate degree

South Dakota School of Mines & Technology (Rapid City, SD)
605/394-5268
http://graded.sdsmt.edu/academics/programs
Degrees available: Doctorate (nanoscience and nanoengineering)

For More Information:

American Society of Mechanical Engineers
Nanotechnology Institute
www.nanotechnologyinstitute.org

National Nanotechnology Initiative
info@nnco.nano.gov
www.nano.gov/html/facts/whatIsNano.html

National Nanofabrication Infrastructure Network
www.nnin.org

Interview: Alissa Agnello

Alissa Agnello is an instructor of nanotechnology at North Seattle Community College in Seattle, Washington. The College is just one of a few postsecondary institutions in the United States to offer a degree in nanotechnology. Ms. Agnello discussed her school's program with the editors of *They Teach That in College!?*

Q. Please tell us about your program.

A. The Nanotechnology Program at North Seattle Community College is a two-year program that culminates in the award of an associate of applied science (AAS)-T degree in nanotechnology. To obtain the degree, students complete seven nanotechnology courses (including two internships) and a variety of other courses, including courses in the physical and biological sciences.

North Seattle Community College also offers a certificate in nanotechnology, which can be completed in one year and consists of six nanotechnology courses, including one quarter of internship. This certificate has been designed to accommodate interested members of the community who have previously taken many science courses, completed an associate's or bachelor's degree in a different science discipline, or have considerable experience working in related industry. This opportunity provides a specialization in nanotechnology without requiring the student to retake courses that he or she might have taken in the past.

Q. What makes your program an appealing option for students interested in nanotechnology?

A. Our program is an appealing option for students interested in nanotechnology since it is unique; few schools in the country have nanotechnology programs and even fewer offer a degree in nanotechnology. We have chosen to approach nanotechnology from a broad perspective, embracing the interdisciplinary nature of the field and introducing students to a variety of aspects of nanotechnology. Most programs choose to focus on only one application of nanotechnology, for example, energy or microelectromechanical systems. Since we believe that the Pacific Northwest has industry to support a variety of different types of nanotechnology, we want to prepare students to take on whichever field of nanotechnology interest them the most. Although we focus on breadth, we do not overlook the importance of depth. Internships are an integral part of the nanotechnology program, allowing students the opportunity to specialize and acquire real-world knowledge of the techniques or fields of their choice.

Q. What type of internship opportunities are provided by your program?

A. There are a number of different industries that are performing nanotechnology-related work or microtechnology work currently. North Seattle Community College has created a nanotechnology Technical Advisory Committee (TAC), on which sit members from local industry, educators, and other consultants. The TAC provides guidance in shaping our program to ensure that each graduate is equipped with the skills needed to be a successful nanotechnology employee. The industry members of the TAC also provide insight into the status of local industry, as well as offer internships to our students. It is not uncommon for these companies to pursue the employment of students who performed internship work for them.

North Seattle Community College also collaborates with the Washington Technology Center and the Nanotechnology User Facility (Center for Nanotechnology), both national centers that are located on the University of Washington campus in Seattle. These collaborations provide our students with the opportunity to gain hands-on experience with a large variety of very high-tech fabrication and characterization techniques. We are also in contact with a number of other resources, including the California Institute of Nanotechnology and a few other community colleges across the country.

There is also opportunity for students to work with instruments in our facility. The nanotechnology lab at North Seattle Community College contains some instrumentation to make and characterize nanostructures, including a scanning electron microscope. We intend to build up the facilities at North Seattle Community College, especially through instrument acquisition. Students in the nanotechnology program may help in this goal, by researching and piecing together instrumentation or by writing standard operating procedures for our on-campus instrumentation.

Q. What are the most important personal and professional qualities for nanotechnology majors?

A. Nano- and microtechnicians must are held to very high standards of responsibility, especially regarding safety and contamination. Many of the techniques performed in procedures related to nanotechnology involve very expensive equipment, so the ability to follow directions precisely and carefully is crucial. Additionally, as with many scientific disciplines, the chemicals used can be hazardous if handled improperly. An issue that is somewhat unique to the field of nanotechnology is that not only must the technician protect himself from the samples, but the samples must be protected from the technicians. This is a major consideration and is the basis for creating clean rooms, especially as micro- and nanofabrication facilities. These expensive clean room facilities, including one at the Washington Technology Center, have a large number of users, from both industry and academia. Proper protocol must be followed in order to prevent a clean room from being contaminated, since one misstep may affect the work of everyone using the facility.

Since nanotechnology is an interdisciplinary field, the limitations for collaboration and research are only limited by creativity! This interdisciplinary attitude suggests that someone studying nanotechnology must have a willingness to learn about a large variety of areas of science and draw connections to understand how each scientific discipline may relate to a specific application.

Nanotechnology is active; one must not be afraid to push buttons, twist knobs, and flip switches. Sometimes nanotechnology looks more like chemistry or biology, so someone working in this field must be able to perform appropriately in those lab settings and follow procedures. After receiving training and experience through internships, our graduates are prepared to use instruments, follow laboratory protocols, and acquire new skills as needed.

Communication skills are also important. Most labs depend on collaboration between technicians, operators, engineering, research scientists, funding sources, regulatory agencies, and other groups. Being able to communicate the ideas of nanotechnology to the public is not a trivial task; the buzz about nanotechnology has been created and many people have a misconception of the risks and rewards that are possible through nanotechnology currently and in the future.

Q. Where do nanotechnology graduates find employment?

A. The current nanotechnology program certainly will prepare students for employment as technicians or operators in industry. The program allows students to work in industry as interns and students who have completed the program have been hired immediately, sometimes even before the completion of the two-year program.

Nanotechnology is an interdisciplinary field, so the graduates of our program are provided with the skills necessary to pursue a career in any scientific field of their choice, including biology research, biotechnology, medicine and pharmaceuticals, electronics, microfabrication, neuroscience, chemical engineering, mechanical engineering, materials science, and environmental science, to name a few.

Additionally, since nanotechnology is a current "buzz" word, we are interested in having students pursue other fields less directly related to scientific research, perhaps in technical writing or educational outreach, to provide true information about nanotechnology to the public.

Q. What is the employment outlook for the field of nanotechnology? How will the field change in the future?

A. The field is relatively new and will grow dramatically. Consumer products containing nanotechnology are already on the market, including cosmetics, stain-resistant clothing, and batteries. As the need for alternative energy arises, nanotechnology will become more prevalent in solar cells. In the field of electronics, the drive to make devices smaller is significant; the techniques currently being used for fabricating devices will soon be obsolete and nanotechnology will need to be used to overcome the obstacles of creating things on such a small scale. Much research is being performed in the medical field to find better ways to treat disease in a targeted and less invasive manner, to avoid side-effects and to improve healing. Also, novel nanomaterials can be used in biological implants.

Many aspects of life are and will continue to be affected by advances in nanotechnology. For this reason, many different parties are interested in nanotechnology research, from the government to industry to academic institutions to venture capitalists, worldwide. The advances made by these various groups will allow for the field of nanotechnology to continue to change as it grows and becomes more prevalent in all fields. As evidenced by our close connection with local industry through our Technical Advisory Committee, as well as our emphasis on internships, North Seattle Community College is dedicated to preparing students in nanotechnology, wherever the field may go.

Ocean Engineering

Ever wonder who developed the technology that discovered and explored the deep sea wreckage of the *Titanic*, as seen in the 1997 film of the same name? Or who is called on for expertise when a submarine is in trouble, in need of a rescue mission? Developing the technology used in such instances is the job of the *ocean engineer.* This fascinating field not only focuses on this undersea technology, but also any engineering applications that deal with the effects of the ocean on ships of all sizes at the surface level. And like any field relying on modern technology to advance its mission, ocean engineers are constantly adapting modern technological innovations to create and design systems that can further the advancement of the ocean engineering field. Students in most programs will be exposed to current research studies, whether it be in classroom study or in practical internships. Students considering a career in ocean engineering should have a strong aptitude for math and science as well as an inquisitive nature and a desire to work with cutting-edge technological industry. Degrees in ocean engineering are available at the baccalaureate, master's, and doctoral levels.

Typical Courses:

- Marine Hydrodynamics
- Marine Engineering
- Foundations of Ship Design
- Thermodynamics
- Physics and Chemistry
- Fluid Dynamics
- Marine Systems Manufacturing
- Marine Systems Production Strategy and Operations Management
- Environmental Ocean Dynamics
- Principles of Ocean Systems Engineering

Potential Employers:

- Governmental agencies
- Defense contractors
- Private industry
- Consulting firms
- U.S. Navy

Available At:

There are only about 20 ocean engineering programs in the United States. Approximately 15 of these programs are accredited by the Accreditation Board for Engineering and Technology. Visit www.abet.org for a complete list of programs.

Florida Atlantic University (Boca Raton, FL)
561/297-3430
www.oe.fau.edu
Degrees available: Bachelor's degree, master's degree, doctorate

Florida Institute of Technology (Melbourne, FL)
321/674-8096
dmes@marine.fit.edu
www.fit.edu/AcadRes/dmes/ocean.html
Degrees available: Bachelor's degree, master's degree, doctorate

University of Florida (Gainesville, FL)
352/392-9537
www.eng.ufl.edu/about/departments/index.php
Degrees available: Master's degree

University of Hawaii at Manoa (Honolulu, HI)
808/956-8111
www.manoa.hawaii.edu
Degrees available: Master's degree

Massachusetts Institute of Technology (Cambridge, MA)
617/253-4330
discoveroe@mit.edu
http://oe.mit.edu/discover
Degrees available: Bachelor's degree, master's degree

University of Michigan (Ann Arbor, MI)
734/764-6470
name-info@umich.edu
www.engin.umich.edu/dept/name/name.html
Degrees available: Bachelor's degree, master's degree, doctorate

University of Rhode Island-Narragansett Bay Campus
(Narragansett, RI)
401/874-6139
grilli@oce.uri.edu
www.oce.uri.edu
Degrees available: Bachelor's degree, master's degree, doctorate

Texas A&M University (College Station, TX)
979/845-4515
http://oceaneng.civil.tamu.edu
Degrees available: Bachelor's degree, master's degree, doctorate

U.S. Naval Academy (Annapolis, MD)
410/293-6420
naoeweb@usna.edu

www.usna.edu/NAOE/index.html
Degrees available: Bachelor's degree

Virginia Tech University (Blacksburg, VA)
540/231-6611
www.aoe.vt.edu
Degrees available: Bachelor's degree, master's degree, doctorate

For More Information:

American Society for Engineering Education
202/331-3500
www.asee.org

American Society of Naval Engineers
703/836-6727
www.navalengineers.org

Junior Engineering Technical Society
703/548-5387
info@jets.org
www.jets.org

Interview: Stephan Grilli

Stephan Grilli is a Distinguished Professor and Chair of the Department of Ocean Engineering at the University of Rhode Island in Narragansett, Rhode Island. He discussed his program and the education of ocean engineering students with the editors of *They Teach That in College!?*

Q. Please tell us about your program.

A. Ocean engineering applies a wide range of engineering disciplines to the ocean and coastal environments. Ocean engineering includes such topics as: design and construction of offshore structures; submarine soil mechanics; coastal engineering; design and fabrication of underwater vehicles (AUVs, ROVs); coastal and offshore wave and marine hydrodynamics and environmental implications; underwater instrumentation; underwater acoustics; and marine resources.

Q. What are the most important personal and professional qualities for ocean engineering majors?

A. Like other engineering students, ocean engineering students should enter the program well educated, with good math and engineering science skills, and an ability for problem solving.

Engineering students should also be creative, persistent, and have a strong interest in making the world a better place to live. Also, ocean engineering students should have a keen interest in and be drawn to the ocean environment, which represents more than two-thirds of the planet.

Q. What advice would you offer students as they graduate and look for jobs?

A. To apply the skills and knowledge gained in the program in a professional and ethical manner and to continue to develop these through experience and continuing education.

Q. What educational level is typically required for ocean engineering graduates to land good jobs in the industry?

A. Although an M.S. degree is increasingly advisable for maximizing long-term growth in the engineering profession, both our undergraduate and graduate students land good jobs in the U.S. and abroad. Our students graduate and work for consulting companies, large companies, government laboratories, and universities. Of particular interest at URI is our award-winning International Engineering Program (IEP) in which engineering students simultaneously complete a B.S. in a foreign language (currently German, French, Spanish, or Chinese). IEP students complete a six-month to one-year stay abroad, which includes both attending classes at a foreign university and completing an internship in a foreign company.

Q. How will the field change in the future?

A. The field will likely expand in several areas: redesign of coastal protections due to sea level rise (induced by global warming), assessment and mitigation of natural hazards in the coastal zone (such as storms/hurricane, tsunamis); prediction and mitigation of environmental pollutants (e.g., sewage, oil/chemical spills); construction of offshore structures and pipelines for resource development in the deep ocean; and development of offshore alternative and renewable energy sources (wind, waves).

Packaging Science

Nearly every product we purchase comes in some sort of packaging. And every package has to serve one or more purposes—it must keep the product adequately protected and/or fresh and it must be pleasing to the eye of the consumer. The packaging scientist must have an aptitude for both science and technology, a keen eye for design, and creative marketing business sensibility. This $100+ billion-a-year industry continues to grow in a society that purchases more than 500 billion packages annually in the United States alone, and there are currently only a handful of college programs helping to fill the increasing demand for graduates in this field. Degrees in packaging science are available at all academic levels.

Typical Courses:

- Principles of Packaging
- Consumer Products Packaging
- Packaging, Society and Environment
- Food Packaging
- Computer Tools for Packaging
- Distribution and Transport Packaging
- Packaging Production and Processing
- Package Decoration
- Analytical Methods in Packaging
- Senior Design in Packaging

Potential Employers:

- Packaging material manufacturers
- Converters (e.g., Sealed Air Corporation, Mitsubishi, Sonoco, International Paper, Georgia-Pacific, Smurfit-Stone, etc.)
- Packaging users (major food and medical companies)
- Parcel services
- Government agencies

Available At:

This list of schools offering programs in packaging science is not exhaustive. For more programs, visit the following website: http://users.erols.com/niphle/Schools.html.

Christian Brothers University (Memphis, TN)
901/321-3418
www.cbu.edu/engineering/packaging
Degrees available: Certificate

Clemson University (Clemson, SC)
864/656-3390
www.clemson.edu/packaging
Degrees available: Bachelor's degree, master's degree

University of Florida (Gainesville, FL)
352/392-4092
www.pkg.ufl.edu
Degrees available: Bachelor's degree

Indiana State University (Terre Haute, IN)
812/237-3353
www.indstate.edu/imt
Degrees available: Bachelor's degree

Michigan State University (East Lansing, MI)
517/353-4384
package@packaging.msu.edu
http://packaging.msu.edu
Degrees available: Bachelor's degree, master's degree, doctorate

Rochester Institute of Technology (Rochester, NY)
585/475-2411
www.rit.edu/cast/mmetps/PROGRAMS/BS/ps.htm
Degrees available: Bachelor's degree, master's degree

San Jose State University (San Jose, CA)
408/924-2550
http://info.sjsu.edu/web-dbgen/catalog/departments/NUFS-section-4.html
Degrees available: Bachelor's degree

University of Wisconsin-Stout (Menomonie, WI)
715/232-1246
www.uwstout.edu/programs/bsp
Degrees available: Bachelor's degree

For More Information:

Institute of Packaging Professionals
630/544-5050
www.iopp.org

National Institute of Packaging Handling and Logistics Engineers
866/464-7453
www.niphle.com

Packaging Machinery Manufacturers Institute
888/275-7664
www.pmmi.org

Interview: Ron Thomas

Clemson University has one of the most successful packaging science programs in the nation. The University offers bachelor's and master's degree programs in packaging science. Professor Ron Thomas, Ph.D. and Chair of Clemson's Department of Packaging Science, was kind enough to discuss his program with the editors of *They Teach That in College!?*

Q. Please briefly describe your program.

A. Packaging science is a blend of science and technology, design, marketing, and business principles. We consider the program to be highly applied in nature, and our goal is to produce industry-ready graduates.

Q. What types of students enter your program? What are their career goals and interests?

A. Students with aptitude in math (especially physics) and science (especially chemistry) and/or engineering are typically interested in this program. These students are typically interested in applied science and engineering and are looking for practical careers in industry.

Q. What types of companies employ packaging science graduates?

A. Packaging is a $115 billion business in the United States, and jobs are quite plentiful for our graduates. We consider that most all companies are in the packaging business since everyone who has a product packages it for distribution. These are "user" companies. All major food and medical companies fall into this category. The producers, or "converters," such as Sealed Air, Mitsubishi, Sonoco, International Paper, Georgia-Pacific, Smurfit, etc., are not as well known by name, but are also major employers. Starting salaries are $45,000 to $50,000.

Q. What are the key skills that packaging science students need to learn in your program to be successful in their careers?

A. As mentioned earlier, the key skill for success is the ability to blend many different disciplines. This is a significant niche that most companies have difficulty filling, and this is one of the major reasons the industry sought to get a program going at Clemson.

Q. Does your school offer any co-op opportunities?

A. Co-ops are mandatory in our program. They are typically of six months' duration, and we assist students in finding their co-ops by hosting co-op fairs on campus. Industries come to campus and interview the students. The students are paid $16 to $20 per hour on average.

Q. What advice do you offer students as they complete their degrees and look for jobs?

A. Students seeking jobs should be flexible about location and quickly get some experience. With a couple years of experience, the job market is even better. Also, there is a global market out there, and students should be prepared and willing to travel.

Q. What is the future for your program and packaging science in general?

A. Our program continues to grow, and packaging science is established as a legitimate academic discipline. There are many schools now offering courses and concentrations in packaging throughout the country, and I expect more schools to become involved. Clemson University considers our program to be of great significance and continually promotes our programs and provides the faculty we need to be successful.

Paper Science and Engineering

Papermaking is one of the oldest industries known to man—wood-based papermaking can be traced to ancient China. Today, it is considered a science and involves more than the manufacture of raw paper. Paper scientists and engineers are responsible for finding new uses for paper products, and better and more affordable ways to produce paper, tissue, and other natural fiber products. As *process engineers,* they may work to perfect the recycling of paper and water and other materials used in the papermaking process. As *research scientists,* they may extract and work with the various components found in wood or generated by the papermaking process that can be used to create medicines, detergents, and many other goods. Or perhaps they can create new paper products that are compatible with today's high speed, four-color printers. Graduates of paper science and paper engineering programs may also work in the paper industry in sales, management, and marketing. Degrees in paper science and engineering are available at all academic levels. There are fewer than 12 paper science and engineering programs in the United States.

Typical Classes:

- Pulp and Paper Manufacturing
- Paper Physics Fundamentals
- Converting and Coating
- Water Quality and Regulations
- Recycling
- Wastewater Engineering
- Surface and Wet End Science
- Solid Waste Treatment
- Process Engineering and Design
- Vector and Multivariate Calculus
- Carbohydrate and Lignin Chemistry

Potential Employers:

- Paper companies
- Chemical suppliers
- Consultants
- Equipment suppliers
- Governmental agencies

Available At:

The following programs are accredited by the Accreditation Board for Engineering Technology (www.abet.org/accrediteac.asp):

Miami University (Oxford, OH)
513/529-2200
paper@muohio.edu
www.eas.muohio.edu/departments/pce
Degrees available: Bachelor's degree, master's degree

State University of New York (Syracuse, NY)
315/470-6500
paperscience@esf.edu
www.esf.edu/pse
Degrees available: Bachelor's degree, master's degree, doctorate

North Carolina State University (Raleigh, NC)
919/515-5807
http://natural-resources.ncsu.edu/wps/pp
Degrees available: Bachelor's degree, master's degree, doctorate

University of Washington (Seattle, WA)
206/543-3077
www.cfr.washington.edu/Acad/undergrad/pse/pse_reqs.htm
Degrees available: Bachelor's degree, master's degree, doctorate

Western Michigan University (Kalamazoo, MI)
269/276-3500
www.wmich.edu/ppse
Degrees available: Bachelor's degree, master's degree, doctorate

Did You Know?

Paper, according to the American Forest and Paper Association, is used in a variety of products, including writing paper, tissue, paper bags, cardboard boxes, milk cartons, masking tape, car filters, tea bags, camera film, and construction products (insulation, gypsum wallboard, roofing paper, flooring, padding, and sound-absorbing materials).

Additional postsecondary programs in paper science and paper engineering are listed below. For more programs, visit www.www.paperonweb.com/school.htm.

Georgia Institute of Technology (Atlanta, GA)
404/894-5700
www.ipst.gatech.edu/degree_progs
Degrees available: Master's degree, doctorate

University of Minnesota (St. Paul, MN)
612/625-7733
www.bbe.umn.edu/teaching/grad/index.html
Degrees available: Certificate, master's degree

Tacoma Community College (Tacoma, WA)
253/566-5000
www.tacomacc.edu/inst_dept/science/programs.asp
Degrees available: Associate degree (prepares students to transfer to a paper science or engineering program at a four-year school)

University of Wisconsin-Stevens Point (Stevens Point, WI)
715/346-3928
papersci@uwsp.edu
www.uwsp.edu/papersci
Degrees available: Bachelor's degree, advanced certificate

For More Information:

American Forest and Paper Association
800/878-8878
info@afandpa.org
www.afandpa.org

Society of Wood Science and Technology
608/231-9347
www.swst.org

Perfusion Technology

One of the most important medical advances in history was the invention of the heart-lung machine, which serves as a patient's heart and lungs by artificially circulating their blood when the function of the patient's own heart is stopped during surgery. The operation of this lifesaving machine is the responsibility of the *perfusionist,* also known as a *cardiovascular perfusionist,* a technician who sets up and monitors the machine during surgery. Perfusionists may also be responsible for other life-support devices, and generally assist the surgical team as necessary. Because of the nature of their work, perfusionists must be trained in the biological science of artificial circulation, as well as in the mechanical functioning of the heart-lung machine and any other device they operate and monitor during medical procedures. Training to become a perfusionist is available from one of 20 schools in the United States; these schools are accredited by the Commission on Accreditation of Allied Health Education Programs.

Typical Courses:

- Basic Surgery and Monitoring
- Cardiac Anatomy and Physiology
- Immunotoxicology
- Biostatistics
- Principles of Pharmacology
- Perfusion Techniques
- Systems Physiology
- Cardiovascular Pharmacology
- Science, Society, and Ethics

Potential Employers:

- Hospitals
- U.S. military

Available At:

The following colleges are accredited by the Commission on Accreditation of Allied Health Education Programs. (Visit the Commission's website, www.caahep.org, for a complete list of programs.

University of Arizona (Tucson, AZ)
520/626-6494

www.perfusion.arizona.edu
Degrees available: Master's degree

Barry University (Miami Shores, FL)
800/756-6000, ext. 3214
www.barry.edu/snhs/BSprograms/cardioPerfusion
Degrees available: Bachelor's degree

Medical University of South Carolina (Charleston, SC)
843/792-3328
www.musc.edu/chp/cp
Degrees available: Bachelor's degree

Milwaukee School of Engineering (Milwaukee, WI)
800/332-6763
www.msoe.edu/grad/msp
Degrees available: Master's degree

University of Nebraska Medical Center (Omaha, NE)
402/559-4000
www.unmc.edu/dept/alliedhealth/cpe/index.cfm?conref=11
Degrees available: Master's degree

State University of New York Upstate Medical University (Syracuse, NY)
315/464-6933
CVP@upstate.edu
www.upstate.edu/chp/cp
Degrees available: Bachelor's degree

Ohio State University (Columbus, OH)
614/292-7261, ext. 2
http://amp.osu.edu/ct/1348.cfm
Degrees available: Bachelor's degree, master's degree, advanced certificate

Quinnipiac University (Hamden, CT)
800/462-1944
www.quinnipiac.edu/x810.xml
Degrees available: Master's degree

Rush University (Chicago, IL)
312/942-2305
www.rushu.rush.edu/perfusion
Degrees available: Master's degree

For More Information:

American Academy of Cardiovascular Perfusion
www.theaacp.com

American Society of ExtraCorporeal Technology
www.amsect.org

Perfusion.com
www.perfusion.com

Personal Fitness Training

Personal trainers are key players in the fitness industry, helping clients achieve personal exercise goals, lose weight, and rehabilitate from injury. But there is a great variance in training and skill levels in this fast-growing occupation. While physical education majors have been offered at colleges and universities for years, no baccalaureate training for personal trainers has been available—until now. Purdue University-West Lafayette is the first four-year degree program in the United States to offer a concentration in personal training. The goal of the program, which was founded in 2005, is to improve the professional standing of personal trainers and prepare students for certification examinations offered by the American College of Sports Medicine. In addition to studying biomechanics, physiology, neurology, functional anatomy, and related concepts, students also focus on business and career development skills, which will help them to improve their management abilities and start their own personal training businesses. Employment of fitness workers is expected to grow by nearly 27 percent through 2016, according to the U.S. Department of Labor.

Typical Courses:

> Human Anatomy and Physiology
> Essentials of Nutrition
> Methods of Health Promotion and Education
> Health and Fitness Program Management
> Health Screening and Fitness Evaluation and Prescription
> Anatomical Foundations of Human Performance
> Principles of Motor Learning and Development
> Exercise Testing and Prescription for Special Populations
> Exercise Physiology
> Sport and Exercise Physiology
> Clinical Practice in Personal Training
> Business Issues for Personal Trainers

Potential Employers:

> Private and commercial health clubs
> Corporate fitness centers
> Aerobics studios
> Rehabilitation centers
> Hospitals

- Colleges and universities
- Community wellness programs
- Personal training studios
- Physical therapy clinics
- YMCAs

Available At:

Purdue University-West Lafayette (West Lafayette, IN)
http://tholian.sla.purdue.edu/academic/hk/hkadvising/PFT.htm
Degrees available: Bachelor's degree

For More Information:

American College of Sports Medicine
317/637-9200
www.acsm.org

American Council on Exercise
888/825-3636
www.acefitness.org

American Fitness Professionals and Associates
609/978-7583
afpa@afpafitness.com
www.afpafitness.com

IDEA Health and Fitness Association
www.ideafit.com

Petroleum Engineering

Travel storm-tossed oceans, frozen tundra, steep mountainsides, and unending deserts of the world in search for the black gold that is known as petroleum. Petroleum engineers explore, drill, and produce the production of oil, as well as gas and other natural resources, that are imperative to the functioning of our transportation systems and industries. As a petroleum engineer, you'll not only work to meet the demand for safe affordable energy, but you may also work in perfecting petroleum by-products such as plastics, textiles, and medicine. Placement of bachelor of science graduates (the minimum educational requirement for a career as a petroleum engineer) is almost 100 percent, and the average starting salary, according to the National Association of Colleges and Employers, was $58,000 in 2005. A master's degree in petroleum engineering or a related field is required for top positions in this field.

Typical Courses:

- Chemistry, Physics, and Geology
- Petrophysics
- Applied Reservoir Analysis
- Drilling Engineering
- Production Systems Engineering
- Natural Gas Engineering
- Transient Pressure Analysis
- Drilling and Completion Fluids
- Rock and Fluid Properties
- Principles of Well Testing and Analysis

Potential Employers:

- Major oil companies
- Independent oil exploration, production, and service companies
- Colleges and universities
- Consulting companies
- Governmental agencies

Available At:

There are fewer than 30 petroleum engineering programs in the United States—16 of which (listed starting on the next page) are accredited by the Accreditation Board for Engineering and Technology (www.abet.org).

University of Alaska-Fairbanks (Fairbanks, AK)
907/474-7734
fyipete@uaf.edu
www.uaf.edu/petrol
Degrees available: Bachelor's degree, master's degree, doctorate

Colorado School of Mines (Golden, CO)
800/446-9488
www.mines.edu/index_js.shtml
Degrees available: Bachelor's degree, master's degree, doctorate

University of Kansas (Lawrence, KS)
785/864-4965
cpe@ku.edu
www.cpe.engr.ku.edu
Degrees available: Bachelor's degree, master's degree, doctorate

University of Louisiana-Lafayette (Lafayette, LA)
337/482-5750
petroleum@lousiana.edu
http://petroleum.louisiana.edu
Degrees available: Bachelor's degree

Louisiana State University (Baton Rouge, LA)
225/578-5215
www.pete.lsu.edu
Degrees available: Bachelor's degree, master's degree, doctorate

Marietta College (Marietta, OH)
740/376-4775
petr@marietta.edu
www.marietta.edu/~petr
Degrees available: Bachelor's degree

University of Missouri-Rolla (Rolla, MO)
573/341-4616
rocks@umr.edu
http://gse.umr.edu
Degrees available: Bachelor's degree, master's degree, doctorate

Montana Tech of the University of Montana (Butte, MT)
406/496-4197
www.mtech.edu/mines/pet%5Feng
Degrees available: Bachelor's degree, master's degree

New Mexico Tech (Socorro, NM) (officially known as New Mexico Institute of Mining and Technology)
575/835-5412
www.nmt.edu/mainpage/catalog/degrees.html
Degrees available: Bachelor's degree, master's degree, doctorate

University of Oklahoma (Norman, OK)
800/522-0772, ext. 2921
mpge@ou.edu
http://mpge.ou.edu
Degrees available: Bachelor's degree, master's degree, doctorate

Pennsylvania State University (University Park, PA)
814/865-3437
www.pnge.psu.edu
Degrees available: Bachelor's degree, master's degree, doctorate

Texas A&M University (College Station, TX)
979/845-2241
info@pe.tamu.edu
www.pe.tamu.edu
Degrees available: Bachelor's degree, master's degree, doctorate

Did You Know?

Oil isn't used just as an energy source for our homes and vehicles. In fact, according to the American Petroleum Institute, it's used in ways you've never imagined! Indeed, oil is used to make antihistamines, clothing, computers, garbage bags, heart valve replacements, life jackets, perfumes, roofing, soft contact lenses, telephones, toothpaste, and umbrellas.

University of Texas-Austin (Austin, TX)
512/471-3161
www.pge.utexas.edu
Degrees available: Bachelor's degree, master's degree, doctorate

Texas Tech University (Lubbock, TX)
806/742-3573
www.pe.ttu.edu
Degrees available: Bachelor's degree, master's degree, doctorate

University of Tulsa (Tulsa, OK)
918/631-2533
www.pe.utulsa.edu
Degrees available: Bachelor's degree, master's degree, doctorate

West Virginia University (Morgantown, WV)
304/293-7682
www.pnge.cemr.wvu.edu
Degrees available: Bachelor's degree, master's degree, doctorate

The following programs are not accredited by ABET, but are known for offering students a quality education. For a list of all petroleum engineering programs in the United States, Canada, and the world, visit www.spe.org.

University of Pittsburgh (Pittsburgh, PA)
412/624-9630
ChE@engr.pitt.edu
www.engr.pitt.edu/chemical/index.html
Degrees available: Bachelor's degree, master's degree, doctorate

University of Southern California (Los Angeles, CA)
213/740-0322
peteng@usc.edu
http://chems.usc.edu/admission/petroleum_engineering.htm
Degrees available: Bachelor's degree, master's degree, advanced certificate

Stanford University (Stanford, CA)
650/723-4744
peteng@pangea.stanford.edu
http://ekofisk.stanford.edu
Degrees available: Bachelor's degree, master's degree, doctorate

For More Information:

American Petroleum Institute
info@api.org
www.api.org

American Society for Engineering Education
202/331-3500
www.asee.org

Junior Engineering Technical Society, Inc.
703/548-5387
www.jets.org

Society of Petroleum Engineers
972/952-9393
www.spe.org

Interview: Robert Chase

Dr. Robert Chase, Professor and Chair of the Department of Petroleum Engineering and Geology at Marietta College in Marietta, Ohio, discussed his program and the education of petroleum engineering students with the editors of *They Teach That in College!?*

Q. Tell us about your program.

A. Marietta College offers a bachelor of science degree in petroleum engineering. Marietta is one of only 16 ABET-accredited petroleum engineering programs offered in the United States and is the only one housed at a small private liberal arts college. All the other programs are at large universities. Class sizes across the campus are typically small (less than 30 students) compared to large universities, so students get a lot of personal attention.

Q. What makes your program an appealing option for students interested in petroleum engineering?

A. The most appealing aspect of our program is the success of our graduates in obtaining jobs in a truly dynamic petroleum industry. We have enjoyed 100 percent placement of our graduating seniors since the early 1990s. Starting salaries this year range as high as $81,000 per year with $15,000 signing bonuses to complement the offers. Placement of our underclassmen in summer internships is almost as high with over 85 percent of our students getting internships in the oil and gas industry. Salaries are high for these positions, too, and the experience gained in the summertime is a great compliment to the education students receive in the classroom. After graduation, students are able to find jobs here in the Appalachian Basin (Ohio, West Virginia, Kentucky, Pennsylvania, New York) as well as in places like Texas, the Rocky Mountain states, California, Michigan, and offshore in the Gulf of Mexico. After a few years of training in the U.S., engineers may elect to take international positions.

One of the great things about jobs in our field is that a petroleum engineer gets to spend a lot of time in the great outdoors working on wells that are being drilled or on wells that are producing oil and gas. If a student wants to see the world, this is a profession that affords that opportunity. Most companies are eager to place students in positions that take them to the far corners of the earth.

One overlooked benefit of coming to Marietta College versus a large university is that students who enjoy athletic sports can come to Marietta College and play varsity sports. Marietta is an NCAA Division III school and offers no athletic scholarships. However, a student who normally couldn't play sports at a big university could come to Marietta and play any number of sports we offer in one of the toughest Division III conferences in the country—the Ohio Athletic Conference.

Q. What high school subjects/activities should students focus on to be successful in this major?

A. High school students need to be strong in math and science. They should take the highest level of mathematics they can as well as chemistry and physics. Earth science courses are a great addition to the mix, too. Engineers use programs like Excel, Word, and PowerPoint in their work constantly, so computer skills are important. Equally important are communication skills. Engineers have to be able to do a lot of technical calculations, but they must also be able to communicate their ideas, too.

Q. What are the most important personal and professional qualities for petroleum engineering students?

A. The most important personal and professional qualities for petroleum engineering students are work ethic, technical capability, and the ability to communicate your ideas. The job sometimes requires you to be out in the field for long hours under less than perfect working conditions, so a strong work ethic is critical.

Q. What advice would you offer petroleum engineering majors as they graduate and look for jobs?

A. There are a wide variety of companies you can go to work for after graduation (major companies like Chevron or ExxonMobil; large independent companies like Anadarko Petroleum or Encana Corporation; large gas companies like Chesapeake Energy, Equitable Resources, or Columbia Gas; oil-field service companies like Schlumberger, Halliburton Services, or BJ Services; government agencies like the Department of Energy or the Minerals Management Service; or small independent producers all around the country). Choose a company that fits your personal lifestyle and long-term employment goals.

Q. How will the field change in the future?

A. In the future, the U.S. energy industry will probably focus more on natural gas production rather than oil because natural gas is the cleanest burning fossil fuel. Over 50 percent of the petroleum engineering work force is also expected to retire in the next 10 years, so job prospects are excellent for the future. Global energy demand is going to continue to increase due to the economic growth in countries like China and India, thus ensuring strong demand for people working in the international side of the oil business as well.

Plastics Engineering and Science

Look around and you will see plastics in almost every aspect of your life. Plastics are used in health care (e.g., surgical gloves, open MRI machines, prosthetic devices), waste treatment, electronics, construction, agriculture, and in everyday life (e.g., bottles, food storage, product packaging, and countless other uses). Someday, according to Plastics-car.org, plastics may make up a large percentage of the interior and exterior of cars and other vehicles. In short, the sky's the limit for students interested in careers in plastics. *Plastics engineers,* who design and develop plastic products, typically have associate or bachelor's degrees in plastic or polymer engineering, materials engineering, chemical engineering, industrial engineering, manufacturing engineering, or a related field. *Plastics technicians,* who assist plastics engineers, typically have some postsecondary training or an associate degree.

Typical Courses:

> Overview of the Plastics Industry
> Polymer Processing Survey
> Mathematics
> Chemistry
> 3D CAD and Modeling
> Manufacturing Processes
> Injection Molding
> Mold Design/Maintenance
> Industrial Blow Molding
> Extrusion
> Polymer Testing

Potential Employers:

> Aerospace industry
> Building and construction industry
> Electronics industry
> Packaging industry
> Transportation industry
> Virtually any industry that uses plastics in its products

Available At:

The following list of schools offering programs in plastics engineering and related fields is not exhaustive. For more programs, visit the following websites: www.plasticsindustry.org/outreach/institutions and www.abet.org (ABET accredits materials and polymers science program, including those in plastics engineering and related areas.)

Clemson University (Clemson, SC)
864/656-3176
www.ces.clemson.edu/psu/cesmajors/materialSciEng.html#pfc
Degrees available: Bachelor's degree

University of Massachusetts-Lowell (Lowell, MA)
978/934-3420
robert_malloy@uml.edu
http://plastics.caeds.eng.uml.edu
Degrees available: Bachelor's degree, master's degree, doctorate

Pennsylvania College of Technology (Williamsport, PA)
570/327-4520
plastics@pct.edu
www.pct.edu/schools/iet/#plastics
Degrees available: Associate degree, bachelor's degree

Pennsylvania State University (Erie, PA)
814/898-6482
www.pserie.psu.edu/academic/engineering/degrees/plet
Degrees available: Bachelor's degree

Pittsburg State University (Pittsburg, KS)
620/235-4350
etech@pittstate.edu
www.pittstate.edu/etech/plast/index.html
Degrees available: Bachelor's degree, master's degree

University of Southern California (Los Angeles, CA)
213/740-4339
http://chems.usc.edu/admission
Degrees available: Bachelor's degree, master's degree, doctorate

University of Southern Mississippi (Hattiesburg, MS)
601/266-4868
www.usm.edu/polymer
Degrees available: Bachelor's degree, master's degree, doctorat

Western Washington University (Bellingham, WA)
360/650-3380
www.etec.wwu.edu
Degrees available: Bachelor's degree

University of Wisconsin-Stout (Menomonie, WI)
www.uwstout.edu/programs/bset
Degrees available: Bachelor's degree

For More Information:

American Plastics Council
www.plastics.org

Plastics Institute of America
http://pia.caeds.eng.uml.edu

Society of Plastics Engineers
www.4spe.org

Society of the Plastics Industry
www.socplas.org

Interview: Robert Malloy

Dr. Robert Malloy is the Chairman of the Department of Plastics Engineering at the University of Massachusetts Lowell. He discussed the program and the education of plastics engineering students with the editors of *They Teach That in College!?*

Q. Please provide an overview of your program.

A. The Plastics Engineering Department is an internationally recognized leader in plastics engineering education. Founded in 1954, we offer the only B.S. Plastics Engineering program in the United States that is accredited by the Accrediting Board for Engineering and Technology Programs. More than 3,000 graduates are working in the plastics industry in leadership positions worldwide. Programs of study include:

✓ Bachelor of Science Degree in Plastics Engineering
✓ Bachelor of Science in Plastics Engineering with a Business Administration Minor
✓ Five-Year Bachelor of Science/Master of Science Program in Plastics Engineering
✓ Master's Degree Program in Plastics Engineering
✓ Doctor of Engineering Degree in Plastics Engineering

The program combines hands-on laboratory experiences relevant to the industry, with the fundamental theory found in courses of mathematics, science, and engineering to produce a well-rounded curriculum. Constant feedback from industry and alumni enable us to stay on the cutting edge of plastics manufacturing and design technologies.

The Department has 15,000 square feet of dedicated laboratory space. Students are exposed to all of the major plastics manufacturing, design, and testing technologies.

Q. What high school subjects/activities should students focus on to be successful in this major?

A. Students who have an interest in chemistry, physics, and math usually do well in the plastics engineering major. Students should participate in design- or materials-related projects whenever possible.

Q. What are the most important personal and professional qualities for plastics engineering majors?

A. Some subtle differences from traditional engineering programs are: 1) willingness to really do things; students need to be comfortable with both practical and theoretical sides of a problem more than other majors; 2) a more diverse set of academic interests—especially an interest in understanding the connection between chemistry and mechanical engineering. As a family of materials, I consider plastics the most "versatile" materials on earth. Our plastics engineering program has a great deal of chemistry so that students develop an understanding of why plastics materials behave or perform as they do. Our students should be able to look at the chemical structure of a plastic and understand how it will behave (i.e., predict its properties).

Q. How will the field change in the future?

A. The plastics industry is very dynamic. New materials and processes are being developed all the time. We are beginning to see more commercial plastics being developed from renewable resources and growth in the area of biodegradable plastics and plastics recycling, especially for packaging applications. The area of medical plastics is also growing rapidly. New medical devices for less-invasive surgery are largely made from plastics. Other items such as bio-absorbable bone repair screws and artificial joints continue to evolve. More plastics in automobiles reduces weight leading to improved fuel economy.

Globalization is always a concern when it comes to product manufacturing; however, plastics part design and manufacturing in the U.S. maintains good long term prospects.

Two other trends: 1) an increasing emphasis on product leadership and project management (engineers are needed to manage entire commercial processes), and 2) a ratcheting of skills up the technology ladder (to lower costs, to improve consistency, and to enable more advanced products and thereby avoid commoditization).

For more information on our programs, visit http://plastics.uml.edu.

Producer, Film and Television

Actor, director, cinematographer, special effects artist . . . these are the typical options people think of when considering careers in film or television. But the career of producer should also be considered by students with business acumen, ambition, a love of film and/or television, and an artistic sensibility. According to the Producers Guild of America, producers "initiate, coordinate, supervise, and control . . . all aspects of the motion-picture and/or television production process, including creative, financial, technological, and administrative [duties]." In the past, producers typically learned their trade via on-the-job experience or by working their way up through a variety of other positions in the industry. Today, college programs have been created to train producers to enter this demanding, yet exciting, career. Although bachelor's degree programs are available in producing, most industry experts feel that a graduate degree in production offers students the best opportunity to break into this highly competitive field.

Typical Courses:

> Film History
> Film and Television Production
> Film and Television Post Production
> Planning the Independent Film Production
> Production Management
> Film and Television Financing
> Entertainment Law
> Marketing/Distribution/Exhibition
> Independent Feature Filmmaking
> Business

Potential Employers:

> Television production companies
> Film production companies
> Film and television studios

Available At:

University of California-Los Angeles (Los Angeles, CA)
info@tft.ucla.edu
www.tft.ucla.edu/producers/start.htm
Degrees available: Master's degree

Chapman University (Orange, CA)
714/997-6765
http://ftv.chapman.edu/prospective/undergraduate/production.cfm
http://ftv.chapman.edu/prospective/grad/producing.cfm
Degrees available: Bachelor's degree, master's degree

Columbia University (New York, NY)
212/854-2815
wwwapp.cc.columbia.edu/art/app/arts/film/index.jsp
Degrees available: Master's degree

University of Southern California (Los Angeles, CA)
213/740-3317
www-cntv.usc.edu/programs/production
Degrees available: Bachelor's degree, master's degree

For More Information:

Producers Guild of America
www.producersguild.org

Interview: Denise Mann

Denise Mann is an Assistant Professor and Head of the Producers Program at the University of California-Los Angeles (UCLA). Students who complete this unique two-year program receive a master of fine arts and are well prepared for careers as producers in the film and television industries. Mann discussed her program and the career of producer with the editors of *They Teach That in College!?*

Q. Tell us about your program.

A. One of the defining features of the University of California-Los Angeles Producers Program and a central reason for its national and international prominence is its prestigious faculty comprised largely of established industry professionals. Our faculty members include studio heads, heads of agencies, networks, and major producers, attorneys, and other prominent industry leaders. The unique strength of the Producers Program is its ability to provide rigorous and up-to-date creative and business courses on a range of topics having to do with the contemporary Hollywood entertainment industry.

Q. What personal qualities do students need to be successful in your program?

A. We encourage those who apply to the Producers Program to come to the table with a strong educational background and good grades; however, that is true of most graduate programs. Given how demanding our program is and how competitive it is to secure jobs in the Hollywood entertainment industry, we are also looking for individuals who bring a great deal of energy and ambition to the table. Additionally, prospective students should have made every effort to educate themselves about this complex and demanding field by reading the industry trades (*Daily Variety* or *Hollywood Reporter*), watching as many films as possible, reading as many screenplays as possible, and taking film history survey courses (American film history, German film history, French film history, etc.) at their university so that they are familiar both with Hollywood films made before the 1980s and also with as many films made outside the United States as possible.

When they are juniors or seniors in college, students are encouraged to intern at one of the hundreds of Hollywood-based development-production companies, at one of the major talent agencies, at a management company, at a studio (in development, marketing, distribution, or some other department), at one of the networks, or at one of the cable companies. Most students without a background in film think the only way to proceed is to work in production as a production assistant on the set of a film, television show, commercial, or music video. By all means, knowing production is an important part of a producer's learning curve; however, additionally, students who are considering a career in producing should consider interning in development at one of the major production companies, management companies, or literary agencies that represent writers. By supporting the efforts of the executives and producers who work long hours inside these offices to find and develop great material, students start to acquire the necessary story sense and strategic business skills that go into producing. (To help familiarize yourself with the range of companies engaged in development, you may wish to explore one of the many published or online directories devoted to listing studios, networks, production companies, and the company credits, such as the *Hollywood Creative Directory,* Internet Movie Database, etc.). Interning at these companies not only gives students a basic understanding of who's who in the industry and the hierarchies involved, but it also gives them a sense of the volume of screenplays submitted that never see the light of day. By reading and evaluating large numbers of screenplays, students start to assess what makes certain screenplays stand out and start to gather the attention of established producers, talent, directors, financiers, and distributors. Most of the film and television companies offering internships are located in either Los Angeles or New York, but occasionally you can find them in other major cities that are involved in feature film production. Most of the major universities offering film programs in Los Angeles and

New York, in particular, offer internship opportunities to nonresidents during their summer sessions.

Finally, students who want to enter producing can continue to learn on their own by reading as many screenplays as they can get their hands on and by evaluating what makes them work. We are not looking for "closet writers" in the Producers Program, but rather, we are looking for producers with a keen eye for great stories. You should be educating yourself not only about how the marketplace functions, but about how you can become a more productive collaborator and support figure for talented new writers and directors. Develop a sense of which projects you'd like to produce if you were given the chance. To support this effort, start making friends with screenwriters now and learn how to help them become better at what they do best—writing. Start watching movies and reading screenplays and look for ways in which they both adhere to and/or provide innovative departures from the Hollywood conventions of genre and story structure.

Q. What advice would you offer students as they complete your program and look for jobs?

A. The advice I offer students after they complete the Producers Program is to continue honing the story and strategic-thinking skills they acquired while in the graduate program. Most students who graduate from the Producers Program pursue assistant-level jobs at agencies, production companies, studios, and networks. The advantage of going to graduate school is that you will be much more likely to advance up the ranks efficiently because you will have a more in-depth understanding of the whole industry. Students in the Producers Program have an advantage over individuals who go into jobs immediately because they are gleaning insights from industry professionals who have spent several decades sharpening their craft. The other thing I tell both current and graduating students from the Producers Program is that producers are only as good as the material to which they are attached. Some students make the mistake of thinking all they have to do is come up with a great idea for a movie. That's only the first step. The really hard work begins when you start working with a writer to turn the idea into a viable screenplay, one that will attract talented actors to play the key roles and that will inspire a talented director to commit several years of his or her life to turning it into a movie. Finally, producers must always be thinking about the audience. They must ask themselves "who will pay the price to go see my film?" Inevitably, producing represents a balance of artistic and commercial agendas.

Prosthetics and Orthotics

Prosthetists and *orthotists* are allied health professionals who work with prostheses and orthoses—such as braces, helmets, and artificial limbs—that help improve the lives of individuals in need of such assistive devices. They work as members of a patient's rehabilitation team, along with physicians, nurses, physical and/or occupational therapists, dieticians, and social workers. The prosthetist/orthotist may be involved with evaluating the individual in need of an orthosis or prosthesis, and the original design, building, and fitting of the device for that individual. Prosthetists and orthotists often have the opportunity to work in varied environments, spending time with individuals in need of assistive devices, as well working in the lab to create new orthoses and prostheses. In addition, this allied health profession offers a variety of exciting employment opportunities available at different levels—including practitioners and technicians—depending on a person's educational background. Practitioners require a bachelor's degree, post-baccalaureate certificate, or a master's degree. Technicians require an associate degree. More than 4.1 million Americans use orthoses (braces) for disabling conditions such as stroke, multiple sclerosis and Parkinson's Disease, as well as for orthopedic impairments due to sports activities, other physical trauma, birth defects, and advanced arthritis, according to the Centers for Disease Control and Prevention.

Typical Courses:

> Health Care Systems and Perspectives
> Orthotics and Prosthetics
> Public Health
> Pathophysiology for Prosthetics and Orthotics
> Health Behavior
> Biomechanics and Kinesiology for Prosthetics and Orthotics
> Below and Above Knee Prosthetics
> Normal and Pathological Gait
> Materials Science and Applied Anatomy in Prosthetics & Orthotics
> Upper Limb Prosthetics
> Research in Health Sciences

Potential Employers:

> Hospitals
> Rehabilitation centers
> U.S. military

Available At:

Only 12 prosthetic and orthotic education programs (listed below) are accredited by the National Commission on Orthotic and Prosthetic Education and the Commission on Accreditation of Allied Health Education Programs (another school, St. Petersburg College in St. Petersburg, Florida is currently developing a baccalaureate program in the field).

Orthotic and Prosthetic Practitioner Programs

California State University (Aliso Viejo, CA)
800/344-5484
oandp@csudh.edu
www.csudh.edu/oandp
Degrees available: Bachelor's degree, advanced certificate

Century College (White Bear Lake, MN)
651/779-3311
www.century.edu/futurestudents/areasofstudy/orthoticsandprosthetics.aspx
Degrees available: Advanced certificate

Eastern Michigan University (Ypsilanti, MI)
734/487-1849
www.emich.edu/hphp/oandp/index.html
Degrees available: Advanced certificate (This program is still in the development stage. Check with the University regarding its status.)

Georgia Institute of Technology (Atlanta, GA)
404/894-7658
joy.daniell@ap.gatech.edu
www.ap.gatech.edu/mspo
Degrees available: Master's degree

Newington Certificate Program in Orthotics and Prosthetics (Newington, CT)
860/667-5304
ncp@hanger.com
www.hanger.com/ncp
Degree level available: Advanced certificate

Northwestern University (Chicago, IL)
312/238-8006
v-rachel@northwestern.edu
www.medschool.northwestern.edu/depts/nupoc
Degrees available: Advanced certificate

University of Texas Southwestern Medical Center (Dallas, TX)
214/645-8254
po.sahss@utsouthwestern.edu
www8.utsouthwestern.edu/utsw/cda/dept28640/files/51716.html
Degrees available: Bachelor's degree

University of Washington (Seattle, WA)
206/543-3600
rehab@u.washington.edu
http://depts.washington.edu/rehab
Degrees available: Bachelor's degree

Orthotic and Prosthetic Technician Programs

Baker College of Flint (Flint, MI)
810/766-4194
www.baker.edu
Degrees available: Certificate, associate degree

Century College (White Bear Lake, MN)
651/773-1700
www.century.edu/futurestudents/areasofstudy/orthoticsandprosthetics.aspx
Degrees available: Associate degree, diploma

Francis Tuttle (Oklahoma City, OK)
405/717-7799
www.francistuttle.com/classes/ctp/details.aspx?PRGID=13
Degrees available: Associate degree

Oklahoma State University-Okmulgee (Okmulgee, OK)
918/293-4678
www.osu-okmulgee.edu/academics/health_and_environmental/orthotics_and_prosthetics
Degrees available: Associate degree

Spokane Falls Community College (Spokane, WA)
clayw@spokanefalls.edu
509/533-3732
www.spokanefalls.edu/TechProf/OrthoticsProsthetics/Home.aspx
Degrees available: Certificate, associate degree

For More Information:

American Academy of Orthotists and Prosthetists
703/836-0788
www.oandp.org

American Orthotic and Prosthetic Association
571/431-0876
info@aopanet.org
www.aopanet.org

National Commission on Orthotic and Prosthetic Education
703/836-7114
info@ncope.org
www.ncope.org

Interview: Clayton Wright

Clayton Wright is the Director of the Orthotics and Prosthetics Technician Program at Spokane Falls Community College in Spokane, Washington. He is also a board certified prosthetist with 13 years of clinical experience. He discussed the school's technician program and the education of students in this field with the editors of *They Teach That in College!?*

Q. Please tell us about your program.

A. SFCC offers a two-year program to teach fabrication of custom artificial limbs (prosthetics) and braces (orthotics). One year is spent in each discipline. Successful completion of the program results in an associate of applied science degree. This is a technical arts (vocational) non-transfer degree. Students may choose to take only one discipline instead of both, resulting in a certificate of completion. Graduates work in private facilities and hospitals under the supervision of orthotic prosthetic practitioners. Our program is accredited by the National Commission on Orthotic Prosthetic Education. A degree or a certificate from our program grants the student eligibility to participate in the American Board for Certification technician registration exam(s).

Q. What high school subjects/activities should students focus on to be successful in this major?

A. A high school diploma or GED is required. Successful technician students need to have good hand skills. Strong math skills are not required, but a modest background in chemistry and physics are a plus. Good communication skills are very important. Some artistic aptitude is necessary. A student who excels in wood/metal shop and is comfortable in an art class would be an excellent candidate.

Q. How will the field change in the future?

A. The field will continue to expand as the population ages and the issues of obesity and diabetes increase. The field will adopt more computer-aided fabrication methods.

Railroad Operations

If you ever dreamed of becoming a railroad conductor, this is the program for you! Designed to provide students with general knowledge and skills for entry-level employment in the railroad industry, this major introduces students to the history of railroading and the various railroad crafts—conducting, mechanics, electronics, and welding. Railroad operations, safety, environment, and quality are additional areas of focus. Business and technical electives provide additional opportunity for students to specialize or prepare for additional study. Most programs require students to specialize in one or more areas such as conducting, mechanics, electronics, or welding. Programs typically award certificates and associate degrees. Only a few colleges in the United States offer training in railroad operations.

Typical Courses:

- History of Railroading
- Railroad Safety, Quality, and Environment
- Physics
- Mechanical Operations
- Construction Management
- Electromechanical Systems
- Industrial Safety
- Metallurgy
- Business Management

Potential Employers:

- Railroads

Available At:

Dakota County Technical College (Rosemount, MN)
651/423-8232
www.dctc.edu/prospStudents/programs/rrConductor.cfm
Degrees available: Certificate

Johnson County Community College (Overland Park, KS)
913/469-3857
www.jccc.edu/home/depts/4614
Degrees available: Certificate, associate degree

Modoc Railroad Academy (Madison, CA)
916/965-5515

Over the next decade, America's railroads will face an urgent shortage of qualified, well-trained men and women to operate and manage today's modern railroads. Industry experts predict that an additional 80,000 workers will be needed through 2012. (Photo courtesy of Photos.com Select/Photos To Go Unlimited)

mra@modocrailroadacademy.com
www.modocrailroadacademy.com
Degrees available: Certificate

Sacramento City College (Sacramento, CA)
916/558-2491
www.scc.losrios.edu/programs/railroad.html
Degrees available: Certificate, associate degree

St. Philip's College-Southwest Campus (San Antonio, TX)
210/921-4603
www.accd.edu/spc/acad/multi%2Dmodal/railroad
Degrees available: Certificate

Tarrant County Junior College (Fort Worth, TX)
817/515-7271
www.tccd.edu/programs/dp.asp?dpid=229
Degrees available: Certificate

For More Information:

Association of American Railroads
202/639-2100
information@aar.org
www.aar.org

Range Management

More than 40 percent of the Earth's surface is covered by rangelands (grasslands, prairies, alpine, savanna, deserts, marshes, and certain types of forests). According to the Society for Range Management, rangeland is one of the most productive and biodiverse types of land on Earth. Range management professionals ensure that these critical ecosystems remain viable and capable of supporting livestock and wildlife, as well as provide renewable natural resources and recreation opportunities to people. This career requires knowledge of soil science, plant physiology, climatology, land management, land reclamation, and land restoration. A minimum of a bachelor's degree in range management or range science is required to work in this field. Although many schools offer coursework in range management, only about 35 colleges and universities in the United States offer degrees in range management or range science.

Typical Classes:

> Ranch Economics
> Range Management
> Watershed Management
> Range Improvements
> Range Analysis
> Soils
> Wildlife Management
> Range Grasses
> Range Plants
> Range Communities
> Range Ecology
> Habitat Management

Potential Employers:

> Federal agencies (such as the Natural Resources Conservation Service, Bureau of Land Management, National Park Service, Fish and Wildlife Service, and U.S. Forest Service)
> State and local government (such as fish and wildlife departments, natural resources departments, park departments, and state land agencies)
> Colleges and universities

> Private industry (such as ranch managers, mining companies, land management companies, agricultural companies)
> Nonprofit conservation organizations (such as The Nature Conservancy, the Land Trust Alliance, and The Trust for Public Land)

Available At:

The following range management and range science programs are accredited by the Society for Range Management. Other colleges offer good training for the field. For a complete list of programs, visit www.rangelands.org/education_universities.shtml.

University of Arizona (Tucson, AZ)
520/621-7260
http://ag.arizona.edu/srnr/academicprograms
Degrees available: Bachelor's degree, master's degree, doctorate

Did You Know?

There are more than one billion acres of rangeland in the United States—primarily in Alaska and the western states.

Colorado State University (Fort Collins, CO)
970/491-6911
frws_info@cnr.colostate.edu
http://welcome.warnercnr.colostate.edu/frws-home/index.php
Degrees available: Bachelor's degree, master's degree, doctorate

University of Idaho (Moscow, ID)
208/885-6536
range@uidaho.edu
www.cnrhome.uidaho.edu/range
Degrees available: Bachelor's degree, master's degree

Oregon State University (Corvallis, OR)
541/737-3341
http://oregonstate.edu/dept/range
Degrees available: Bachelor's degree

New Mexico State University (Las Cruces, NM)
505/646-2514
ascience@nmsu.edu
http://cahe.nmsu.edu/academics/anrs
Degrees available: Bachelor's degree, master's degree, doctorate

Texas A&M University (College Station, TX)
979/845-2755
http://rangeweb.tamu.edu/extension/Index.htm
Degrees available: Bachelor's degree

Texas Tech University (Lubbock, TX)
806/742-2841
www.rw.ttu.edu/dept
Degrees available: Bachelor's degree, master's degree, doctorate

University of Wyoming (Laramie, WY)
307/766-2263
http://uwadmnweb.uwyo.edu/UWRENEWABLE/Renewable_Rangeland_Ecology.asp
Degrees available: Bachelor's degree, master's degree, doctorate

Utah State University (Logan, UT)
435/797-3219
FRWS@cnr.usu.edu
www.cnr.usu.edu/front.asp
Degrees available: Bachelor's degree, master's degree, doctorate

For More Information:

Society for Range Management
303/986-3309
info@rangelands.org
www.rangelands.org

U.S. Department of Agriculture
Natural Resources Conservation Service
www.nrcs.usda.gov

U.S. Department of Agriculture
U.S. Forest Service
www.fs.fed.us

U.S. Department of the Interior
Bureau of Land Management
www.blm.gov

U.S. Department of the Interior
National Park Service
www.nps.gov

Recreation Leadership/ Outdoor Education

Calling all nature lovers! Imagine this normal workday: guiding a white water trip through a Class V river run, teaching backpacking safety to a group of first-time campers, or marking a new path for backcountry skiing. A major in outdoor education will prepare you for these tasks and much more—and a career in one of the fastest growing segments of the recreation industry. Programs, whether a two-year associate degree, or traditional four-year bachelor's degree, are based on a theoretical foundation, as well as practical experience ranging from kayaking to avalanche awareness. Most programs focus on the adventure or the environmental aspects interdependently, but students should look into each program in depth to discover programs that focus on one more than another, according to their interests. Programs emphasize outdoor program administration, team building, problem solving, adventure leadership, and natural resource management. Degrees in outdoor education are available at the two- and four-year level.

Typical Courses:

> Organization and Management of Adventure Programs
> Environmental Health and Safety
> Mountaineering
> Ecotourism and Natural Resource Management
> Scuba Diving
> Wilderness Survival and First Aid
> Marine Survival
> Fly Fishing
> Backpacking
> Cross Country Skiing
> Sociology of Sport

Potential Employers:

> National Park Service
> National Forest Service
> State and local parks and recreation agencies
> Outward Bound
> College/university outdoor programs
> Adventure-based residential treatment programs for at-risk youth

Available At:

The following programs are just a sampling of the opportunities that are available to students interested in recreation leadership/outdoor education. Visit the websites of schools in your area to see if they offer study options in the field.

Feather River College (Quincy, CA)
530/283-0202, ext. 275
www.frc.edu/ORL/index.html
Degrees available: Associate degree

Georgia College and State University (Milledgeville, GA)
478/445-5004
www.gcsu.edu/kinesiology/majors.html#outdoor
Degrees available: Bachelor's degree

Ithaca College (Ithaca, NY)
607/274-3011
www.ithaca.edu/academics/programs/outdoor
Degrees available: Bachelor's degree

Malone College (Canton, OH)
800/521-1146
www.malone.edu/2183
Degrees available: Bachelor's degree

University of Minnesota-Duluth (Duluth, MN)
218/726-8000
cehsp@d.umn.edu
www.d.umn.edu
Degrees available: Bachelor's degree

Western State College of Colorado (Gunnison, CO)
970/943-2010
www.western.edu/recreation/program.html
Degrees available: Bachelor's degree

For More Information:

Outdoor Industry Association
303/444-3353
info@outdoorindustry.org
www.outdoorindustry.org

Recreation Therapy

People don't often stop to consider the link between recreation and health. Studies have proven that both children and older adults enjoy stronger mental and physical capacity and better social interaction if they recreate. Certified recreation therapists use ingenuity and imagination to enhance people's physical, cognitive, and emotional well-being through leisure activities. According to Temple University's Therapeutic Recreation (TR) Program, TR interventions include adapted aquatics, adapted fitness activity, adventure programming, animal assisted therapy, aquatics therapy, creative arts, exercise programs, horticulture, journaling, leisure education, medical play, music, social skills training, stress management, T'ai Chi Chuan, therapeutic horseback riding, wheelchair sports, and Yoga. While all of the listed educational programs focus on using recreation as a therapeutic medium, some programs offer recreation therapy in the department of education as an option in secondary education while other programs focus primarily on a health sciences curriculum and/or a parks and recreation curriculum. Recreation Therapy is sometimes referred to as Therapeutic Recreation.

Typical Courses:

- Introduction to Health Professions
- Contemporary Aspects of Disability
- Professional Seminar
- Research and Evaluation
- Teaching Health Promotion through Leisure Education
- Health Psychology and Human Behavior
- Sport and Recreation for Individuals with Disabilities
- Foundations of Professional Therapeutic Recreation Practice
- TR Assessment and Documentation
- Clinical Procedures in Therapeutic Recreation
- Modalities in Therapeutic Recreation Practice
- Therapeutic Recreation Administration

Potential Employers:

- Hospitals
- Nursing homes
- Adult day programs
- Outpatient centers
- Retirement communities

> Developmental disability centers
> Substance recovery programs
> Schools
> Mental health agencies
> Home health care agencies
> Correctional facilities
> Municipal recreation centers

Available At:

The following list of schools offering programs in therapeutic recreation is not exhaustive. For more programs, visit www.atra-tr.org/curriculumguide.htm or www.recreationtherapy.com/trcollg.htm.

Eastern Washington University (Cheney, WA)
509/359-2486
www.ewu.edu/x16380.xml
Degrees available: Bachelor's degree

Indiana University (Bloomington, IN)
812/855-4711
www.indiana.edu/~iutr
Degrees available: Bachelor's degree, master's degree

Ithaca College (Ithaca, NY)
607/274-3237
www.ithaca.edu/hshp/programs/tr
Degrees available: Bachelor's degree

University of North Carolina-Wilmington (Wilmington, NC)
910/962-3250
www.uncw.edu/hahs/academics-therapeuticrec.htm
Degrees available: Bachelor's degree

San Jose State University (San Jose, CA)
408/924-3000
www.sjsu.edu/hrtm/rt
Degrees available: Bachelor's degree

Temple University (Philadelphia, PA)
215/204-6278
www.temple.edu/chp/departments/tr
Degrees available: Bachelor's degree, master's degree, doctorate

University of Utah (Salt Lake City, UT)
801/581-8215
www.health.utah.edu/prt
Degrees available: Bachelor's degree

Winston-Salem State University (Winston-Salem, NC)
336/750-2370
www.wssu.edu/WSSU/UndergraduateStudies/School+of+Education
Degrees available: Bachelor's degree

University of Wisconsin-La Crosse (La Crosse, WI)
608/785-8207
www.uwlax.edu/sah/rmtr
Degrees available: Bachelor's degree, master's degree

For More Information:

American Therapeutic Recreation Association
atra@atra-tr.org
www.atra-tr.org

Therapeutic Recreation Directory
www.recreationtherapy.com

Interview: Catherine Coyle

Dr. Catherine Coyle is an Associate Professor of Therapeutic Recreation at Temple University in Philadelphia, Pennsylvania. She discussed the program and the education of therapeutic recreation students with the editors of *They Teach That in College!?*

Q. Please provide a brief overview of your program.

A. The therapeutic recreation (TR) program at Temple University is a 121-credit, bachelor of science degree. It prepares students to become recreation therapists who work collaboratively with doctors, nurses, teachers, psychologists, social workers, occupational therapists, and physical therapists to facilitate health, recovery, and wellness in persons with disabilities or chronic illnesses. While this team of health professionals works collectively to achieve these outcomes, recreation therapists have a unique way of contributing—they use recreation, play, and leisure activities. While their practice may seem 'trivial' to the lay person, it isn't. Recreation therapists do much more than 'play and recreate' with people; they understand the connection between health and recreation, and use this understanding to promote recovery and wellness in persons with disabilities. Recreation therapists realize that children cope better with being hospitalized when given a chance to play; that people recovering from illnesses or adapting to disability adjust and stay healthier longer when they are physically and socially active; and, that older adults maintain a sharper mind and a higher level of social involvement when they recreate.

At Temple, you will come to learn, understand, and value the unique role of recreation therapists in the health and human service system—to promote play, recreation, and leisure as a means to psychological and physical recovery, health, and well-being among individuals with disabilities, including children, adolescents, adults and older adults. In this curriculum, you will learn how to use counseling techniques, recreation activities, and other activity-based interventions to help individuals with physical, cognitive, emotional or social impairments recover basic motor functioning and reasoning abilities, adapt psychologically, build confidence, socialize effectively, and live fully in their communities.

Because of this, we place a heavy emphasis on assuring that students have a solid foundation in the social and physical sciences, as well as in related areas of health and counseling. The primary goal of any undergraduate TR program is to prepare entry level recreation therapists who can deliver rehabilitation, health promotion, and disease prevention programs to individuals with disabilities across the lifespan and in diverse health and human service settings.

Temple's TR department not only has a distinguished tradition of preparing recreation therapists; it is also uniquely different from other programs throughout the nation. First, Temple is the only university in the nation that has a department dedicated exclusively to the discipline of therapeutic recreation. This means that the instruction and experiences you get are focused solely on preparing you to be a recreation therapist. Secondly, the department is housed within the College of Health Professions; therefore you will interact with future colleagues—students majoring in other disciplines like nursing, occupational therapy, physical therapy, health information management, exercise science, and public health. In fact, recreation therapy students at Temple University have the opportunity to earn a certificate in interdisciplinary studies as a part of their coursework. Additionally, you will be taught not only by nationally recognized scholars and researchers, but by individuals with diverse backgrounds and clinical practice experiences, which means you benefit from our knowledge, professional connections, and commitment to preparing the next generation of leaders. Finally, Philadelphia is an ideal setting for anyone interested in the health professions. Strategically located between Washington, D.C. and New York, it is a large metropolitan area rich in diversity and cultural experiences. You will have easy access to a wealth of varied internship and volunteer opportunities during your academic career. For instance, within the immediate vicinity of Temple University, there are five different, free-standing pediatric hospitals, four free-standing physical rehabilitation hospitals, four free-standing behavioral health hospitals, as well as numerous nursing homes, day programs, schools, and residential facilities that employ recreation therapists. At Temple, you will complete a set of specific courses in the major and two credit-earning, field-based clinical internships that allow you to gain hands-on practical experience as a recreation therapist. The Temple TR program is held in high regard nationally and locally. This recognition results directly from the leadership provided by alumni of our program. Temple Owls are everywhere and have been past presidents of national and local professional organizations as well as recipients of awards and recognitions for their clinical and service activities.

Q. What high school subjects/activities should students focus on to be successful in this major?

A. Students should take college preparatory courses, especially math and science courses. If your school offers psychology or anatomy courses, take them as well because these courses will also be helpful. Being involved in extracurricular activities is also important. Skills developed through your participation in sports, art, music, dance, photography, computers, the debate team, or the community service club will be assets in your career as a recreation therapist. If you are adept at foreign languages, continue them. The ability to be bilingual is increasingly important for health care professionals.

Q. What are the most important personal and professional qualities for therapeutic recreation (TR) majors?

A. This major is a good fit if you are interested in a health-related career, enjoy being physically and socially active, have strong leisure pursuits, and have a strong interest in helping others. Because you will use recreation activities in the course of your work, you should have a varied assortment of active and creative leisure pursuits. As a recreation therapist you will be working with children, adolescents, adults, and/or older adults who have a chronic illness or disability; therefore, you should be comfortable interacting with people, and interested in helping others. Additionally, you will often be asked to lead groups of people in activities. Therefore, effective leadership and communication skills are important, as are enthusiasm, creativity, and ingenuity. Finally, students interested in majoring in therapeutic recreation must truly believe that they can "learn more about someone in an hour of play than in a lifetime of conversation" (Plato).

Q. Where do TR graduates find employment?

A. The diversity in employment settings and populations is one of the most exciting things about becoming a recreation therapist. For instance, some recreation therapists work with the elderly in intermediate and extended nursing facilities, in adult day centers, or in senior centers. Others work with children and adults in physical rehabilitation or behavioral health hospitals, residential facilities, schools or group homes. Others find employment opportunities with municipal recreation centers providing support and services for participants with disabilities.

Q. How will the field of therapeutic recreation change in the future?

A. Predicting future change is never easy. However, there are some demographic and health care trends emerging that will provide recreation therapists with new opportunities. The graying of the baby boomers is one such trend. Many of these individuals will retire without giving much thought to how they will fill their retirement time. Accumulating research evidence indicates healthy aging is related to staying active and finding meaning in life after work. Clearly, an emerging role for recreation therapists might be to expand their practice to offer pre- and post-retirement leisure counseling. Another trend is the growing recognition of health promotion and the role of physically and socially active lifestyles in maintaining the health of all individuals, including individuals with disabilities and chronic illnesses. As the only health and human service profession exclusively dedicated to promoting and assuring that individuals with disabilities have the skills and abilities to pursue physically and socially active leisure pursuits, therapeutic recreation professionals have an opportunity to be leaders in designing and delivering health promotion services to persons with disabilities.

Renewable Energy

Energy use in the United States increased by 17 percent between 1991 and 2000, according to the National Energy Policy Development Group. However, our energy production increased by only 2.3 percent. Public concerns about pollution from fossil fuels, increasing costs for conventional energy sources, and our overdependence on foreign energy supplies have created strong interest in renewable energy resources such as wind energy, solar energy, hydropower energy, geothermal energy, and bioenergy. The National Renewable Energy Laboratory estimates that renewable-energy industries will provide at least 300,000 new jobs for American workers over the next two decades. Courses in renewable-energy-related topics can be found at two- and four-year colleges throughout the United States, but only a few institutions offer certificate and degrees in the field.

Typical Courses:

- Physics
- Mathematics
- Introduction to Renewable Energy
- Introduction to Energy Management
- Renewable Energy Applications
- Photovoltaic Theory and System Design
- Photovoltaic Installation
- Electrical Systems
- Introduction to Wind Energy
- Introduction to Solar Energy
- Introduction to Hydropower
- Introduction to Geothermal Energy
- Introduction to Bioenergy

Potential Employers:

- Manufacturing companies
- Research and development companies
- Utility companies
- Government agencies (such as the National Renewable Energy Laboratory and the Energy Efficiency and Renewable Energy Clearinghouse)
- Nonprofit groups and agencies
- Colleges and universities

> Trade associations
> Engineering firms
> Architecture firms

Available At:

The following list of colleges that offer courses and majors in renewable energy and related fields is not exhaustive. Visit www.irecusa.org and www1.eere.energy.gov/education/higher_education.html for more programs. (Note: Programs are in general renewable energy unless otherwise noted.)

Bismarck State College (Bismarck, ND)
800/445-5073
www.bismarckstate.edu/energy/students/prop
Degrees available: Certificate, diploma, associate degree (all in process plant technology)

Cincinnati State Technical and Community College (Cincinnati, OH)
513/861-7700
http://cincinnatistate.edu/FutureStudent/Academics/AcademicDivisions/EngineeringTechnologies/EngineeringTechnologiesDivision.htm
Degrees available: Certificate, associate degree (both in electromechanical engineering technology renewable energy)

Ellsworth Community College (Iowa Falls, IA)
www.iavalley.cc.ia.us
Degrees available: Associate degree (renewable energy technology)

Henry Ford Community College (Dearborn, MI)
313/845-6336
www.hfcc.edu
Degrees available: Certificate

Hocking College (Nelsonville, OH)
877/462-5464
www.hocking.edu
Degrees available: Certificates (alternative energy, advanced alternative energy, fuel cells technology), Associate degree (fuel cells and alternative energy)

Iowa Lakes Community College-Emmetsburg Campus (Emmetsburg, IA)
712/852-5295
www.iowalakes.edu/programs_study/agriculture/biomass_energy
Degrees available: Certificate, associate degree (both in biomass energy processing)

Iowa Lakes Community College-Estherville Campus
(Estherville, IA)
800/521-5054
www.iowalakes.edu/programs_study/industrial/wind_energy_turbine
Degrees available: Diploma, associate degree (both in wind energy and turbine technology)

Iowa State University (Ames, IA)
515/294-6555
www.biorenew.iastate.edu/academics.html
Degrees available: Master's degree, doctorate (noth in biorenewable resources and technology)

Lane Community College (Eugene, OR)
541/463-5034
http://lanecc.edu/instadv/catalog/science/programs/energy.htm
Degrees available: Associate degree

Lansing Community College (Lansing, MI)
517/483-1957
www.lcc.edu/manufacturing/alternative_energy
Degrees available: Certificates (customer energy specialist, stationary energy technology), associate degree (alternative energy technology, customer energy specialist)

Minnesota West Community and Technical College-Canby Campus (Canby, MN)
800/658-2535
www.mnwest.edu
Degrees available: Diploma (wind energy mechanic), associate degree (wind energy technology)

Minnesota West Community and Technical College-Granite Falls Campus (Granite Falls, MN)
800/657-3247
www.mnwest.edu
Degrees available: Certificate (renewable energy base-ethanol production), associate degree (renewable energy technology)

Missouri Southern State University (Joplin, MO)
417/625-9341
www.mssu.edu/ecolonomics
Degrees available: Certificate (ecolonomics)

University of Northwestern Ohio (Lima, OH)
419/998-3120
www.unoh.edu/academics/collegetechnologies/alt_fuels.shtml
Degrees available: Diploma (alternate fuels technician)

Oregon Institute of Technology (Klamath Falls, OR)
503/725-5924
www.oit.edu
Degrees available: Bachelor's degree

St. Clair County Community College (Port Huron, MI)
810/989-5754

www.sc4.edu
Degrees available: Certificate (alternative energy technology)

San Juan College (Farmington, NM)
505/566-3003
munsont@sanjuancollege.edu
www.sanjuancollege.edu/reng
Degrees available: Associate degree, advanced certificate (both in photovoltaic system design and installation)

Sonoma State University (Rohnert Park, CA)
707/664-2430
www.sonoma.edu/ensp/academic_plan_energy.htm
Degrees available: Bachelor's degree

For More Information:

American Solar Energy Society
www.ases.org

American Wind Energy Association
www.awea.org

Association of Energy Engineers
www.aeecenter.org

Geothermal Education Office
www.geothermal.marin.org

Geothermal Energy Association
www.geo-energy.org

Interstate Renewable Energy Council
518/458-6059
www.irecusa.org

Midwest Renewable Energy Association
715/592-6595
www.the-mrea.org

National Hydropower Association
202/682-1700
www.hydro.org

National Renewable Energy Laboratory
303/275-3000
www.nrel.gov

Renewable Fuels Association
202/289-3835
www.ethanolrfa.org

Solar Energy Industries Association
www.seia.org

U.S. Department of Energy
Energy Efficiency and Renewable Energy
www.eere.energy.gov

Interview: Tom Munson and Carl Bickford

San Juan College in Farmington, New Mexico, was the first community college in the United States to offer an associate degree in renewable energy. The editors of *They Teach That in College!?* discussed renewable energy and the education of renewable energy students with Tom Munson, Coordinator of the College's Renewable Energy program, and Carl Bickford, Professor of Engineering and Renewable Energy and one of the founders of the program.

Q. Please tell us about your program.

A. The renewable energy program at San Juan College gives the student a solid foundation in the science and in the design/installation techniques required to work with renewable energy technologies. We offer Photovoltaic System Design and Installation either as an associate of applied science (A.A.S.) degree or as a one-year certificate. The certificate is designed for students who already have a college degree or who currently work in a related industry. Students gain the knowledge and skills necessary to design and safely install electrical energy systems based on current photovoltaic and power conditioning equipment. The curriculum includes hands-on electrical training both in a computer-based laboratory and outdoors doing projects and installations. Training in and compliance with the National Electrical Code is emphasized both in the classroom and during installation practice. For additional information, please visit our website at www.sanjuancollege.edu/reng.

Q. What types of students enter your program? What are their career goals and interests?

A. The students who enter the program are looking for a career change and want to make a positive difference in the world. They often want to translate academic knowledge into real-world physical projects.

Q. What type of career path does the average student take upon graduating from your program?

A. Most students end up working in the PV (photovoltaic) industry in varying capacities. Some get jobs working as designers and installers for solar companies that do installation and repair services. Others get jobs working for distributors both in technical support capacities and in sales positions. A few have started their own businesses.

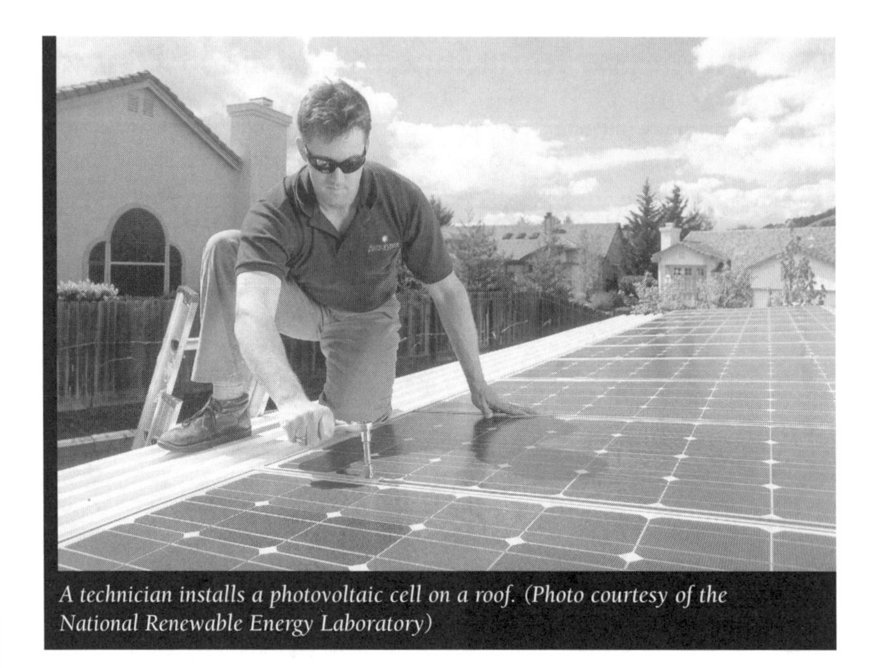

A technician installs a photovoltaic cell on a roof. (Photo courtesy of the National Renewable Energy Laboratory)

Q. What personal qualities do students need to be successful in your program and in their post-college careers?

A. A concern about the environment, wanting to make a difference, and a desire to make this world a better place to live in are qualities that will help students to be successful in the program.

Basic science and math skills and basic tool skills will be helpful in completing the program. Although it isn't required, skill in working with one's hands and prior electrical knowledge and wiring experience are also beneficial.

Q. What is the future for your program and renewable energy?

A. Our program will grow along with the renewable energy industry, which continues to grow in both this country and the world at large. We are looking to expand our program to accept more students and also will be adding solar thermal training. This is an industry that will be on the leading edge as the consciousness of the society increases.

Interview: David Wilson

David Wilson is the Program Coordinator of the Alternative Energy Engineering Technology Program at Lansing Community College in Lansing, Michigan. He discussed his school's program with the editors of *They Teach That in College!?*

Q. What is Alternative Energy Technology?

A. Alternative energy technology involves the study of abundant and renewable alternative energy sources such as the sun, the wind, from soybeans and other food crops, and even from the natural heat below the earth's surface. Using such energy sources is good for the environment—and for the economy. Advances in technology are making alternative energy more practical and economical for mass use. Students at Lansing Community College (LCC) learn about many common and not so common forms of alternative energy, their uses, costs and origin as well as an understanding of conventional energy sources.

Q. Tell us about your program.

A. LCC has two A.A.S. degrees; Alternative Energy Technology, and Customer Energy Specialist; along with two certificates; Stationary Energy Technology, and Customer Energy Specialist. Several other new degrees and certificates are under development in collaboration with our Architectural, Automotive, Building Technology, Electrical, Entrepreneurial, HVAC, Welding/Fabrication, Precision Machining, and Landscape Design Programs. This variety of degrees and certificates will provide students with the option of choosing general studies in alternative energy, or focusing on a specific career field.

Q. What type of internship opportunities are provided by your program?

A. Eligible LCC students can participate in paid and unpaid internships. Past assignments have been primarily in automated building systems efficiency and management. Internships with the U.S. Green Building Council, Consumers Energy, Dowding Industries, The Great Lakes Renewable Energy Association, and the Lansing Board of Water & Light are in the works.

Q. What are the most important personal and professional qualities for alternative energy technology majors?

A. The most important personal qualities a person can have include a genuine interest in sustainability with an emphasis on renewable and alternative forms of energy. This quality is exhibited in one's lifestyle and personal habits as they relate to all forms of energy. Taking this interest in sustainability to the professional level must include being well-informed with a focus on facts rather that opinion.

Q. Where do alternative energy technology graduates find employment?

A. Graduates from LCC's Alternative Energy Engineering Technology Program can find employment in welding/fabrication, precision machining/manufacturing, building and building systems design and construction, electric utility companies, wind farm developers, solar photovoltaic manufacturing, with many more being added regularly.

Q. What is the employment outlook for the field?

A. Presently (Fall, 2007) the Michigan economy is mired in near double-digit unemployment due primarily to the downsizing of the automotive industry over the past few years. But the future looks very good as many manufacturing companies are re-tooling to meet the needs of an increase in demand for solar photovoltaic systems and a booming wind energy industry. For example, an international solar photovoltaic manufacturer (based in Michigan) has recently built two new factories and has talked of building another to meet the demand for its products. Another company that has manufactured automotive parts for several decades is building a new $8 million facility to manufacture parts for large wind turbines.

The Governor of Michigan, the Honorable Jennifer Granholm, has recently proposed a very ambitious plan to turn Michigan's weak economy around by focusing on and investing in sustainable, renewable, alternative energy. Alternative energy technology graduates should have little difficulty in finding good paying jobs in their chosen field over the next few years, not only in Michigan, but all across the country.

Risk Management

Risk managers help businesses protect their assets by controlling risks and losses. They also help businesses maintain optimal levels of production. Some examples of how risk management workers accomplish these goals is by keeping workers properly trained, reviewing and analyzing work procedures to make sure they are safe, ensuring that the supply chain command operates efficiently, and maintaining a work environment where theft and fraud are kept to a minimum, or eliminated. Risk managers can find employment in a variety of settings, including industrial, service, nonprofit, and public-sector organizations. The field of risk management is closely intertwined with the traditional insurance industry, and with business in general, so students interested in a career in risk management will likely see some overlap in their coursework with these fields of studies. Risk management students may participate in internship programs that afford them the opportunity to work in such areas as underwriting, management, or finance.

Typical Courses:

- Introduction to Risk Management
- Business Law
- Life/Health/Employee Benefits
- Investments
- Introduction to Economics
- Statistics
- Mathematics
- Accounting for Decision Making
- Finance

Potential Employers:

- Insurance companies
- Corporations
- Airlines
- Financial institutions
- Manufacturers
- Government agencies
- Hospitals
- School districts
- Colleges and universities

Available At:

Illinois Wesleyan University (Bloomington, IL)
309/556-1000
http://titan.iwu.edu/~business/risk.htm
Degrees available: Bachelor's degree

University of Wisconsin-Madison
608/262-1550
www.bus.wisc.edu/asrmi
Degrees available: Bachelor's degree, master's degree, doctorate

For More Information

American Risk and Insurance Association
610/640-1997
www.aria.org

Public Risk Management Association
703/528-7701
www.primacentral.org

Risk and Insurance Management Society
212/286-9292
www.rims.org

Rubber Engineering

Rubber is used in countless products—from tires for motor vehicles, to shoes and rubber balls, to tires and rubber gloves, to the gaskets used in automobiles and spacecraft. In short, life would be a lot harder without rubber. Approximately one million people are employed in the rubber industry in the United States. Rubber engineers design and help create products out of natural and synthetic rubber materials. Ferris State University offers the only rubber engineering technology bachelor's degree program in the United States. Students in the program receive hands-on experience with the latest rubber industry technology. They are also required to serve two 10-week internships with rubber manufacturing companies in order to gain experience in the field and make professional contacts—which could lead to job offers after graduation. Graduates of the program enter the field as process, product or project engineers, quality control engineers, or technical sales representatives.

Typical Courses:

- Controls for Automation
- Plastics Engineering Management Systems
- Plastics and Elastic Materials and Additives
- Introduction to Industrial Engineering
- Introduction to Plant Engineering
- Rubber Product Design
- Rubber Compounds/Compounding
- Advanced Rubber Processing
- Statistical Quality Control

Potential Employers:

- Rubber production plants
- Government research facilities

Available At:

Ferris State University (Big Rapids, MI)
231/591-2640
http://catalog.ferris.edu/programs/290
Degrees available: Bachelor's degree

For More Information:

International Institute of Synthetic Rubber Producers
713/783-7511
www.iisrp.com

Rubber Manufacturers Association
202/682-4800
www.rma.org

Satellite Communications

Today, we expect ready access to information, and the ability to communicate to and from anywhere in the world. Thanks to the work of those in satellite communications, all this is possible. Career opportunities as technicians, operators, installers, and managers for work in different aspects of satellite technology are available throughout the world. Technicians may be dispatched by cable television companies to set up broadband services to new customers. Installers may be contracted to establish communication links in remote areas or emerging "Third World" countries. Operators may be hired by different vendors and businesses to set up encryption equipment used to conduct credit card transactions or inventory control. Still other workers may specialize in the delivery of video, audio, music, and text services. Interested students should be proficient in mathematics and science. Other important skills needed to succeed in this industry are the ability to communicate with others and solve problems abstractly. The demand for satellite communications experts will grow as we continue to rely heavily on high tech ways to communicate with others, gather news, and conduct business. Mitchell Technical Institute in Mitchell, South Dakota, is the only school in the United States to offer a two-year associate of applied science degree in satellite communications.

Typical Courses:

- Earth Station Transmitter Systems
- Satellite Communications Lab
- Teleport Regulations
- Earth Station Receiver Systems
- Principles of Satellite & Wireless Communication
- Television Technology
- Electronics Theory
- Microcomputer Software Applications
- Electronics Mathematics

Potential Employers:

- Television networks
- Satellite companies
- Television stations

Available At:

Mitchell Technical Institute (Mitchell, SD)
800/MTI-1969
www.mitchelltech.com/programs/sat.php
Degrees available: Associate degree

For More Information:

Satellite Broadcasting and Communications Association
800/541-5981
info@sbca.org
www.sbca.com/index.asp

Interview: Dave VerSteeg

Dave VerSteeg is a Satellite Communications Instructor at Mitchell Technical Institute in Mitchell, South Dakota. He discussed his school's program and the education of students in this field with the editors of *They Teach That in College!?*

Q. Please tell us about your program.

A. Mitchell Technical Institute (MTI) is the only school in the nation to offer a two-year associate of applied science degree in satellite communications. This program provides training in installation, operation, maintenance, and management of satellite communication systems. This includes working with transmission and reception of broadcasts, uplinks and downlinks, between satellites and remote or in-house studios.

In addition to the A.A.S. degree from MTI, the Society of Broadcast Engineers will award our graduates who meet their specific grade point criteria a broadcast technologist certificate.

Q. What high school subjects/activities should students focus on to be successful in this major?

A. As you might expect, my first response to that question is always math and science. The science aspect is fairly obvious, but many students are initially surprised at the amount of math required for our industry. We use trigonometry to analyze the resistive and reactive components in AC circuits, and we use logarithms to solve decibel equations related to the gain of amplifiers and the attenuation of feed lines.

Each of the various programs at our school conducts an advisory meeting each semester to meet with the leaders in our industry. The primary purpose of the meetings is to discuss the state of the industry and how it relates to our curriculum. We pride ourselves in our ability to react to the dynamic needs of our employers on a timely basis. I've noticed that lately we often talk about the "soft skills" of our incoming freshman and their lack of written and verbal communication skills. That may become a higher priority for our high school students.

Another subject that is becoming more significant is the ability to speak and read a foreign language. Our students work in an industry that spans the globe at the speed of light, and multi-linguistic skills could be a valuable commodity.

Did You Know?

Sputnik I, the first man-made Earth satellite, was launched by the Soviet Union on October 4, 1957. It was about the size of a beach ball and weighed only 183.9 pounds. Thus began the space race. The United States countered by launching *Explorer I* on January 31, 1958. Today, nearly 40 countries own satellites, and there are nearly 3,000 orbiting the earth.

Q. What advice would you offer students as they graduate and look for jobs?

A. One of the more difficult concepts we try to get across to our students is the fact that we are preparing them for jobs in the future that might not exist at this moment. They need to think "out-of-the-box" and not subconsciously limit their possibilities. The students often come to us with a pre-conceived notion of what they would like to do—maybe they saw an uplink truck at a state basketball tournament—but fail to realize there is so much more for them to do. A few of our students have found great jobs working for Union Pacific Railroad. Most people don't realize it has one of the largest communication networks in the country. Other students are working on cruise ships to provide television, telephone, and high-speed Internet access to their customers. Another unique opportunity that has surfaced recently is the need for the services I just mentioned on the oil platforms in the Gulf of Mexico. Credit card transactions and inventory control is often communicated via a satellite communications link of some kind.

Another piece of advice I would offer is to NOT burn any bridges. Our students intern with various companies just prior to graduation. When they leave those positions they might not expect to ever see those people again, only to find out they may be back with a different branch of the same company in just a few years.

Q. Where do graduates find employment?

A. Our students are able to find employment in almost every corner of the planet. I remember when the United States first entered the Desert Storm conflict we had a high demand for civilian satellite communication technicians to establish communication links in the Middle East. More recently the tragedy in New Orleans brought a surge for SNG (Satellite News Gathering) truck operators to provide uplinks for network media coverage.

Janet Greenway, the career services coordinator here at Mitchell Tech, provides detailed reports on the employment status, salaries, and employers of MTI students in all programs. The following is a portion of her data on last year's SATCOM graduates:

Company	*State*	*Job Description*
IntelSat	GA	Radio Frequency Broadcast Engineer
PetroCom	LA	Field Technician
ViaCom	CA	Uplink Technician
Lodgenet	SD	Video Operations Technician
DirectTV	CO	Mobile Truck Operator
Crawford Commun.	GA	International Access Operator
PSSI Global	CA	Satellite Uplink Operator
LiveOnSite	MD	Information Technology Technician

Q. What is the employment outlook for the field of satellite communications? How will the field change in the future?

A. I'm happy to report the employment outlook for satellite communication technicians is excellent. There are many more job opportunities throughout the country than we have students, and we don't anticipate the demand to decrease anytime soon. The children of today will grow up in a world where they expect all of their personal data to be available to them wherever they are. They will also expect to be able to communicate with their friends through multiple mediums (voice/video/text) no matter where they are located. These expectations will only increase the need for a reliable communications backbone and the technicians with the skills to maintain it.

The most prevalent change occurring in our industry at this time is the transition from analog to digital modulation techniques. Analog is disappearing and digital equipment is everywhere. Most of the digital systems use a computer interface to allow the operator maximum control, so computer proficiency is extremely important. Voice over Internet Protocol (VoIP) and Internet Protocol video schemes are fast becoming the norm.

Screenwriting

If you've ever dreamed of winning an Academy Award, and you have a talent for writing, a major in screenwriting might help you develop your skills and give you the background and contacts in the film industry to get your career started. Or maybe your interests lie in writing for television. In television screenwriting programs, you can learn to develop scripts for dramatic forms ranging from action-adventure, to social drama, to situational comedy. No matter your interests you will learn about the elements of character, dialogue, scene, setting, texture, style, and tone via intensive workshop classes. Writing scenes, short scripts, treatments, and finally full-length feature screenplays—ready to be pitched to agents—is what a student majoring in screenwriting can expect. A combination of creative talent, storytelling ability, and college study (associate, bachelor's, and master's degrees are available in screenwriting), will give you a leg up over others in this highly competitive industry.

Typical Courses:

- Dramatic Structure
- Editing
- Visual Storytelling
- Film and Television Aesthetics
- Introduction to Screenwriting
- History of Film and Television
- Acting for Non-Actors
- Seminar in Television and Film Writing
- Narrative Theory and Practice for Screenwriters
- Writing Screenplay Adaptations
- Film and Television Genres

Potential Employers:

- Movie studios
- Self-employment (freelance writer)
- Production companies
- Talent agencies
- Advertising agencies

Available At:

University of the Arts (Philadelphia, PA)
800/616-ARTS
www.uarts.edu/academics/cmac/wr/bfawriting.html
Degrees available: Bachelor's degree

University of California-Los Angeles (Los Angeles, CA)
310/825-5761
info@tft.ucla.edu
www.tft.ucla.edu/ftv_mfa/index.cfm?action=screen
Degrees available: Bachelor's degree (general, with an emphasis in screenwriting), master's degree

Chapman University (Orange, CA)
714/997-6765
DodgeCollege@chapman.edu
http://ftv.chapman.edu/prospective/undergraduate/screenwriting.cfm
Degrees available: Bachelor's degree

Columbia College Chicago (Chicago, IL)
312/663-1600
www.colum.edu/undergraduate/filmvideo/screenwriting/screenwritconcreqs.html
Degrees available: Bachelor's degree

Columbia University (New York, NY)
212/854-2815
film@columbia.edu
wwwapp.cc.columbia.edu/art/app/arts/film/index.jsp
Degrees available: Master's degree

Hollins University (Roanoke, VA)
540/362-6575
hugrad@hollins.edu
www.hollins.edu/grad/film/screenwriting.htm
Degrees available: Master's degree

Metropolitan State University (St. Paul, MN)
651/793-1300
www.metrostate.edu/catalog/index.cfm?check=1&id=8
Degrees available: Bachelor's degree

Minneapolis Community & Technical College (Minneapolis, MN)
612/659-6000
www.minneapolis.edu/academics/areaofstudy.cfm?aos_id=40
Degrees available: Associate degree

New York University (New York, NY)
212/998-1940
http://ddw.tisch.nyu.edu/page/undergraduate.html
http://ddw.tisch.nyu.edu/page/graduate.html
Degrees available: Bachelor's degree, master's degree

University of Southern California (Los Angeles, CA)
213/740-3303
writing@cinema.usc.edu
www-cntv.usc.edu/programs/writing
Degrees available: Bachelor's degree, master's degree

For More Information:

American Screenwriters Association
866/265-9091
asa@goasa.com
www.asascreenwriters.com

Sundance Institute
310/360-1981
institute@sundance.org
www.sundance.org

Writers Guild of America
East Chapter
212/767-7800
info@wgaeast.org
www.wgaeast.org

Writers Guild of America
West Chapter
800/548-4532
http://www.wga.org

Screenwriter's Utopia
www.screenwritersutopia.com

Interview: Alan Miller

Alan Miller teaches in the expanded Cinema Program at Minneapolis Community & Technical College in Minneapolis, Minnesota. Students who complete the program earn an associate degree in screenwriting or other aspects of film and video, with courses in directing, producing, production management, and sound. Mr. Miller has been teaching for 30 years. He discussed the education of students in this field with the editors of *They Teach That in College!*

Q. What high school classes should students focus on to be successful in this major?

A. High school students should place a big emphasis on English, history, and the social sciences.

Did You Know?

The American Screenwriters Association offers the High School Screenwriting Initiative, a one-day seminar for high school students interested in screenwriting. Visit www.goasa.com for more information.

Q. What are the most important personal and professional qualities for screenwriting students?

A. Students must have dedication and be able to handle arduous tasks on deadline. They obviously need to be creative and imaginative, but at the same time be able to work within specific rules and guidelines, often working with other professionals.

Q. Where do your screenwriting graduates find employment?

A. Throughout the film industry and other allied creative fields, from advertising firms and agencies to whomever deals in film, video, production, or the like.

Q. What is the employment outlook for graduates of your program?

A. Film is a burgeoning field, particularly with the advent of many production companies, the Internet, and cable television. It is the medium students are probably most familiar with and offers a great opportunity for those willing to work hard, to be prompt in fulfilling their responsibilities, and be prepared to overcome rejection, which is built into the industry, as well as competition from many others striving for the same goals.

Ski Resort Management

Combine your passion with snow sports with a top-notch college education! Ski resort managers are employed at mountain operations and resorts throughout the United States in positions such as resort director, ski instructor, and equipment and operations manager. In postsecondary ski management programs, technical and academic instruction is provided, coupled with practical experience in the form of an internship or fieldwork. Degree choices range from a certificate to a bachelor's degree.

Typical Courses:

- Resort Budgeting and Organization
- Resort Master Planning
- Resort Merchandising
- Resort Mountain Operations
- Snow Science
- Ski Business Management
- Methods for the Professional Ski Teacher
- Ski Lift Construction and Design
- Ski Equipment Mechanics
- Internship in Ski Business and Resort Management

Potential Employers:

- Ski resorts

Available At:

Gogebic Community College (Ironwood, MI)
800/682-5910, ext. 207
www.gogebic.edu/academics/SAM
Degrees available: Associate degree (transferable courses to Northern Michigan University's bachelor's program in ski business management)

Lyndon State College (Lyndonville, VT)
802/626.6413
www.lyndonstate.edu/academics/majors/skiresortmanagementBS/tabid/190/Default.aspx
Degrees available: Bachelor's degree

University of Maine-Farmington (Farmington, ME)
207/778-7050
www.farmington.edu/academics/ski-industries.php
Degrees available: Certificate program (must be combined with a bachelor's degree in any discipline)

Northern Michigan University (Marquette, MI)
906/227-1000
http://webb.nmu.edu/Colleges/Business
Degrees available: Bachelor's degree (Joint program with Gogebic Community College. Some courses must be taken at Gogebic Community College.)

Sierra Nevada College (Incline Village, NV)
775/831-1314
www.sierranevada.edu/803
Degrees available: Bachelor's degree

Western State College of Colorado (Gunnison, CO)
970/943-2010
www.western.edu/recreation/program.html
Degrees available: Bachelor's degree

Did You Know?

During the 2006-2007 season, there were 485 ski areas in operation in the United States, according to the National Ski Areas Association. States with the highest number of ski areas included New York, Michigan, Wisconsin, Pennsylvania, California, Colorado, Vermont, New Hampshire, Maine, Minnesota, Montana, and Idaho.

For More Information:

National Ski Areas Association
303/987-1111
nsaa@nsaa.org
www.nsaa.org

Professional Ski Instructors of America
www.psia.org

Speech Pathology

Speech pathologists work to diagnose and treat speech and language disorders, as well as swallowing disorders. They work with children and adults whose speech is compromised due to physical or neurological disorders, developmental delays, or injury. Many speech pathologists also work with geriatric clients whose language and speech is affected due to sickness, such as a stroke. In fact, according to the *Occupational Outlook Handbook*, the biggest demand for speech pathologists will be from the growing elderly population who will need services to help adjust to chronic illness. The minimum educational requirement to work in this profession is a master's degree.

Typical Courses:

- Clinical Methods
- Organic Disorders
- Communication Problems of the Aged
- Evaluation and Treatment of Dysphagia in Adults
- Augmentative Communication
- Motor Speech Disorders and Cerebral Palsy
- Developmental Speech Disorders
- Acquired Speech and Language Disorders
- Articulation Disorders
- Stuttering
- Evaluation of Children

Potential Employers:

- Schools
- Health maintenance organizations
- Hospitals
- Public health departments
- Research agencies
- Colleges and universities
- Private practice
- Long-term care facilities
- Rehabilitation centers
- Government agencies
- Industrial audiology
- Corporate speech-language pathology programs

Available At:

The following list offers a selection of schools that award degrees in speech pathology. For a complete listing, visit the American Speech-Language-Hearing Association's website at www.asha.org/gradguide.

Arizona State University (Tempe, AZ)
480/965-2374
www.asu.edu/clas/shs
Degrees available: Bachelor's degree, master's degree, doctorate

California State University-Fresno (Fresno, CA)
559/278-2423
www.csufresno.edu/csd
Degrees available:: Bachelor's degree, master's degree

University of Colorado-Boulder (Boulder, CO)
303/492-3043
www.colorado.edu/slhs
Degree available: Bachelor's degree, master's degree, doctorate

University of Florida (Gainesville, FL)
352/392-2113
http://web.csd.ufl.edu
Degrees available: Bachelor's degree, master's degree, doctorate

University of Georgia (Athens, GA)
706/542-4561
www.coe.uga.edu/csse
Degrees available: Bachelor's degree, master's degree, doctorate

Howard University (Washington, DC)
202/806-7690
www.howard.edu/schoolcommunications/CSD/About.htm
Degrees available: Bachelor's degree, master's degree

University of Illinois-Urbana-Champaign (Champaign, IL)
217/333-2230
www.shs.uiuc.edu
Degrees available: Bachelor's degree, master's degree, doctorate

University of Kansas (Kansas City, KS)
913/588-5937
www.ku.edu/~splh/ipcd
Degrees available: Bachelor's degree, master's degree, doctorate

University of Maine-Orono (Orono, ME)
207/581-2006
www.umaine.edu/comscidis
Degrees available: Bachelor's degree, master's degree

University of Massachusetts-Amherst (Amherst, MA)
413/545-0131
www.umass.edu/sphhs/comdis
Degrees available: Bachelor's degree, master's degree, doctorate

University of Minnesota (Minneapolis, MN)
612/624-3322
www.slhs.umn.edu
Degrees available: Bachelor's degree, master's degree, doctorate

University of Oregon (Eugene, OR)
541/346-2480
http://education.uoregon.edu/cds
Degrees available: Bachelor's degree, master's degree, doctorate

University of North Texas (Denton, TX)
940/565-2481
www.sphs.unt.edu
Degrees available: Bachelor's degree, master's degree, doctorate

Did You Know?

Speech-language pathologists who worked in health care earned salaries that ranged from $53,000 to $68,000 in 2005, according to the American Speech-Language-Hearing Association. Those employed in administration earned between $72,900 and $80,000.

University of Southern Mississippi (Hattiesburg, MS)
601/266-5216
www.usm.edu/shs
Degrees available: Bachelor's degree, master's degree, doctorate

Western Michigan University (Kalamazoo, MI)
616/387-8045
www.wmich.edu/hhs/sppa
Degrees available: Bachelor's degree, master's degree, doctorate

University of Wyoming (Laramie, WY)
307/766-6427
www.uwyo.edu/comdis
Degrees available: Bachelor's degree, master's degree

For More Information:

American Speech-Language-Hearing Association
actioncenter@asha.org
www.asha.org

National Student Speech Language Hearing Association
301/296-8705
nsslha@asha.org
www.nsslha.org

Interview: Sid P. Bacon

Dr. Sid P. Bacon is the former Chairman of the Department of Speech and Hearing Science at Arizona State University (ASU) in Tempe, Arizona. He currently is Dean of Natural Sciences in the College of Liberal Arts and Sciences at ASU. He discussed his program and the education of speech pathology students with the editors of *They Teach That in College!?*

Q. Please provide a brief overview of your program.

A. Arizona State University offers a bachelor of science degree in speech and hearing science. It focuses on the scientific aspects of normal speech, language, and hearing, and includes a few courses on various disorders of human communication. Our students are very well prepared to pursue graduate training in either speech-language pathology or audiology. Graduate degrees are generally necessary to practice clinically. [Note: The University also offers a master of science degree in communication disorders (with an emphasis in speech-language pathology), an Au.D. degree (Doctorate of Audiology), and a Ph.D. degree (Doctorate of Philosophy).]

Q. What high school subjects/activities should students focus on to be successful in this major?

A. Students would benefit from courses in biology, psychology, child development, physics, and mathematics. They also would benefit from extracurricular activities such as baby-sitting, working in physician's offices or nursing homes, and participating in activities with individuals with special needs.

Q. How will the field change in the future?

A. Advances in science and technology in areas such as brain imaging and genetics will lead to a better understanding of the causes of communication disorders and consequently to better treatments. There is likely to be a greater emphasis on communication at both ends of the age spectrum. On the young end, there will be a growing emphasis on early intervention as it pertains to language and literacy—getting children ready to read and be successful in school. At the older end, there will be a greater emphasis on how to improve communication and avoid or minimize the social isolation that often accompanies the decline in communication abilities in the elderly. The field also will continue to expand to help address communication problems globally, particularly in third-world countries.

Sports Management

Maybe you dreamed of being a major league baseball player, a grand slam tennis tournament winner, or a professional golfer but your talents never quite reached that of the professional athlete. You can still pursue a passion for sports with a degree in sports management! Health and fitness conscious individuals will gain a business and fitness background that will prepare them for careers as fitness club managers, sales and marketing professionals for professional sports teams, and health educators or program directors for their local parks and recreation department. Individuals of all ages engage in sporting activity as a means for social interaction and a step towards healthy living. If you possess good communication skills and a desire to help individuals reach their fitness goals—while having fun playing sports—a degree in sports management is an excellent means to jump-starting your career. Most programs have options that allow you to concentrate on an area that is most important to you—business management, health and science, or recreation leadership.

Typical Courses:

> Sports Marketing
> Public Relations and Advertising for the Sports Industry
> Accounting
> Fitness Facility Management
> Philosophy, Principles, and Organization of Athletics in Education
> Program Planning and Leadership for Recreation and Physical Education
> Sports and Society
> Current Issues in Sports
> Sports Law
> Health and Fitness Electives

Potential Employers:

> Fitness and health clubs
> Community recreation departments
> Professional sports teams
> Colleges and universities

Available At:

The following list of sports management programs is not exhaustive. Check with academic institutions near you to determine if majors, minors, certificates, or concentrations are available in sports management. Additionally, visit www.nassm.com/InfoAbout/SportMgmtPrograms for a comprehensive list of programs.

University of Colorado-Colorado Springs
719/262-3345
www.business.uccs.edu/sport
Degrees available: Bachelor's degree

Indiana University-Bloomington
812/855-5523
www.indiana.edu/%7Ekines/undergraduate/marketing.shtml
www.indiana.edu/%7Ekines/graduate/ms_marketing.shtml
Degrees available: Bachelor's degree, master's degree

Mercyhurst College North East (North East, PA)
800/825-1926
http://northeast.mercyhurst.edu
Degrees available: Associate degree

University of New Haven (West Haven, CT)
www.newhaven.edu/show.asp?durki=1939
Degrees available: Bachelor's degree, master's degree

New Hampshire Technical Institute (Concord, NH)
603/271-6426
www.nhti.edu/academics/academicprograms/degsprtmgmt.html
www.nhti.edu/academics/academicprograms/certsportsmgmt.html
Degrees available: Certificate, associate degree

New York University (New York, NY)
212/998-7200
www.scps.nyu.edu/areas-of-study/tisch
Degrees available: Bachelor's degree, master's degree

North Carolina State University (Raleigh, NC)
919/515-3276
http://cnr.ncsu.edu/prtm/academic/index.html
Degrees available: Bachelor's degree, master's degree

North Dakota State University (Fargo, ND)
701/231-9718
http://hnes.ndsu.edu
Degrees available: Bachelor's degree, master's degree

North Iowa Area Community College (Mason City, IA)
641/423-1264
www.niacc.edu/business/sport.html
Degrees available: Associate degree

Football is one of the five most popular sports in the United States. The others? Baseball, basketball, hockey, and soccer. (Photo courtesy of VStock LLC/Photos To Go Unlimited)

Rutgers University (New Brunswick, NJ)
732/932-9525
www.exsci.rutgers.edu
Degrees available: Bachelor's degree

Seton Hall University (South Orange, NJ)
http://business.shu.edu/sports
Degrees available: Bachelor's degree, master's degree, advanced certificate

University of Tennessee (Knoxville, TN)
865/974-1282
http://web.utk.edu/~sals
Degrees available: Bachelor's degree, master's degree, doctorate

Texas A&M University (College Station, TX)
sptmgmt@tamu.edu
http://sm.tamu.edu/sm
Degrees available: Bachelor's degree, master's degree, doctorate

For More Information:

National Association for Sport and Physical Education
800/213-7193
www.aahperd.org/naspe/template.cfm

North American Society for Sport Management
www.nassm.com
www.nassm.com/InfoAbout/SportMgmtPrograms/United_States

Sports Ministry

Sports ministry is a unique approach to sharing the message of Jesus Christ with people everywhere, allowing students to channel their God-given athletic talents and abilities into being effective ministers. The commonality of sports and recreation across so many age groups, institutions, and cultures makes athletic activity an excellent avenue for sharing the word of the Lord and modeling Christian values and experiences, both on and off of the field. Students who enroll in a sports ministry program can expect to study general academics; religious-themed subjects such as the Bible, evangelism, and ministerial skills; and sports-related subjects such as coaching, fitness and wellness, and the mechanics of sports games. A sports ministry program prepares students to work together with athletes, missionaries, churches, and others to spread the Christian message in many different, often multicultural, environments, at home or abroad. For example, some sports ministers work in prisons, schools, churches, community organizations, and international missions.

Typical Courses:

> Christian Theology
> Models of Christian Ministry
> Old Testament/New Testament
> Communicating the Christian Faith
> Theological Foundations for Sports Ministry
> Administration and Organization of Sports Ministry
> Evangelism and Discipleship in Sports Ministry
> Leadership and Staff Dynamics

Potential Employers:

> Nonprofit religious organizations
> Camp ministries
> Churches

Available At:

Huntington University (Huntington, IN)
260/356-6000
www.huntington.edu/rec/sportsministry.htm
Degrees available: Bachelor's degree

Malone College (Canton, OH)
800/521-1146
www.malone.edu/2202
Degrees available: Bachelor's degree

Moody Bible Institute (Chicago IL)
312/329-4451
http://mmm.moody.edu/GenMoody/default.asp?sectionID=BB135E240ED24EEC99617246CE147E84
Degrees available: Bachelor's degree

Washington Bible College (Lanham, MD)
301/552-1400
http://true441.youthsite.org/index.cfm?PAGE_ID=330&EXPAND=319
Degrees available: Bachelor's degree

For More Information:

Athletes in Action
937/352-1000
athletesinaction@aia.com
www.athletesinaction.org

National Association for Sport and Physical Education
800/213-7193
www.aahperd.org/naspe/template.cfm

National Council of Churches USA
212/870-2227
http://ncccusa.org

National Religious Vocation Conference
773/363-5454
nrvc@nrvc.net
www.nrvc.net

Sports/Commercial Turf Equipment Repair

The fields athletes perform on, the parks we play in, and the golf courses on which we swing our clubs . . . all need to be maintained, not only so they are attractive, but also so people are able to safely engage in sporting activities on them. This requires expensive equipment and people who know how to use and maintain it.The growing field of sports/commercial turf equipment repair involves the maintaining, operation, troubleshooting, and rebuilding of commercial power equipment, such as mowers, trimmers and edgers, and rotary tillers. The Ohio State Agricultural Technical Institute is one of the few schools in the United States that offers a certificate in sports/commercial turf equipment repair. For students interested in earning an associate degree, the school offers programs in power and equipment, turfgrass management, and landscape contracting and construction that can be pursued in addition to the certificate.

Typical Courses:

- Introduction to Turfgrass Management
- Engine Basics
- Technical Mathematics
- Landscape, Nursery, and Turf Equipment
- Compact Diesel Engines
- Introduction to Microcomputer Applications
- Power Transmission for Turf Equipment
- Basic Electricity and Electronics
- Basic Hydraulic Systems
- Welding and Metal Fabrication
- Technical Reporting

Potential Employers:

- Equipment dealers
- Manufacturers
- Lawn care companies
- Landscape firms
- Nurseries
- Golf courses
- Parks

> Colleges and universities
> Professional sports teams

Available At:

The Ohio State University (Wooster, OH)
Agricultural Technical Institute
330/264-3911, ext 1327
www-afa.adm.ohio-state.edu/u-majors/pdf/ati/cte.pdf
www-afa.adm.ohio-state.edu/u-majors/pdf/ati/powereq.pdf
Degrees available: Certificate, associate degree (power and equipment)

For More Information:

Junior Engineering Technical Society
703/548-5387
info@jets.org
www.jets.org

Strategic Intelligence

Intelligence professionals gather information about domestic groups and foreign governments in order to safeguard the security and the interests of the United States and its citizens. This information might be economic, political, or military in nature, or it may focus on threats of terrorism or other criminal activities. The National Defense Intelligence College, which is attached to the Defense Intelligence Agency, offers the only accredited academic programs in strategic intelligence in the United States. These programs train those interested in obtaining senior positions in the U.S. armed forces and the national security structure. All students must be U.S. citizens who are members of the U.S. armed forces or federal government employees, be nominated by their parent organization, and possess a Top Secret, Sensitive Compartmented Information security clearance prior to enrollment.

Potential Employers:

- U.S. armed forces
- Government agencies (such as the Central Intelligence Agency, the Defense Intelligence Agency, the Federal Bureau of Investigation, and the Department of Homeland Security)

Available At:

National Defense Intelligence College (Washington, DC)
202/231-3319
JMIC@dia.mil
www.dia.mil/college/academics.htm
Degrees available: Certificate, bachelor's degree, master's degree, doctorate, advanced certificate

For More Information:

Association for Intelligence Officers
www.afio.com

Central Intelligence Agency
www.cia.gov/employment

Defense Intelligence Agency
www.dia.mil/employment

Federal Bureau of Investigation
www.fbi.gov

U.S. Department of Homeland Security
www.dhs.gov

Supply Chain Management

Supply chain management professionals are key players in manufacturing and service industries. According to the Institute for Supply Management, they use their knowledge of purchasing/procurement, transportation/logistics, contract development, negotiation, inventory control, distribution and warehousing, product development, economic forecasting, risk management, and global business to help their companies stay competitive in a global economy. A growing number of colleges and universities are offering degrees in supply chain management (sometimes called logistics and transportation management, global logistics management, operations and supply chain management, transportation and logistics management, and acquisitions management) at the certificate through graduate levels. Other schools offer study in the field via supply chain management concentrations that are part of degrees in business, business administration, business information systems, management, marketing, or other fields.

Typical Classes:

- Introduction to Supply Chain Management
- Economics
- Transportation Management
- Strategic Warehouse Management
- Sales
- Negotiations: Theory and Practice
- Information Technology Tools
- Forecasting in the Supply Chain
- Quality Process Management
- Supply Chain Research and Analysis Techniques
- Inventory Strategies
- E-Commerce and the Supply Chain
- Customer Relationships

Potential Employers:

- Technology companies
- Manufacturing companies
- Service organizations
- Consulting firms
- Any organization that offers products or services

Available At:

The following list of schools offering programs in supply chain management is not exhaustive. For more programs, visit the following website, www.ism.ws.

University of Alaska-Anchorage (Anchorage, AK)
907/786-4100
www.scob.alaska.edu/logistics.asp
Degrees available: Certificate, associate degree, bachelor's degree, master's degree, advanced certificate

Elmhurst College (Elmhurst, IL)
630/617-3500
http://public.elmhurst.edu/business/1275622.html
http://public.elmhurst.edu/scm
Degrees available: Bachelor's degree, master's degree

Georgia Southern University (Statesboro, GA)
912/681-0318
m_and_m@georgiasouthern.edu
http://coba.georgiasouthern.edu/depts/mml
Degrees available: Bachelor's degree

University of Houston (Houston, TX)
713/743-2255
wakudrle@uh.edu
www.tech.uh.edu/Programs/Logistics_Technology
Degrees available: Bachelor's degree, master's degree

Iowa State University (Ames, IA)
515/294-3659
www.bus.iastate.edu/OSCM
Degrees available: Bachelor's degree, master's degree

Michigan State University (East Lansing, MI)
517/355-8377
www.bus.msu.edu
Degrees available: Bachelor's degree, master's degree, doctorate

The Ohio State University (Columbus, OH)
614/292-8808
http://fisher.osu.edu/departments
Degrees available: Bachelor's degree, master's degree, doctorate

Riverside Community College-Norco Campus (Norco, CA)
Rex.Beck@rcc.edu
http://academic.rcc.edu/logisticsmanagement
Degrees available: Certificates, associate degrees

Syracuse University (Syracuse, NY)
315/443-3751
http://whitman.syr.edu/supplychain
Degrees available: Bachelor's degree, master's degree, doctorate

Western Illinois University (Macomb, IL)
309/298-1198
www.wiu.edu/marketing
Degrees available: Bachelor's degree, master's degree

For More Information:

American Society of Transportation and Logistics
202/580-7270
www.astl.org

Council of Supply Chain Management Professionals
630/574-0985
http://cscmp.org

Institute for Supply Management
800/888-6276
www.ism.ws

Interview: Rex Beck

Rex Beck is an Assistant Professor in the Logistics Management Program at Riverside Community College-Norco Campus in Norco, California. He has more than 20 years of experience in logistics management, including materials management, logistics analysis and administrative support, logistics customer field and call center support, warehouse management system implementation, reverse logistics, warehouse management, and quality system implementation and management. Mr. Beck discussed Riverside's logistic management program and the education of students in this field with the editors of *They Teach That in College!?*

Q. What educational options are available to students in your program?

A. We offer two certificates (in Logistics Management, and Business Administration with a Logistics Management Concentration) and two A.S. degrees (also in Logistics Management, and Business Administration with a Logistics Management Concentration).

Q. What high school subjects/activities should students focus on to be successful in this major?

A. Although vocational-level coursework related to the logistics industry would be helpful, such coursework is usually not available at the high school level. Coursework, both available and necessary, would include classes that develop the strong written, verbal, mathematical, and computer skills demanded by both industry and our academic program.

As an educator of future managers, we would find high school activities providing opportunity to develop leadership skills an excellent starting point. During the high school years, students may also find opportunities for entry-level work within the industry. Such hands-on experience is always a positive.

Q. What are the most important personal and professional qualities for logistics management students?

A. The most important thing to us is that our graduates have the skills necessary to thrive as managers in the demanding environment of our logistics industry. One of the exciting things about this industry is the opportunity to utilize a broad base of knowledge and skills. A wide variety of technical and managerial skills are necessary to be a competent contributor. To go beyond this and join the ranks of the best managers requires much more than technical skills and the application of management skills such as planning, organizing, and controlling. These things are table stakes. True excellence requires great commitment and a highly motivational leadership style.

Did You Know?

U.S. News & World Report recently selected supply chain management as a hot track career field.

Q. What educational level is typically required for logistics management graduates to land good jobs in the industry?

A. The history of our industry tells us individuals with excellent potential as managers can rise from entry-level positions to responsible management positions with nothing beyond a high school diploma. These days are behind us for all but a few employers. It is now common for employers to require a general bachelor's degree before promoting an individual into a management position. Because our program is unique in educating students specifically as logistics managers, we are finding our associate degree graduates to be very competitive.

Q. Where do logistics management graduates find employment?

A. Logistics management graduates find employment in positions involving warehousing, purchasing, contract management, transportation and traffic, inventory management, and numerous other activities related to the movement and delivery of goods from the point of origin to the final consumer. Logistics management has become so critical to commerce that many logistics practitioners are making the jump to general executive management.

Q. How will the field of logistics management change in the future?

A. Logistics management often involves finding the right tradeoff between technology, labor, and facilities. Since technology is becoming increasing economical over time, while labor and facilities only rise in cost with the passage of time, we will continue to see technology used more extensively. This will likewise create a future in which the logistics manager will work in an environment which is increasingly driven by technology. Pressures for these future managers to be formally educated will logically continue to increase as well.

Sustainable Agriculture/Organic Farming

In the 20th century, agriculture was revolutionized with an industrial approach focusing on mass-production on large farms, making food widely available and seemingly inexpensive. However, this approach has "hidden costs" that include the degradation of water and soil needed to grow future crops. In contrast, sustainable agriculture strives to develop systems for raising crops and livestock that are self-sustaining—that is, systems that do not pollute the environment or deplete the earth's limited resources. Sustainable agriculture methods focus not only on economic viability, but on social responsibility and environmental management. Sustainable agriculture practices are more typically employed by smaller farms who sell their products locally. Students of sustainable agriculture programs can focus on different aspects of sustainable agriculture/organic farming: production, the actual hands-on farming experience; sales and marketing, working for wholesalers or retailers to buy or sell food produced by sustainable agricultural practices; or government agencies and private organizations that might focus on research, development, and/or applications of sustainable agriculture practices.

Typical Courses:

- Introduction to Sustainable Agriculture and Organic Farming
- Soil Physics
- Soil Microbiology
- Soil Chemistry
- Soil Fertility
- Soil Analysis
- Biology
- Botany
- Chemistry
- Ecology
- Environmental Conservation
- Introduction to Crop Development Techniques
- Agricultural Ethics
- Plant and Animal Systems in Sustainable Agriculture
- General Farm Management
- Greenhouse Management

Potential Employers:

> Government agencies such as the Agricultural Research Service, U.S. Department of Agriculture, and the Natural Resource Conservation Service
> Commercial agencies and companies
> Private consulting firms

Available At:

Only a few colleges and universities offer programs in sustainable agriculture. For more information on college programs, visit www.attra.org/other.html#University.

Colorado State University (Fort Collins, CO)
970/491-6501
http://organic.colostate.edu
Degrees available: Bachelor's degree

University of Maine in Orono (Orono, ME)
207/581-2913
www.sag.umaine.edu
Degrees available: Bachelor's degree

University of Missouri (Columbia, MO)
573/882-8301
http://cafnr.missouri.edu/academics/sustainable-ag.php
Degrees available: Bachelor's degree

Washington State University (Pullman, WA)
Center for Sustaining Agriculture and Natural Resources
509/335-3385
http://futurestudents.wsu.edu/academics/fos/study.asp?ID=S_AG
Degrees available: Bachelor's degree, master's degree

For More Information:

Alternative Farming Systems Information Center
US Department of Agriculture
301/504-6559
http://afsic.nal.usda.gov

National Sustainable Agriculture Information Service
800/346-9140
www.attra.org

Sustainable Agriculture Research and Education
www.sare.org

Interview: Kristy Ott

Kristy Ott is the Sustainable Agriculture Education Coordinator at the Center for Sustaining Agriculture and Natural Resources at Washington State University (WSU) in Pullman, Washington. She discussed the field with the editors of *They Teach That in College.*

Q. Please tell us about your program.

A. The first Organic Agriculture Systems major to be offered in the country is part of a larger Agriculture and Food Systems (AFS) degree program. This is an exciting, college-wide, interdisciplinary program that offers a bachelor of science degree with five majors: Agriculture Business and Technology Systems, Agriculture Education, Organic Agriculture Systems, Pest Management Systems, and Plant and Soil Systems. In each major, emphasis is placed on gaining a solid background in the agricultural sciences, including learning to work with and in the complexity of agriculture and food systems. All students take a core set of classes in order to develop a broad interdisciplinary background while also studying specific subjects that prepare graduates for their chosen fields. There are multiple opportunities for students to interact personally and professionally with faculty, staff, and other students outside of class through a wide range of activities, including numerous student clubs, field and/or lab jobs in research programs, and other events. Additionally, WSU is home to a three-acre Organic Teaching Farm in which students can participate in growing vegetables for the local Community Supported Agriculture program and have hands-on learning with organic farming practices. For more information visit http://afs.wsu.edu, www.css.wsu.edu/organicfarm, and http://csanr.wsu.edu.

Additionally, several graduate programs of study are available for organic agriculture. Contact Lynne Carpenter-Boggs at 509/335-1553 or lcboggs@wsu.edu or visit http://csanr.wsu.edu.

Q. Can you tell us about the internship opportunities provided by your program?

A. Internships are a very important part of education as they allow the student to spend time working in their field of study, while gaining valuable hands-on education away from the university. The internship is designed between the internship host, student, and faculty advisor. Because we feel that this experience is so essential to overall learning, many of the AFS degrees, including the Organic Agriculture Systems major, require that the student do an internship for completion of their degree. The internship program is very open and can focus on anything from working on a large- or small-scale farm, food production systems, food packaging/storage facilities, organic certification processes, or more.

Q. What high school subjects should students take to be successful in this major?

A. Students coming into this major should be proficient in math and science. Although a background in farming may be helpful, many of our students have no experience farming and find the program to be very rewarding and valuable. University core requirements and major-specific courses can be viewed on the AFS's website.

Q. What are the most important personal and professional qualities for students in your program?

A. Sustainable and organic agriculture positions lend themselves to being community- and people-based professions. Sustainable agriculture professionals and students must be open-minded, adaptable, and willing to consider other people's points of view. A sustainable and organic agriculture professional must also be able to understand alternative types of agriculture and farming practices.

Q. What advice would you give sustainable agriculture majors as they graduate and look for jobs?

A. Be open! Consider many opportunities and even if your first job isn't your dream job, the connections of people in sustainable and organic agriculture are so tight, that it is likely one door can open another.

Q. What is the employment outlook in sustainable agriculture?

A. Sustainable and organic agriculture are emerging fields in the U.S., and jobs are going to continue to open up. People interested in sustainable and organic agriculture often find jobs in government, nonprofit agencies, scientific research, industry, farming, certification, processing, social and community groups, hospitality and restaurant management, education, and international opportunities.

Sustainable Business

Sustainable business practices aim to build profitability and economic stability while being mindful of the environment and promoting local communities. By using materials and/or operations that are less harmful to the environment, not only does the local community and physical environment benefit, but the company employing sustainable business practices can benefit too: for example, by saving expenses from not having to handle potentially harmful raw materials and/or byproducts, or by possibly creating a superior product. Sustainable business practices embrace such concepts as *biomimicry* (studying nature and then imitating or adapting it to solve human problems), recycling, a "triple-bottom line" mindset (measuring success by not only traditional "bottom line" benchmark of economic profit, but also evaluating social justice and environmental "profit"), and whole-system thinking. Sustainable business programs attract socially and environmentally conscious students with an interest in business and a desire to help others acquire an understanding of the natural world's role in our lives.

Typical Courses:

- Principles of Accounting
- Principles of Management
- Principles of Marketing
- Financial Management
- Ethics and the Ecology of Commerce
- Cases in Sustainable Business
- Spreadsheets
- Microeconomics
- Introduction to Environmental Studies
- Environmental Chemistry
- Industrial Ecology
- Environmental Business Management
- Sustainable Energy Systems
- Environmental Regulatory Compliance
- Environmental Economics and Policy

Potential Employers:

- Energy industry
- Manufacturing industry

> Service industry
> Nonprofit organizations
> Government agencies
> Virtually any business

Available At:

Aquinas College (Grand Rapids, MI)
616/632-8900
tuethmat@aquinas.edu
www.aquinas.edu/sb
Degrees available: Certificate, bachelor's degree, master's degree

Arizona State University (Tempe, AZ)
480-727-6963
http://schoolofsustainability.asu.edu/degrees/index.php
Degrees available: Bachelor's degrees, master's degrees, doctorate

Catawba College (Salisbury, NC)
704/637-4110
www.catawba.edu/academic/sustainablebusiness/majors.asp
Degrees available: Bachelor's degree

Missouri Southern State University (Joplin, MO)
417/625-9341
www.mssu.edu/ecolonomics
Degrees available: Certificate (ecolonomics)

For More Information:

Center for Sustainability at Aquinas College
www.centerforsustainability.org

Lowell Center for Sustainable Production
http://sustainableproduction.org

The World Business Council for Sustainable Development
www.wbcsd.org

Interview: Matthew Tueth

Dr. Matthew Tueth, Professor and Sustainable Business Department Chairman at Aquinas College in Grand Rapids, Michigan, discussed his program with the editors of *They Teach That in College!?*

Q. What is sustainable business?

A. Sustainable business (SB) is a strategy for making and distributing goods and services in a way that simultaneously increases long-term profits, the health of the natural world, and human community health. Since August 2003, Aquinas College has offered a bachelor of science degree in sustainable business, a minor in sustainable business, and a six-course certificate in sustainable business.

Q. What type of internship opportunities are provided by your program?

A. Each student working toward a B.S. in sustainable business is required to complete an internship. A requirement of the internship is to engage the interning student in activities that allow them to apply SB theory to practical business situations. Internships may be arranged outside the West Michigan region.

Q. What classes should high school students take to prepare for study in this major?

A. High school students intending to major in sustainable business should take classes in conventional business, environmental studies, environmental science, chemistry, biology, and physics.

Q. Where do sustainable business graduates find employment?

A. Sustainable business graduates are employed in virtually every business sector and type—energy, manufacturing, service; private businesses, non-profits, and government; small, medium, and large-sized businesses. The broad application of SB practices and principles may surprise the typical student.

Q. How will the field of sustainable business change in the future?

A. Sustainable business will increase exponentially as more businesses learn about the competitive advantage that it provides as it produces long-term value for the community, the natural world, and for business itself. SB decreases production costs while delivering these benefits.

Television, Film, and Radio Production

Every time you turn on your television and watch your favorite sitcom, nightly newscast, pay-per-view movie, or television commercial, an entire team of behind-the-scenes production personnel was involved in the creation of what you see on the screen. Lighting and sound technicians, camera operators, and video editors are just a few positions on this team of professionals who work together to make what we see and hear a visual and auditory success. Students in television, film, and radio production technology programs can expect to get significant hands-on experience, as much of the mastery of these types of skills comes from practice. This is a competitive field, so students should be strong-willed, hardworking, and willing to do a lot of grunt work in the beginning. You may find yourself on-location at a video shoot for a commercial, in the studio mixing sound or editing film, or on assignment shooting a live news report. Graduates will find work inside and outside the studio, and individuals who seek flexibility in their work environment will find a career in television, film, and radio production a perfect match.

Typical Courses:

- Directing for Television and Film
- Remote Production/Video Editing
- Television Studio Production for Business
- Audio for Motion Pictures and Television
- Physics of Sound
- Cinematography
- Pre-Production for Motion Pictures and Film
- Film/Video Production Aesthetics and History
- Radio Production
- Post-Production Techniques
- Lighting for Television and Video
- Practicum/Fieldwork

Potential Employers:

- Television and radio stations
- Motion picture studios
- Video production companies
- Large corporations with in-house advertising departments

Available At:

The following list of television, film, and radio production programs is not exhaustive. Check with academic institutions near you to determine if majors, minors, certificates, or concentrations are available in television, film, and radio production.

Borough of Manhattan Community College-City University of New York (New York, NY)
212/220-8090
www.bmcc.cuny.edu/speech/VAT/VAT.html
Degrees available: Associate degree (video arts and technology)

University of California-Los Angeles (Los Angeles, CA)
info@tft.ucla.edu
www.tft.ucla.edu/dof.cfm
Degrees available: Bachelor's degree (film production, television and video production)

Colby Community College (Colby, KS)
888/634-9350
http://colbycc.edu/?m=4&s=62
Degrees available: Associate degrees (radio, radio/television, television)

Columbia College Chicago (Chicago, IL)
312/663-1600
www.colum.edu
Degrees available: Bachelor's degrees (radio, television)

College of DuPage (Glen Ellyn, IL)
630/942-2047
www.cod.edu/academic/acadprog/occ_voc/ComArtSc.htm
Degrees available: Certificate (motion picture/television), associate degrees (film/video production, television production)

Ferris State University (Big Rapids, MI)
231/591-2712
http://catalog.ferris.edu/programs/179
Degrees available: Bachelor's degree (television and digital media production)

Grand Valley State University (Allendale, MI)
616/331-5000
www.gvsu.edu/filmvideo
Degrees available: Bachelor's degree (film and video production)

University of Iowa (Iowa City)
319/335-0330
www.uiowa.edu/%7Eccl
Degrees available: Bachelor's degree (cinema), master's degree (film and video production)

Kent State University (Kent, OH)
330/672-2468
www.jmc.kent.edu/students/prospective/mjr04.htm
Degrees available: Bachelor's degree (electronic media production)

Madonna University (Livonia, MI)
800/852-4951
www.madonna.edu/pages/tvc.cfm
Degrees available: Associate degree, bachelor's degree (both in television and video communications)

Marquette University (Milwaukee, WI)
414/288-7250
www.marquette.edu/comm/departments/brec.html
Degrees available: Bachelor's degree (broadcast and electronic communication)

Minneapolis Community and Technical College (Minneapolis, MN)
612/659-6133
www.minneapolis.edu/academics/areaofstudy.cfm?aos_id=38
Degrees available: Diploma, associate degree (both in audio-video digital media)

Montgomery College-Rockville Campus (Rockville, MD)
301/279-5000
www.montgomerycollege.edu/curricula/descriptions/cdcommunications.htm#tv
and
www.montgomerycollege.edu/curricula/descriptions/cdcommunications.htm#tvcert
Degrees available: Certificates (radio and television production), associate degrees (communication and broadcasting technology-radio and television)

Ohio University (Athens, OH)
740/593-4870
www.tcomschool.ohiou.edu/ug/seq_video.html
Degrees available: Bachelor's degree (video production)

Palm Beach Community College (Lake Worth, FL)
561/207-5421
www.pbcc.edu/programs/programsheet.asp?id=72
Degrees available: Certificates (motion picture and television production technology: production management technology, production technology, post-production technology), associate degree (motion picture & television production technology)

Piedmont Community College (Yanceyville, NC)
336/694-5707
www.pccfilm.com
Degrees available: Associate degree (film and video)

Southeast Missouri State University (Cape Girardeau, MO)
573/651-2241
www.semo.edu/communication

Degrees available: Bachelor's degree (radio, video production)

University of Southern Indiana (Evansville)
812/464-8600
www.usi.edu/libarts/comm/RTV
Degrees available: Bachelor's degree (radio and television)

Southern Maine Community College (South Portland, ME)
207/741-5500
www.smccme.edu
Degrees available: Associate degree (video and audio production)

Suffolk County Community College-Ammerman Campus (Selden, NY)
631/451-4000
www3.sunysuffolk.edu/Curricula/306.asp
Degrees available: Associate degree (radio and television production)

Western Kentucky University (Bowling Green, KY)
270/745-0111
www.wku.edu/Journalism/Broadcasting/index.htm
Degrees available: Bachelor's degree (broadcasting)

For More Information:

International Alliance of Theatrical Stage Employees, Moving Picture Technicians, Artists and Allied Crafts
www.iatse-intl.org

National Association of Broadcast Employees and Technicians
http://nabetcwa.org

Society of Broadcast Engineers
www.sbe.org

Society of Motion Picture and Television Engineers
www.smpte.org

Textile Engineering

A major in textile engineering prepares students to work in a global industry that not only includes traditional apparel and home furnishing applications, but also cutting-edge applications in the plastics, packaging, biomedical, marine, construction, environmental, automotive, aerospace, industrial, safety, and other industries. Textile engineers draw on diverse science and engineering principles, and have an abundance of career opportunities available to them. Degrees in textile engineering are available at all academic levels.

Typical Courses:

- Calculus
- Chemistry
- Physics
- Yarn Engineering
- Weaving and Knitting; Nonwovens
- Polymer Synthesis and Processing
- Dyeing and Finishing
- Statistics
- Industrial Textiles
- Textile Production Control

Potential Employers:

- Chemical manufacturers
- Global textile retail companies
- Automotive companies
- Government forensic science agencies

Available At:

The Accreditation Board for Engineering and Technology (www.abet.org) accredits two textile engineering programs: at North Carolina State University and Philadelphia University. These and several other programs are listed below.

Auburn University (Auburn, AL)
334/844-2308
www.eng.auburn.edu/programs/txen/about
Degrees available: Bachelor's degree, master's degree, doctorate

Clemson University (Clemson, SC)
864/656-1512
www.clemson.edu/mse/index.htm
Degrees available: Bachelor's degree, master's degree, doctorate

Georgia Institute of Technology (Atlanta, GA)
404/894-2490
webadmin@ptfe.gatech.edu
www.ptfe.gatech.edu
Degrees available: Bachelor's degree, master's degree, doctorate

North Carolina State University (Raleigh, NC)
919/515-6637
www.tx.ncsu.edu/departments/tecs
Degrees available: Bachelor's degree, master's degree, doctorate

Philadelphia University (Philadelphia, PA)
215/951-2700
www.philau.edu/engineering/BStextileengineeringtech
Degrees available: Bachelor's degree, master's degree, doctorate

For More Information:

American Apparel and Footwear Association
www.apparelandfootwear.org

National Council of Textile Organizations
202/822-8028
www.ncto.org

Toy Design

The business of toys is for the truly multitalented individual—serious and analytical on the one hand, and young-at-heart, carefree, and creative on the other. Toy design students must be technologically inclined and business minded as they study the manufacturing of plastic and non-plastic toys, computer-aided industrial design, safety and regulatory requirements, and elements of consumer motivation. Yet the successful toy designer must also be able to maintain the mindset of the ultimate consumer—the child. According to the Fashion Institute of Technology (one of only two toy design schools in the United States), graduates go on to become product managers, inventors, toy research and development specialists, and designers of plush toys, dolls, action figures, vehicles, games, construction sets, and other playthings.

Typical Courses:

- Soft Toy and Doll Design
- Drafting for Toy Design
- Product Materials and Safety Considerations
- Games
- Hard Toy: Engineering
- Model Making
- Interactive Media for Toy Design
- Marker Rendering
- Licensed Product Design
- Computer Graphics in Toy Design

Potential Employers:

- Toy manufacturers (such as Hasbro, Gund, Mattel/Fisher-Price, LucasArts, Lego, LeapFrog, Wild Planet, and VTech)

Available At:

Fashion Institute of Technology (New York, NY)
212/217-7133
fitinto@fitnyc.edu
www.fitnyc.edu/aspx/Content.aspx?menu=Future:SchoolsAndPrograms:ArtAndDesign:ToyDesign
Degrees available: Bachelor's degree

The world toy market is a $67 billion industry, according to the Toy Industry Association. Growing markets include Latin America, Asia, and Europe. (Photo courtesy of VStock LLC/Photos To Go Unlimited)

Otis College of Art and Design (Los Angeles, CA)
310/665-6985
toydesign@otis.edu
www.otis.edu
Degrees available: Bachelor's degree

For More Information:

Industrial Designers Society of America
703/707-6000
idsa@idsa.org
www.idsa.org

Toy Industry Association
info@toyassociation.org
www.toy-tia.org

Playthings Magazine
www.playthings.com

Valuation Sciences

For as long as there has been some medium of exchange employed—be it stones, hides, trading beads, or one of the many currencies used today, like the euro, yen, or the dollar—people have attempted to assign value to personal objects and property. Valuation sciences focus on the study of appraisal, or estimating the value of something. *Appraisers* are sought after to estimate the value of many types of things, such as jewelry, antiques, art, collectibles, land, buildings, and an individual's share in a business. Students in valuation sciences programs learn how to appraise a wide variety of objects by studying the history, theory, and practical skills necessary, taking into consideration such factors as affects of consumer behavior and local and global influences on an item's value. The base of valuation sciences programs tend to draw from areas such as accounting, business law, economics, and finance, and then offer specialization in chosen areas of interest, such as business valuation, art, or real estate. Because appraisal skills are used in many situations, graduates of valuation sciences programs can work in a variety of settings.

Typical Courses:

- Principles of Accounting
- Appraisal Principles and Practice
- Value Influences and Analysis
- Market Influences and Analysis
- Financial Accounting Concepts
- Managerial Accounting
- Financial Concepts
- Financial Policy
- Appraisal Documentation
- Research Methods and Design

Potential Employers:

- Accounting firms
- Antique shops
- Art galleries
- Auction houses
- Financial institutions
- Government agencies such as U.S. Customs and Border Protection.
- Real estate companies

Available At:

The following colleges and universities offer certificate or degree programs in valuation sciences. Additionally, contact schools in your area to see if they offer study options in the field.

Lindenwood University (St. Charles, MO)
admissions@lindenwood.edu
www.lindenwood.edu/academics/deg_prog.asp
Degrees available: Bachelor's degree, master's degree

Northwestern University (Chicago, IL)
847/491-5611
www.scs.northwestern.edu/pdp/npdp/appraisal
Degrees available: Advanced certificate (fine and decorative art valuation)

Pratt Institute (New York, NY)
212/647-7199
www.pratt.edu/ccps-cert/personal_property_appraisal
Degrees available: Certificate (fine and decorative art valuation)

Rhode Island School of Design (Providence, RI)
800/364-RISD
www.risd.edu/pdf/curricula/cert_appraisal.pdf
Degrees available: Certificate

For More Information:

American Society of Appraisers
703/478-2228
asainfo@appraisers.org
www.appraisers.org

The Appraisal Foundation
202/347-7722
info@appraisalfoundation.org
www.appraisalfoundation.org

Appraisal Institute
www.appraisalinstitute.org

National Association of Independent Fee Appraisers
312/321-6830
info@naifa.com
www.naifa.com

National Association of Jewelry Appraisers
naja.appraisers@netzero.net
www.najaappraisers.com

Web Design/Development

Every website you visit, whether it's a company or personal site, was designed by someone. Some are trained professionals and others are not. If you've been to a website that contained hard-to-find information, out-of-date links, and visually chaotic graphics, you understand the importance of good design in attracting people to a site. The advent of the Internet for the mainstream population created an instant demand for individuals to create aesthetically pleasing, user-friendly websites for businesses of all sizes. *Website developers and designers* create and maintain highly professional and complex websites for corporations, associations, schools, and more. The website designer plays an integral role in an organization's ability to communicate a message, attract and maintain customers, and disseminate pertinent information. He or she must have an eye for design and an aptitude for computer technology. The U.S. Department of Labor notes that among design occupations, there will be an increase in graphic design jobs through 2016, particularly for graphic designers with website design experience. However, competition in this field is significant, and individuals entering the field must be prepared for a competitive marketplace upon graduation.

Typical Courses:

- Design Process and Technology
- Drawing for Graphic Designers
- Multimedia Technology
- HTML
- Photoshop
- InDesign
- Dreamweaver
- Internet Graphics
- Fireworks
- Flash
- 3-D Modeling & Animation

Potential Employers:

- Advertising agencies
- Corporations with in-house designers
- Graphic design firms

> Internet service providers
> Consulting agencies
> Freelance opportunities (self-employment)

Available At:

The following list of Web design/development programs is not exhaustive. Check with academic institutions near you to determine if majors, minors, certificates, or concentrations are available in Web design/development.

Bergen Community College (Paramus, NJ)
201/447-7100
www.bergen.edu/ecatalog
/programview.asp?program.cbn=22&semester.rm=1
Degrees available: Associate degree

Cecil Community College (North East, MD)
410/287-1000
information@cecilcc.edu
www.cecilcc.edu/programs
Degrees available: Certificate, associate degree

Did You Know?

According to NetRatings, the average person spent nearly 32 hours surfing the Internet in October, 2007. The average person visited more than 1,500 unique sites.

Cincinnati State Technical and Community College
(Cincinnati, OH)
513/861-7700
www.cinstate.cc.oh.us
Degrees available: Associate degree

Dawson Community College (Glendive, MT)
800/821-8320
www.dawson.edu
Degrees available: Associate degree

Delaware County Community College-Marple Campus
(Media, PA)
610/359-5050
www.dccc.edu/catalog/career_programs.html#web_development
Degrees available: Associate degree

Eastern Idaho Technical College (Idaho Falls, ID)
800/662-0261
www.eitc.edu/pdf/catalog/Web%20Development%20Specialist.pdf
Degrees available: Associate degree

Hudson Valley Community College (Troy, NY)
518/629-7225
business@hvcc.edu
www.hvcc.edu/bus/cwd
Degrees available: Associate degree

Mohawk Valley Community College (Utica, NY)
315/792-5348
www.mvcc.edu/academics/departments/bit/wbdsgnmngmt.cfm
Degrees available: Certificate, associate degree

Portland Community College (multiple campuses, Portland, OR)
866/922-1010
www.pcc.edu/pcc/pro/progs/wsd
Degrees available: Certificate, associate degree

Spokane Falls Community College (Spokane, WA)
888/509-7944
http://tech.spokanefalls.edu/AppliedVisualArts/default.asp?menu=2&page=AASWebDesign
Degrees available: Associate degree

Community College of Vermont (multiple campuses, Vermont)
802/241-3535
www.ccv.edu/degree/AAS/web_design
Degrees available: Associate degree

Williston State College (Williston, ND)
888/863-9455
www.wsc.nodak.edu
Degrees available: Certificate, associate degree

For More Information:

International Webmasters Association
626/449-3709
www.iwanet.org

World Organization of Webmasters
916/989-2933
info@joinwow.org
www.joinwow.org

Western Clinical Herbalism

As the public's interest in the use of various types of alternative medicine has increased, so have students' interests in academic programs that incorporate such subject matter. Practitioners of herbal medicine use herbs to promote well-being and treat illness. The oldest type of medicine known to man, herbal medicine is still used in some form by the majority of people in the world. Although knowledge of herbs and how they are used to promote health and well-being is the focus of an herbal medicine program, modern science is also stressed: knowledge of human anatomy and physiology, plant biology, nutrition, medical terminology all come into play. Students with an interest in holistic health, especially the study of herbs and their medicinal properties, are attracted to herbal medicine programs.

Typical Courses:

- History of Herbalism
- Foundations of Western Clinical Herbalism
- Nutrition
- Human Biology
- Anatomy
- Plant Biology
- Western Herbal Medicine Making
- Application of Clinical Herbalism
- Integration of Herbs Into Healthcare Practice
- Herbal Integration Internship

Potential Employers:

- Health food retailers
- Dietary supplement manufacturers
- Pharmaceutical companies
- Colleges and universities
- Health care organizations
- Private practice

Available At:

Minneapolis Community and Technical College
(Minneapolis, MN)
612/659-6102
www.minneapolis.edu/academics/areaofstudy.cfm?aos_id=94
Degrees available: Associate degree

For More Information:

American Association of Acupuncture and Oriental Medicine
866/455-7999
www.aaaomonline.org

American Botanical Council
512/926-4900
abc@herbalgram.org
www.herbalgram.org

American Herbal Products Association
301/588-1171
ahpa@ahpa.org
www.ahpa.org

American Herbalists Guild
203/272-6731
ahgoffice@earthlink.net
www.americanherbalistsguild.com

Herb Research Foundation
303/449-2265
www.herbs.org

The Herb Society of America
440/256-0514
herbs@herbsociety.org
www.herbsociety.org

Wood Science and Technology

When most people think of forest products, they think of paper or the wood that is used to build furniture or construct houses. But there is a lot more to forest products than just paper and wood. Did you know that forest products, according to the Society of Wood Science and Technology, are used to create an anti-cancer drug, rayon clothing, molded panels in automobiles, vanilla flavoring in ice cream, and other products? *Wood science technology workers* study the physical, chemical, and biological properties of wood and the methods of growing and processing it for use in everyday life. To meet the growing demand for professionals in this industry, colleges and universities are offering undergraduate and graduate programs in wood science and technology—many of which are accredited by the Society of Wood Science and Technology.

Typical Classes:

- Introduction to Forest Biology
- Introduction to Forest Resources
- Introduction to Wood Science and Technology
- Wood Anatomy and Structure
- Physical and Mechanical Properties of Wood
- Wood Chemistry
- Adhesion and Adhesives Technology
- Harvesting Forest Products
- Wood Composites
- Wood Deterioration and Preservation
- Forest Products Business Management
- Forest Resource Economics

Potential Employers:

- Mills
- Manufacturers of wood products
- Wood suppliers
- Forest products associations
- Pulp and paper companies
- Government agencies
- Colleges and universities

Available At:

The following program in wood science and technology is accredited by the Society of Wood Science and Technology (SWST):

University of Idaho (Moscow, ID)
208/885-9663
forprod@uidaho.edu
www.cnrhome.uidaho.edu/forp
Degrees available: Bachelor's degree, master's degree, doctorate

Mississippi State University (Mississippi State, MS)
662/325-2116
www.cfr.msstate.edu/forestp/index.asp
Degrees available: Bachelor's degree, master's degree, doctorate

North Carolina State University (Raleigh, NC)
919/515-7709
www.ncsu.edu/wood
Degrees available: Bachelor's degree, master's degree, doctorate

Oregon State University (Corvallis, OR)
541/737-4257
woodscience@oregonstate.edu
http://woodscience.oregonstate.edu
Degrees available: Bachelor's degree, master's degree, doctorate

Pennsylvania State University (University Park, PA)
814/865-7541
ForestResources@psu.edu
www.sfr.cas.psu.edu/WoodProd/WoodProducts.html
Degrees available: Bachelor's degree, master's degree, doctorate

State University of New York (Syracuse, NY)
315/470-6880
jabarton@esf.edu
www.esf.edu/wpe
Degrees available: Bachelor's degree, master's degree, doctorate

University of Maine (Orono, ME)
800/WOOD-UNIV
woodscience@maine.edu
www.forest.umaine.edu/education/WSC
Degrees available: Bachelor's degree, master's degree, doctorate, advanced certificate

University of Minnesota (St. Paul, MN)
612/625-7733
bbe@umn.edu
www.cnr.umn.edu/BP
Degrees available: Bachelor's degree, master's degree, doctorate

Virginia Polytechnic Institute and State University (Blacksburg, VA)
540/231-8853

vtwood@vt.edu
www.woodscience.vt.edu
Degrees available: Bachelor's degree, master's degree, doctorate

West Virginia University (Morgantown, WV)
304/293-2941
www.forestry.caf.wvu.edu/wvu_woodscience
Degrees available: Bachelor's degree, master's degree, doctorate

The following schools offer programs in wood science and technology, but are not accredited by the SWST. The SWST offers a list of accredited and unaccredited schools at its website, www.swst.org/schooldirectory.html.

Auburn University (Auburn, AL)
334/844-1007
https://fp.auburn.edu/sfws
Degrees available: Bachelor's degree, master's degree, doctorate

Clemson University (Clemson, SC)
864/656-3013
http://virtual.clemson.edu/groups/CAFLS
Degrees available: Bachelor's degree, master's degree, doctorate

Iowa State University (Ames, IA)
515/294-1458
www.nrem.iastate.edu
Degrees available: Bachelor's degree, master's degree, doctorate

Purdue University (West Lafayette, IN)
765/494-4600
www.fnr.purdue.edu
Degrees available: Bachelor's degree, master's degree, doctorate

University of Wisconsin-Stevens Point
715/346-4617
www.uwsp.edu/cnr
Degrees available: Bachelor's degree, master's degree

For More Information:

Society of Wood Science and Technology
608/231-9347
vicki@swst.org
www.swst.org

Zoo Science

Academic programs in zoo science prepare students for one of the many positions working in zoos or working in a zoo-related field. Aquarium studies are often offered in tandem with zoo science programs, providing students with the knowledge and experience necessary to work with marine life or manage aquaria. Students enrolled in zoo science programs gain knowledge of one or more zoo-related areas, such as animal training, maintenance, and care; management of employees and facilities; design of exhibits and animal habitats; and the rules and regulations that zoos and aquariums adhere to. Some programs allow students to specialize in a specific area, such as working with exotic animals or animal husbandry. Internships at zoos or aquariums provide students with an overview of the daily routine at such facilities. Since zoo science workers often interact with the public who come to visit their facilities, good communication skills and a desire to share their love and knowledge of animals is important.

Typical Courses:

- Introduction to Zoo and Aquarium Science
- Care of Wild Animals in Captivity
- Captive Animal Health
- Captive Animal Training and Enrichment
- Zoo Exhibit Design and Horticulture
- Animal Physiology
- Animal Ecology
- Animal Behavior
- Animal Nutrition
- Animal Breeding
- Animal Records
- Genetics
- Biological Studies in Zoos and Aquaria
- Park Maintenance and Operations Management

Potential Employers:

- Zoos
- Aquaria
- Nature centers
- Research organizations

Unique Program

Moorpark College is the only postsecondary institution in the United States that offers a hands-on program in the training of exotic (and domestic) animals. Students learn the principles and techniques of animal training at its five-acre America's Teaching Zoo, which is located on campus. The EATM program, which lasts 22 months, offers students three options: a General EATM option, an Animal Behavior Management option, and a Wildlife Education option. Graduates of the program earn certificates or associate degrees and pursue careers in the film/television industry, zoos, amusement parks, and in wildlife education/outreach. Others pursue a bachelor's degree in an animal-related field. Moorpark has articulation agreements with several colleges including California State University-Bakersfield (an online bachelor of science program in environmental resource management) and Southwestern Missouri State University (for students who already have a bachelor's degree who are interested in earning a master's of science in reproductive physiology), as well as with select California public universities.

Available At:

Friends University (Wichita, KS)
316/295-5608
www.friends.edu/academics/cbase/Div_nsm/zoo.aspx
Degrees available: Bachelor's degree

Michigan State University (East Lansing, MI)
www.msu.edu
Degrees available: Bachelor's degree, master's degree

Moorpark College (Moorpark, CA)
805/378-1441
www.moorparkcollege.edu/eatm
Degrees available: Certificates, associate degree

Niagra County Community College (Sanborn, NY)
716/614-6424
acobaugh@niagaracc.suny.edu
www.niagaracc.suny.edu/lsd/animal.html
Degrees available: Associate degree

Pensacola Junior College (Pensacola, FL)
888/897-3605
www.pjc.edu/students/programs/allprograms.asp
Degrees available: Associate degree, advanced certificates

The Association of Zoos and Aquariums has 216 accredited members in North America. Its member-zoos and -aquariums have more than 735,000 specimens (including amphibians, birds, fish, invertebrates, mammals [such as the lion pictured above], marine mammals, and reptiles). (Photo courtesy of PHOTICK/Photos To Go Unlimited)

Pikes Peak Community College (Colorado Springs, CO)
800/456-6847
www.ppcc.cccoes.edu/CatalogSchedule/Programs/Program.cfm?Program=NuRp
Degrees available: Associate degree

Santa Fe Community College (Gainesville, FL)
352/395-5604
linda.asbell@santafe.cc.fl.us
http://inst.santafe.cc.fl.us/%7Ezoo
Degrees available: Associate degree

Western Illinois University (Macomb, IL)
309/298-1546
www.wiu.edu/grad/catalog/zooaquastudies.php
Degrees available: Advanced certificate

For More Information:

American Association of Zoo Keepers
www.aazk.org

Association of Zoos and Aquariums
301/562-0777
www.aza.org

Association/Organization Index

A

B

C

D

E

F

G

H

I

J

L

M

N

School Index

D

E

F

G

H

I

J

K

L

M

N

O

P

Q

R

S

T

Schools by State Index

Alabama

Alaska

Arizona

Arkansas

California

Canada

Colorado

Connecticut

Delaware

District of Columbia

Florida

Georgia

Hawaii

Idaho

Illinois

Indiana

Iowa

Kansas

Kentucky

Locations Throughout the United States

Louisiana

Maine

Maryland

Massachusetts

Michigan

Minnesota

Mississippi

Missouri

Montana

Nebraska

Nevada

New Hampshire

New Jersey

New Mexico

New York

North Carolina

North Dakota

Ohio

Oklahoma

Oregon

Pennsylvania

Rhode Island

South Carolina

South Dakota

Tennessee

Texas

Utah

Vermont

Virginia

Washington

West Virginia

Wisconsin

Wyoming